UNDOING CULTURE

Theory, Culture & Society

Theory, Culture & Society caters for the resurgence of interest in culture within contemporary social science and the humanities. Building on the heritage of classical social theory, the book series examines ways in which this tradition has been reshaped by a new generation of theorists. It will also publish theoretically informed analyses of everyday life, popular culture, and new intellectual movements.

EDITOR: Mike Featherstone, *University of Teesside*

SERIES EDITORIAL BOARD
Roy Boyne, *University of Teesside*
Mike Hepworth, *University of Aberdeen*
Scott Lash, *University of Lancaster*
Roland Robertson, *University of Pittsburgh*
Bryan S. Turner, *Deakin University*

Recent volumes include:

Baroque Reason
The Aesthetics of Modernity
Christine Buci-Glucksmann

The Consuming Body
Pasi Falk

Cultural Identity and Global Process
Jonathan Friedman

The Established and the Outsiders
Norbert Elias and John L. Scotson

The Cinematic Society
The Voyeur's Gaze
Norman K. Denzin

Decentring Leisure
Rethinking Leisure Theory
Chris Rojek

Global Modernities
Mike Featherstone, Scott Lash and Roland Robertson

The Masque of Femininity
The Presentation of Woman in Everyday Life
Efrat Tseëlon

The Arena of Racism
Michel Wieviorka

UNDOING CULTURE

Globalization, Postmodernism and Identity

MIKE FEATHERSTONE

SAGE Publications
London • Thousand Oaks • New Delhi

SAGE Publications Ltd
6 Bonhill Street
London EC2A 4PU

SAGE Publications Inc
2455 Teller Road
Thousand Oaks, California 91320

SAGE Publications India Pvt Ltd
32, M-Block Market
Greater Kailash – I
New Delhi 110 048

Published in association with *Theory, Culture & Society*,
School of Human Studies, University of Teesside

British Library Cataloguing in Publication data

A catalogue record for this book is
available from the British Library.

ISBN 0–8039–7605–4
ISBN 0–8039–7606–2 pbk

Library of Congress catalog record available

Typeset by Mayhew Typesetting, Rhayader, Powys
Printed in Great Britain by The Cromwell Press Ltd,
Broughton Gifford, Melksham, Wiltshire

*Dedicated to the memory of
my mother and father*

CONTENTS

PREFACE

The various chapters of this book have been written over the last five or six years. Most of them started their lives as conference papers or essays written for edited collections. They have been selected from the range of papers written in this period because they have a certain coherence in terms of the themes they seek to address. In many ways they represent a deepening and extension of some of the issues developed in *Consumer Culture and Postmodernism* (1991a). Yet, rather than directly addressing postmodernism, they seek to explore the grounds for postmodernism via two main concerns. The first is the formation and deformation of the cultural sphere which addresses the question of the autonomization of culture and the type of autonomous person (the artist and intellectual as hero) associated with this process. The second concerns the process of globalization which I argue provides the wider intellectual context for many of the themes associated with postmodernism.

My work in both areas has been sustained through the support and numerous discussions of these issues with many friends and colleagues. I have a special debt to my friends on the editorial board of the journal *Theory, Culture & Society*: Josef Bleicher, Roy Boyne, Mike Hepworth, Scott Lash, Roland Robertson and Bryan S. Turner, who will recognize many of the concerns addressed here. In particular Bryan Turner, Scott Lash and Roland Robertson have in their own ways worked across the same territory I've been seeking to traverse (Roland Robertson's pioneering work in developing the theory of globalization needs a special mention). I would also like to acknowledge the contribution of Mike Hepworth and Roger Burrows, who both read the whole manuscript, made many helpful editing suggestions and persuaded me to take my own medicine and follow the editor's maxim: the more you cut the better it gets. In addition I must acknowledge the support of my colleagues in the Sociology, Criminology and Social Policy subject group in the School of Human Studies at the University of Teesside for both their encouragement and tolerance for some of my wilder ventures. My immediate colleagues in the Centre for the Study of Adult Life, especially Robin Bunton and Roger Burrows, who have worked together with Bryan Turner and me to found the new associate journal to *TCS*, *Body & Society* have been particularly supportive. I also have a special debt to Barbara Cox, who has worked on *Theory, Culture & Society* for a number of years now and has found ways of channelling all our postmodern styles of work into a miraculous kind of order which has enabled us to hit publication deadlines on schedule. I also much appreciate the patience and support of friends at Sage Publications who have encouraged and helped us in all the various schemes which *TCS* has developed over the years: Stephen Barr, Ian Eastment, Krysia Domaszewicz, David Hill, Jane Makoff, Robert Rojek and Janey Walker.

In the last few years I have had the good fortune to be able to enjoy a taste of the nomadic academic life as a visiting professor in Brazil, Japan and Canada. I would like to thank colleagues and students at Campinas University in São Paulo, Doshisha University in Kyoto, Simon Fraser University in Vancouver, for making my stay so rewarding and hospitable. I would also like to mention the support of a number of colleagues and friends at these and other institutions in the above three countries with whom I discussed many of the ideas which developed into this book: Antonio A. Arantes, Ana Zahira Bassit, Guita Debert, Arnaldo Augusto de Siguera, Gisela Taschner, Makio Morikawa, Yasuhiro Aoki, Katsu Harada, Ken'nichi Kawasaki, Chris King, Toyoie Kitagawa, John Maher, Hideichiro Nakano, Yoko Ogawa, Kazuhiko Okuda, Sab Omote, Shuichi Wada, Sharon Fuller, Rick Gruneau, Stephen Kline, Martin Laba, David Ley, Richard Pinet, Caroline Newton.

I would like to thank the following friends and colleagues who helped in various ways in developing the ideas which emerged into this book: Zygmunt Bauman, Laura Bovone, Massimo Canevacci, David Chaney, Klaus Eder, David Frisby, Christian Lalive d'Epinay, Stephen Mennell, Brian Moeran, Hans Mommaas, Justin O'Connor, John O'Neill, Oswaldo Panaccione, Britt Robillard, John Rex, Chris Rojek, Hermann Schwengel, Lisa Skov, Sam Whimster, Cas Wouters, Derek and Jenny Wynne. I must also acknowledge the help and encouragement I received from friends, who are sadly no longer with us: Norbert Elias, Hans Haferkamp and Friedrich Tenbruck. Finally, thanks are due to my family, especially Edna, Claire and John, for their tolerance and understanding for the person working in the room upstairs.

1

INTRODUCTION: GLOBALIZING CULTURAL COMPLEXITY

Things fall apart; the centre cannot hold.

(W.B. Yeats, 'The Second Coming')

Those who write, travel.
The art of being there is to go there.

(Joseph de Maistre)

Undoing cultural unities

The above quotation from Yeats has been used numerous times, both directly and indirectly, to highlight the current sense of cultural fragmentation and dislocation. It is assumed that culture has become decentred, that there is an absence of coherence and unity; culture can no longer provide an adequate account of the world with which to construct or order our lives. The lines which directly precede the above quotation at the start of Yeats poem run: 'Turning and turning in the widening gyre/The falcon cannot hear the falconer'. This inability to find the way home, to return to the lost point of coherence and order, was of course a well-worked theme in the events surrounding the end of the First World War and its immediate aftermath, the time when Yeats wrote the poem.

Our current sense of cultural fragmentation which is indicated in titles of books such as *Off Center* (Miyoshi, 1991), *Dislocating Masculinity* (Cornwall and Lindisfarne, 1994), *Relocating Cultural Studies* (Blundell *et al.*, 1993), *Border Dialogues* (Chambers, 1990), *Disrupted Borders* (Gupta, 1993), *The Nation and its Fragments* (Chatterjee, 1993), *Decentring Leisure* (Rojek, 1995), then is not new. Indeed people have long been *Undoing Culture*, to add the title of this book to the rapidly growing list. Yet what is noticeable is that late twentieth-century analysts of culture rarely seek to examine other potentially parallel phases of history, such as the time in which Yeats wrote 'The Second Coming' just after the First World War – a phase in which there was a marked sense of cultural relativism and crisis, as the writings of Spengler, Scheler, Weber and others demonstrate. If we wanted to cast further afield the culture of the baroque in the seventeenth century which fascinated Walter Benjamin (1977) and others (Buci-Glucksmann, 1994; Maravall, 1986) also comes to mind. Yet ours would not be the first generation to be accused of harbouring 'men [or today we should say people] without memories', to play off Adorno's phrase.

It can be argued that the sense that there is a cultural crisis, that we need a 'diagnosis of our times', has long been the meat and drink of cultural specialists (artists, intellectuals and various types of cultural intermediaries). In effect they have a professional interest in undoing and reworking the knots of culture. This is not to suggest that cultural specialists are arbitrarily, or capriciously, inventing cultural crises. They are clearly responding to perceptions and images of events happening in the world. Yet it is the relationship between their immediate world, the conditions of intellectual and cultural production and consumption within which they work, and this larger world 'out there' which needs investigation. Noticeable in the post-war era have been the specific shifts within intellectual practices which occurred as tightly controlled establishments, able to monopolize the supply of intellectual goods, gave way to a phase of demonopolization, which has provided a range of opportunities for outsider groups.

This was one of the arguments of my previous book, *Consumer Culture and Postmodernism* (1991a), that postmodernism should not merely be understood as an epochal shift, or new stage of capitalism. Rather, attention should be given to the mediations between the economy and culture by focusing on the activities of cultural specialists and intermediaries and the expanding audiences (the postwar baby boom generation) for a new range of cultural goods. *Contra* some strands of postmodern theory which proclaim the triumph of culture and along with it the end of the social, it argued that we have not so readily moved towards a stage in the development of social life which has broken down completely the power balances and interdependencies which bind together groups of people. At the same time it must be conceded that concepts such as 'the social' and 'society' are no longer able to deliver the theoretical benefits they once promised. As we shall see in some of the later chapters in the book, the process of globalization has been helping to undermine the alleged integrity and unity of nation-state societies. Yet we should be aware of assuming that this is the whole story, because the notion of 'society' has long been as much a projected image of what social life should be like as a reality. It glossed many social processes which were never domesticated, regulated and integrated. One of these processes, the shifting role of travel and mobility in constructing images of social life, is the subject of the final chapter.

A central aim of this book is to explore some of the processes which are alleged to have uncoupled culture from the social and some of the ways in which this particular image itself has been formed. It has, therefore, been argued that culture has gained a more significant role within social life and that today everything is cultural (e.g. Baudrillard, 1993). In effect culture is now beyond the social and has become released from its traditional determinisms in economic life, social class, gender, ethnicity and region. In terms of our reference to the decentring of culture, this could be taken to be a counter-argument: in effect culture has not been decentred, rather, it has become recentred. Certainly, if we take into account the rise in significance accorded to the study of culture within academic life this could well be the case. Culture, long on the periphery of the social science field, has now been moved towards the centre. To take an example: my book *Consumer Culture and Postmodernism* (Featherstone, 1991a) was reviewed by the *British Journal of Industrial Relations* in the early 1990s. For a book on culture and theory to be reviewed by an industrial relations journal would hardly have seemed possible in the 1970s. Today a number of new journals have appeared in the fields of business, management and organizational studies which address many of the theoretical and cultural issues which were taken on board in *Theory, Culture & Society* and other places in the early 1980s. It can be argued that this is part of a wider tendency within academic life which has seen the weakening of the divisions between subject areas alongside a much stronger approval for inter- and trans-disciplinary studies. From this perspective, then, the more general decentring and fragmentation of culture has been accompanied by a recentring of culture within academic life.

An aim, then, of this book, is to investigate the processes both inside and outside the academy and wider field of cultural producers, which form our sense of culture as something unified or fragmented. In one sense we are all cultural producers in that we engage in practices which not only reproduce the cultural repertoires we are provided with and need as we move through social life, but are to some extent able to modify and shape them as they are passed down the unbroken chain of generations which constitutes human life. Yet the extent to which we can all participate in cultural production and consumption clearly varies historically and between societies. It also varies between groups within societies, as almost all societies and social entities possess groups of specialists who engage in the production and dissemination of culture (priests, artists, intellectuals, educators, teachers, academics, cultural intermediaries, etc.). This power potential they possess through their ability to produce and mobilize culture is, of course, not unimpeded, but is itself dependent upon the interdependencies and power balances these groups enjoy with other, usually more powerful, groups such as economic and military specialists. It is possible, then, that our overall sense of the value, meaning and potential unity or crisis-ridden nature of a culture will depend not only on the conditions of social life we find ourselves in, but on the conditions of those who specialize in cultural production as well. Under certain circumstances the power potential of certain groups of cultural specialists may increase to the extent that particular cultural forms gain greatly in autonomy and prestige. This is the subject of Chapter 2, which explores the processes that lead to the formation and autonomization of the cultural sphere. The relatively autonomous cultural sphere which developed alongside the public sphere (Habermas, 1989) since the eighteenth century, was accompanied by a rise in the prestige of artists and intellectuals, to the extent that for some groups in the middle classes art became a heroic way of life, which was seen as more important than life itself.

This subject is taken up in Chapters 3 and 4, which address the ways in which the ordered heroic life has been formed as part of the processes which led to the autonomization of the culture sphere. Max Weber's respect for the sense of unity generated by the ordered life of the Puritan is well known, as is his assumption that it is impossible to reproduce this in modern times. For Weber the artistic, intellectual or erotic lives are necessarily incomplete and lack fundamental coherence, something which became the fate of the individual in modernity. Yet the topic is given an intriguing twist when we consider those accounts of Weber's life which sought to present it as a form of heroic stoicism, perhaps the only viable 'noble' response to the meaninglessness generated by the rationalization of life and the confusion resulting from the clashing of incompatible values in the modern world. Against the possibility of striving for an ordered life we have to place the sacrifice and isolation demanded by this masculine form of heroic self-formation. This theme is taken up in the next chapter, in which everyday life, the world of sociability, maintenance and women is contrasted against the masculine heroic ideal. Yet this ideal, which became such a powerful force in the arts and intellectual life in the late nineteenth century, has since been weakened with the deformation of the cultural sphere and the rise of consumer culture. This should not be taken as merely entailing a tragic loss, but as allowing new forms of identity development to take place amongst previously excluded outsider groups.

It is assumed, then, that in the twentieth century the process of the formation and autonomization of the cultural sphere has given way to deformation. One of the strands associated with postmodernism in the late twentieth century has been that we are witnessing the 'end of art', and the end of the artist as a heroic figure concerned to carve out a distinctive form of life. The extension of consumer culture particularly through the mass production and proliferation of commodity-signs and images is seen to have spelled the end of a separate cultural sphere.

Yeats's 'Second Coming' can again be used to illustrate this process. While the poem has regularly been taught in schools and universities as part of the specialist canon of high culture, it has recently been popularized and packaged for a mass audience. The poem has been used as lyrics for a song recorded by Joni Mitchell on a recent CD. W.B. Yeats might well have approved this popularization of the poem and its capacity to reach wider audiences, yet the problem is complicated because the binary opposition high culture/mass culture no longer seems appropriate. Joni Mitchell writes for intermediate audiences which cannot easily be designated as belonging to popular culture or mass culture – not that they are high culture either. This, then, is an example of a 'cross-over', where previously sealed-off cultural forms more easily flow over what were once strictly policed boundaries, to produce unusual combinations and syncretisms.

This question of the difficulty of categorizing culture which flows across boundaries is a central issue in Chapters 5, 6 and 7. It can be argued that the intensification of the flow of cultural goods and images within consumer culture makes it more difficult to read culture, to attribute a fixed meaning and relationship between a cultural sign or image and the social attributes of the person who uses or consumes the item. As is argued in Chapter 2, on the autonomization of the cultural sphere, there is the assumption, derived from anthropological studies of tightly bounded societies, that the logic of the system of cultural classification is somehow homologous to the distinctions, differences and divisions between social groups who unconsciously use culture as relatively fixed markers in status games. Yet it can be argued that the difficulty in controlling the flow of new goods, images and information, which is generated by the modernist and market impulses within consumer societies, leads to problems of misreading the signs. The problems we encounter in everyday practice because culture fails to provide us with a single taken-for-granted recipe for action introduces difficulties, mistakes and complexity. Culture which once seemed invisible, as it was habitually inculcated into people over time and became sedimented into well-worn social routines, now surfaces as a problem. Taken-for-granted tacit knowledge about what to do, how to respond to particular groups of people and what judgement of taste to make, now becomes more problematic. Within consumer culture newspapers, magazines, television and the radio all offer advice on how to cope with a range of new situations, risks and opportunities – yet this only adds to rather than reduces complexity.

While some would see this as essentially a postmodern problem, we should be aware that Simmel (1968), writing around the turn of the century, identified this as a characteristic feature of modernity, or perhaps we should say 'the modern condition': the difficulties of coping with, and meaningfully assimilating, the overproduction of objective culture. Nearly a century later what we refer to as postmodernism can be associated with a further tightening and intensification of this process. As will be argued in Chapters 6, 7 and 8, the global dimension plays a crucially important part in our attempt to understand this process. It is not sufficient to regard the intensification of the flows of commodities, money, images, information and technology as globalizing the postmodern by exporting its cultural forms and complexity problematic from the Western centres to the rest of the world. This is to assume a neat sequence of social change based upon West European experience via its assumed master concepts of tradition, modernity and postmodernity, largely propelled by economic changes.

It is also important to examine the ways in which globalization has produced both the modern and the postmodern, in the sense that the power struggles between nation-states, blocs and other collectivities gradually became globalized as more and more parts of the world were drawn into the competing figuration of interdependencies and power balances. As is argued in the final chapter, there is an important spatial and relational dimension to modernity which is lost when we conceive it as coming out of one particular time and place with all others necessarily condemned to traverse the same route. Hence it is possible now to see the beginnings of differential reactions to modernity, through the production of a series of different cultural frames, of which the rise in the power potential of non-Western nation-states (in particular the rise of East Asia) is making us in the West increasingly aware. It might, then, be advisable to speak of global modernit*ies*, with the emphasis given to the plural forms.

Global modernities and cultural complexity

The process of globalization suggests simultaneously two images of culture. The first image entails the extension outwards of a particular culture to its limit, the globe. Heterogeneous cultures become incorporated and integrated into a dominant culture which eventually covers the whole world. The second image points to the compression of cultures. Things formerly held apart are now brought into contact and juxtaposition. Cultures pile on top of each other in heaps without obvious organizing principles. There is too much culture to handle and organize into coherent belief systems, means of orientation and practical knowledge. The first image suggests a process of conquest and unification of the global space. The world becomes a singular domesticated space, a place where everyone becomes assimilated into a common culture. In one version this dream of a secular ecumene (Tenbruck, 1990) as the endpoint of historical develop-ment, represents a global culture as the culture of the nation-state writ large. Few today would adhere to this faith in the unfolding of a historical logic to deliver us into a world state with an integrated culture. While there are processes of cultural integration, homogenization and unification at work, it is clear that they are by no means uncontested.

It may well be better to consider a global culture in the first sense to be a form, a space or field, made possible through improved means of communication in which different cultures meet and clash. This points directly towards the second aspect of the globalization of culture and at the same time suggests greater cultural movement and complexity. Yet once the spiral of relativization of culture through increased contact, juxtaposition and clashing has begun, many questions start to surface about long-held formulations of culture in the social sciences and the humanities. We need to consider the question of the perception of complexity: which groups of people represent cultures as more complex and why? What does this assertion of complexity suggest about our image of cultures as more simple and integrated in the past? How were such images possible and sustainable? How far does this point towards the need to develop a new set of cultural concepts with which to reconceptualize the role of culture in social life?

For those who like to detect the play of logics in the historical process, globalization could be seen as entailing a social integration process which runs from tribal groups to nation-state societies, superstate blocs and eventually a world state-society. While many would hesitate to go so far as to see the emergence of a world state-society based upon the global monopolization of violence and taxation, we already find references to a 'global society' (Giddens, 1994: 96–7), suggesting that various modes of global integration and forms of organization are well under way. Such an emergent global society is clearly far from being comparable to the conventional sociological notion of society which is grounded in the nation-state, and as in the case of the influential Durkheimian tradition, emphasizes normative integration and common cultural values.

If there is an emergent global society, the impetus would seem to be coming from technological developments and the economy (and it is important to conceive both in relation to social and cultural frameworks and the activities of specific groups of people and other collective agents such as nation-states, which further these developments in terms of their potential as forms of empowerment). Technological developments such as means of transportation (motor cars, railways and aeroplanes) enable the binding together of larger expanses of time-space not only on an intra-societal level, but increasingly on an inter-societal and global level. The same can be said for the mass media (radio, terrestrial and satellite TV) and new communications technology (telephones, fax, and the emergent computer network, the 'internet'). Unlike the first set of devices, which have generally been designed for monological, or one-way communication, the latter range of devices have a dialogical and interactive capacity which enables distant others across the world to pursue us and make demands on us to hit deadlines, as we strive to manage wider networks with more intense information interchanges. The development of weaponry also provides a further dramatic means of binding people together in conflict over vast areas of time and space.

In a similar way global integration can be conceived as being furthered through the expansion of economic activity to the extent that common forms of industrial production, commodities, market behaviour, trade and consumption also become generalized around the world. The expansion of the modern world system can be conceived in this way, which points to the ways in which particular nation-states and groups within nation-states have sought to expand markets and production systems (Wallerstein, 1974, 1980). To take the parallel case of global consumption, it is clear that certain retailing forms of business, techniques, sites and modes of marketing have rapidly proliferated around the world.

One noticeable example is the tremendous success of fast-food franchises such as McDonald's. George Ritzer (1993) has analysed this process which he refers to as 'McDonaldization', namely 'the process by which the principles of the fast-food restaurant are coming to dominate more and more sectors of American society as well as of the rest of the world'.

Ritzer argues that we are witnessing the McDonaldization of society and the world – something which is to be found not only in food but in car maintenance, education, child care, supermarkets, video rental outlets, cinemas, theme parks and sex. It is part of a massive bureaucratization of everyday life which leads to a progressive standardization, and this, as we shall see, cannot easily be integrated into definitions of the postmodern.

There is a further aspect to McDonaldization which Ritzer does not go into: it not only entails economic (in the form of time/money) 'efficiency' gains through standardization of the product and delivery, but also represents a cultural message. The burger is not only consumed physically as material substance, but is consumed culturally as an image and an icon of a particular way of life. Even though McDonald's do not go in for elaborate imagistic advertising, the burger is clearly American and it stands for the American way of life. It is a product from a superior global centre, which has long represented itself as *the* centre. For those on the periphery it offers the possibility of the psychological benefits of identifying with the powerful. Along with the Marlboro Man, Coca-Cola, Hollywood, Sesame Street, rock music and American football insignia, McDonald's is one of a series of icons of the American way of life. They have become associated with transposable themes which are central to consumer culture, such as youth, fitness, beauty, luxury, romance, freedom. American dreams have become intertwined with those of the good life. The extent to which these images and artefacts are exported around the world has been seen by some to point to the global homogenization of culture in which tradition gives way to American mass consumer culture. In this model of cultural imperialism (Mattelart, 1979; Schiller, 1976) the weight of economic power possessed by US corporations backed by the world's most powerful nation-state is sufficient to provide points of entry into national markets around the globe. In effect culture follows the economy.

This is well documented by travel writers who venture to the world's far-flung and wild places only to discover that the paraphernalia of American culture has got there first. Hence Pico Iyer in his *Video Nights in Kathmandu* subtitled *Reports from the Not-So-Far East*, remarks how he found that 'Everywhere, in fact, dreams of pleasure and profit were stamped "Made in America"' (1989: 23–4). The book's back-cover blurb says: 'Mohawk haircuts in Bali. In Gungzhou – in the new China – a Buffeteria serving dishes called "Yes, Sir Cheese My Baby," and "Ike and Tuna Turner."' Noticeable here too is the fact that the language of global mass consumer culture is English.

Yet even if one believes that cultures flow like water and easily dissolve the differences they encounter, there is a problem with the assumption that the United States is the centre from which everything flows out towards the periphery. This may have been relatively true up until the 1970s, but it is hard to sustain today. The United States still dominates the culture and information industries which transmit globally, but there is a growing sense of multipolarity and the emergence of competing centres. Certainly Japan and East Asia are of growing global significance, currently largely in terms of the flow of consumer goods and finance rather than images and information. The celebration of Japanese national identity, or *Nihonjinron*, has been muted or directed inwards in the postwar era, but this may not always be the case. Japanese consumer goods do not seek to sell on the back of a Japanese way of life. Indeed it can be argued that if the term Japanization of the world means anything it is in terms of a market strategy built around the notion of *dochaku*, or glocalism. The term refers to a global strategy which does not seek to impose a standard product or image, but instead is tailored to the demands of the local market. This has become a popular strategy for multinationals in other parts of the world who seek to join the rhetoric of localism.

In addition to global processes of Americanization and Japanization, or Westernization and Orientalization, it is possible also to speak of 'the Brazilianization of the world: the dual processes of zoning and cultural syncretism. A number of commentators have pointed to the emergence of 'dual cities' (Mollenkopf and Castells, 1991) which provide new juxtapositions of the new rich and the new poor. In his analysis of the development of Los Angeles, Mike Davis (1992: 20) draws attention to the way in which it is a highly segregated zoned city with its fortified core and middle- and upper-class apartment complexes in close proximity, yet separated and protected from contact with lower- and underclass ethnic ghettos and the zones of crime and disorder. Despite being an 'informational city' (Castells, 1994), Davis argues, Los Angeles more closely approximates the urban sprawl described in William Gibson's science fiction novels: a trajectory which means that it has begun to resemble São Paulo more than postmodern Tokyo-Yokohama. This form of Brazilianization based on the model of fortified zoned, divided, dangerous cities (see Banck, 1994 for a discussion of the invasions of the exclusive beach culture by *favela* people), provides an interesting alternative to the *Carmen Miranda* or samba/beach culture image of Brazil (see Enloe, 1989 for a discussion of the globalization of *Carmen Miranda*).

The ease with which people can slip in and out of ethnic identities has been remarked on by a number of commentators (Abu-Lughod, 1991). In contrast to the assimilation, or melting pot, models which worked off strong insider/outsider divisions in which identity was seen as fixed, today there is a greater acknowledgement that people can live happily with multiple identities. Hence both the evaluative stance and the terminology for those people who move around the world as migrants and are caught between culture shifts. Here we think of groups such as third-generation Brazilian Japanese living in São Paulo, who go to Japan to seek employment as migrant workers – the so-called 'Nickeys'. It is no longer adequate to seek to understand such groups through categories such as 'the marginal man', or 'halfies'. Rather, their situation is given a positive impetus in the use of the term 'doubles'.

What this suggests is that an important part of the processes which are leading to intensified globalization has to be understood in terms of the movement of people around the world. More people are living between cultures, or on the borderlines, and European and other nation-states, which formerly sought to construct a strong exclusive sense of national identity, more recently have had to deal with the fact that they are multicultural societies as 'the rest' have returned to the West in the post-1945 era.

In this context we should endeavour to draw lessons from postcolonial theory, which shares a number of the assumptions found in the post-modern critique of identity. From the point of view of postmodernism, modernity has been seen as entailing a quest to impose notions of unity and universality on thought and the world. In effect its mission is to impose order on disorder, to tame the frontier. Yet with the shifting global balance of power away from the West, with more voices talking back to the West, there is a strong sense that modernity will not be universalized. This is because modernity is seen as both a Western project and as the West's projection of its values on to the world. In effect modernity has allowed Europeans to project *their* civilization, history and knowledge as civilization, history and knowledge in general.

Instead of the confident sense that one is able to construct theory and map the world from the secure place of the centre, which is usually seen as higher and more advanced in symbolic and actual terms, postmodernism and postcolonialism present theory as mobile, or as constructed from an eccentric site, somewhere on the boundary. The movement of people from the global boundaries to the centre is coupled with a displacement of theory to the boundary, with a weakening of its authority. There is a lowering of theory's capacity to speak for people in general, to a greater acknowledgement of the limited and local nature of its assertions.

The very notion that we can undertake a comparative analysis based upon homogeneous national cultures, consensual traditions or 'organic' ethnic communities is being challenged and redefined. As Homi Bhabha (1994: 5) argues

> there is overwhelming evidence of a more transnational and translational sense of the hybridity of imagined communities. Contemporary Sri Lankan theatre represents the deadly conflict between the Tamils and the Sinhalese through allegorical references to state brutality in South Africa and Latin America; the Anglo-Celtic canon of Australian literature and cinema is being rewritten from the perspective of Aboriginal political and cultural imperatives; the South African novels of Richard Rive, Bessie Head, Nadine Gordimer, John Coetzee are documents of a society divided by apartheid that enjoin the international intellectual community to mediate on the unequal, asymmetric worlds that exist elsewhere; Salman Rushdie writes the fabulist historiography of post-independence India and Pakistan in *Midnight's Children* and *Shame*, only to remind us in *The Satanic Verses* that the truest eye may now belong to the migrant's double vision; Toni Morrison's *Beloved* revives the past of slavery and its murderous rituals of possession and self-possession, in order to project a contemporary fable of a woman's history that is at the same time the narrative

of an affective, historic memory of an emergent public sphere of men and women alike.

This conscious mixing of traditions and crossing of boundaries highlights the ways in which the rest, now so obviously visible in the West, have always been a part of the West. This destroys the unitary clean and coherent images of modernity that have been projected out of the Western centres. Postcoloniality, as Bhabha (1994: 6) remarks, points to the hybrid and syncretic perspectives of those who were confined to the borders, half inside and half outside of modernity. This for Bhabha suggests a postcolonial *contra-modernity*, visible not only in the South but in the North, not only in the countryside but in the world cities.

This position resonates with Paul Gilroy's (1993: 36) depiction of black culture and music as a distinctive counterculture of modernity in its refusal of 'the modern occidental separation of ethics and aesthetics, culture and politics'. For Gilroy, discussions of modernity rarely mention slavery and the African diaspora; nor, we might add, does colonialism manage to enter the largely intra-societally inspired sociological accounts of modernity of eminent theorists such as Giddens and Habermas. It is not only that modernity is coupled with barbarism through the degradation of shipping African slaves across the Atlantic. It is not that the figure of Columbus does not appear alongside the standard pairing of Luther and Copernicus as key figures of modernity, or that Las Casas's (1992) accounts of the genocide in Latin America are rarely spoken of alongside Auschwitz, which they dwarf. Nor that accounts of slavery are somehow confined to black history and not the intellectual history of the West as a whole. Or that slavery is often viewed sociologically as a part of a plantation economy regarded as a premodern residue fundamentally incompatible with capitalism and modern rationality.

All these factors should be grounds for rethinking the category; yet it is the fact that blacks are both inside and outside the development of Western culture within modernity which is the biggest problem. Gilroy (1993: 54) argues that slavery is the premise of modernity, something which exposes the foundational ethnocentricism of the Enlightenment project with its idea of universality, fixity of meaning and coherence of the subject. The problem is that it has produced members of society who are living denials of the validity of the project, whose existence within society, or capacity to be seen as persons or citizens was long denied. Yet black people are both Americans and black, or Europeans and black, and participate in a culture and set of collective memories which cannot be integrated with or limited to the cultures of the nation-states in which they reside. Their culture is African and Western and their identity lived through a form of 'double consciousness', formed from experiences which are both inside and outside the West, inside and outside modernity.

This clearly demands a concept of culture which can account for such displacements, which have been at the heart of the formation of modernity and which postcolonial theory will increasingly bring to the surface. It demands a conception of culture which not only discovers increasing complexity in the current phase of globalization, but also looks at previous phases of globalization and its relationship to modernity. Here we can think of the need to investigate the ways in which particular European notions of culture were generated within modernity which presented its culture as unified and integrated, which neglected the spatial relationships to the rest of the world that developed with colonialism, in effect the dark side of modernity that made this sense of unity possible.

Sociology has long taken as its subject matter society, a notion which, as is argued in Chapter 8, was developed at a particular point in the late nineteenth century when nations were preoccupied with integration as part of a nation-state formation process. It can also be argued that the focus on intra-societal mechanisms of integration was perceived as especially relevant at a point in time when nation-states were increasingly drawn into a tighter competing figuration, which encouraged the strong assertion of national identity. Today the level of global interdependencies and conflict across and through the boundaries of the nation-state make the heritage of this artificial division of labour harder to justify.

Postmodernism and postcolonialism have pointed to the problem of cultural complexity and the increasing salience of culture in social life through the greater production, mixing and syncretism of cultures which were formerly held separate and firmly attached to social relationships. The radical implications of postmodernism and postcolonial theory are to question the very idea of the social, the unity of modernity and the metanarratives of the Western Enlightenment tradition with its belief in universalism and progress. This suggests a spatial relativization of the West in a world which ceases to be its own projection or mirror image (c.f. Said on Orientalism). Works such as Said's (1978) emerged from the fact that: (a) more people are crossing boundaries and have multiple affiliations which question taken-for-granted stereotypes; and (b) there has been a shift in the global balance of power away from the West to the extent that it cannot now avoid listening to the 'other', or assume that the latter is at an earlier stage of development.

The Western self-image and that of the passive other, are under in-creasing contestation, so it is not surprising that one of the forces associated with postmodernism has been postcolonialism (Spivak, Trin T. Minh-ha, Bhabha, Gilroy, Hall, *et al.*). The changing global circumstance as a result of the process of globalization has provoked a particular Western reaction to this situation in the form of postmodernism, which has engaged in a far-reaching questioning of its own tradition, albeit generally conceived in *internal* terms and not addressed to the spatial relations of the West to the rest of the world.

It is no longer possible to conceive global processes in terms of the dominance of a single centre over the peripheries. Rather there are a number of competing centres which are bringing about shifts in the global balance of power between nation-states and blocs and forging new sets of interdependencies. This is not to suggest a condition of equality between participants but a process which is seeing more players admitted to the game who are demanding access to means of communication and the right to be heard. The expansion and speed of forms of communication means that it is more difficult for governments to police and control the volume of information and image flows that cross their frontiers.

Our image of culture has become more complex. This leads to a number of important questions about the image of culture we have long operated with in the social sciences. This image may have presented an over-simplified view of a culture as something integrated, unified, settled and static; something relatively well-behaved which performed the task of oiling the wheels of social life in an ordered society. If this image is now seen as inadequate to capture the current phase of globalization with its nation-state deformation processes, how did it arise and become so influential? If it was associated with the construction of national cultures alongside state formation, was it always more of an ideal, an intention rather than an actuality? Something which suppressed the various levels of complexity and difference already inherent within modern societies?

Rather than the emergence of a unified global culture there is a strong tendency for the process of globalization to provide a stage for global differences not only to open up a 'world showcase of cultures' in which the examples of the distant exotic are brought directly into the home, but to provide a field for a more discordant clashing of cultures. While cultural integration processes are taking place on a global level the situation is becoming increasingly pluralistic, or polytheistic, a world with many competing gods, along the lines Weber (1948b) discusses in his 'Science as a vocation' essay. This has been referred to as the global babble. It has meant that 'the rest are increasingly speaking back to the West' and along with the relative decline of Western power it has required that the West has increasingly been forced to listen. It is no longer as easy for Western nations to maintain the superiority of adopting a 'civilizational mission' towards the rest of the world, in which the others are depicted as occupying the lower rungs of a symbolic hierarchy, which they are gradually being educated to climb up to follow their betters. Rather, this modernist image, at the heart of modernization theory, is being disputed and challenged. As we shall see, the term 'postmodernism' can be understood as pointing to this process of cultural fragmentation and collapse of symbolic hierarchies which, I would argue, gains much of its impetus from the awareness of a shift in the value of the symbolic power and cultural capital of the West, rather than a move to a new stage of history, 'postmodernity,' itself premised upon a developmental model of tradition and modernity constructed from Western experience. This, then, is one important sense in which postmodernism points to the decentring of culture and the introduction of cultural complexity.

The process of globalization, then, does not seem to be producing cultural uniformity; rather it makes us aware of new levels of diversity. If there is a global culture it would be better to conceive of it not as a common culture, but as a field in which differences, power struggles and cultural prestige contests are played out. Something akin to an underlying form which permits the recognition and playing out of differences along the lines of Durkheim's non-contractual aspects of contract, or Simmel's analysis of the taken-for-granted common ground underpinning social conflict. Hence globalization makes us aware of the sheer volume, diversity and many-sidedness of culture. Syncretisms and hybridizations are more the rule than the exception – which makes us raise the question of the origins and maintenance of the particular image of culture we have long operated with in the social sciences, to which we will now turn.

2
THE AUTONOMIZATION OF THE CULTURAL SPHERE

Max Weber's theory of cultural rationalization and differentiation is well known. For Weber the development of modernity not only involved a long process of differentiation of the capitalist economy and the modern state but also entailed a cultural rationalization with the emergence of separate scientific, aesthetic and moral value spheres. Weber's (1948c) discussion of the differentiation of the cultural sphere from a more rudimentary, holistic, religious cultural core is conducted at a high level of abstraction. Although Weber provides brief glimpses of the way in which each aspect of the cultural sphere is relentlessly driven by its own logic, the way in which values relate to lifestyle and conduct, and the tensions experienced by intellectuals, the 'cultivated man' and the cultural specialists, his prime purpose was to sketch out a typology (Weber, 1948c: 323–4; this aspect of Weber's work will be discussed more fully in the next chapter). While we do find fuller discussions of the cultural sphere in the writings of Bell (1976) and Habermas (1984a), we need to build on these sources if we seek to understand the particular conjunction of culture in contemporary Western societies. In effect we need to investigate the conditions for the development of the cultural sphere by focusing on particular historical sequences and locations. First, we need to understand the emergence of relatively autonomous culture (knowledge and other symbolic media) in relation to the growth in the autonomy and power potential of specialists in symbolic production. We therefore need to focus on the *carriers* of culture and the contradictory pressures that are generated by changing interdependencies and power struggles of the growing fraction within the middle class towards dual processes of (a) the monopolization and separation of a cultural enclave, and (b) the demonopolization and diffusion of culture to wider publics. Second, we need to focus on the development of separate institutions and lifestyles for cultural specialists and examine the relation between value complexes and conduct in the various life orders, not only in terms of a cultural sphere conceived as the arts and the academy ('high culture') but also in terms of the generation of oppositional countercultures (bohemias, artistic avant-gardes and other cultural movements). Third, we need to comprehend the relational dynamic of a parallel development to that of the cultural sphere: the general expansion of cultural production via 'culture industries' and the generation of a wider market for cultural and other symbolic goods to produce what has been termed a *mass culture* or a *consumer culture*. Both tendencies have contributed to the increasing prominence of culture within modern societies – tendencies that threaten to erode and domesticate everyday culture, the taken-for-granted stock of memories, traditions and myths.

This suggests that cultural specialists are often caught in an ambivalent relationship toward the market that may lead to strategies of separation and distancing to sustain and promote the autonomy of the cultural sphere. At the same time, in terms of their interdependencies and power struggles with the other groups (notably economic specialists), this may dispose them to use the marketplace to reach wider audiences to bolster their general societal power and increase the prestige and public value of their specialist cultural goods. Conditions that favour the autonomization of the cultural sphere will better allow cultural specialists to monopolize, regulate and control cultural production, to seek to place cultural production above economic production, and to place art and intellectual pursuits above everyday life, popular uneducated tastes and mass culture. Alternatively, conditions that threaten the autonomy of the cultural sphere, the demonopolization processes that discredit the 'sacred' intellectual and artistic symbolic hierarchies, will tend to allow outsider groups of cultural specialists, or encourage new alliances of particular groups of cultural specialists with other powerful groups of economic specialists, to endorse alternative tastes and seek to legitimize an expanded repertoire that may include the formerly excluded popular traditions and mass cultural goods. Without an attempt to comprehend the rising and declining fortunes of particular groups of cultural specialists and their shifting relation to other groups of power-holders such as economic specialists, it may be difficult to make sense of those who mourn or applaud present-day assertions, such as 'the end of art', 'the end of the avant-garde', 'the end of the intellectuals', and 'the end of culture' (Featherstone, 1991a).

In this chapter we will look at various approaches that have addressed these issues. This will be done via an examination of three major conceptions of the development of an enlarged field of cultural production, which entails analysing the interrelationship of the development of the cultural sphere and a mass consumer culture. First, we examine the production of culture perspective in which a mass culture that is presented as threatening to engulf and debase the culture sphere is seen as the logical outcome of the process of capitalist commodity production. Second, we examine a mode of consumption approach, which draws on anthropological perspectives to argue that there are similarities in the consumption of symbolic goods in all societies and that we should refrain from evaluating mass-produced culture in a negative way. Rather, the classification of cultural goods and tastes (be they everyday consumer durables, lifestyle practices, or high cultural pursuits), must be understood as operating relationally within the same social space. This sociogenetic perspective focuses on how the symbolic aspects of goods and activities are used practically to draw the boundaries of social relationships. Third, we explore a psychogenetic perspective on cultural consumption that examines the genesis of the propensity and desire to consume new goods and experiences. Such a perspective, which focuses upon the middle class and draws upon Weber's notion of ideal interests, also raises the issue of the long-term process of the generation of habitus, dispositions and means of orientation in different interdependent and competing groups of people. Finally, we return to a discussion of the cultural sphere and suggest some of the conditions that favour its formation and deformation and the generation of particular evaluations of mass culture by a set of cultural specialists. This attempt to identify how such issues should be addressed can help us to better understand the process of cultural development and to move beyond statically conceived notions of the cultural sphere, market culture, mass culture, consumer culture, everyday culture, and deeply ingrained cultural traditions and codes.

Producing commodified consumption

The study of consumption has long been regarded as the province of economics, and, although Adam Smith argued that 'consumption is the sole end purpose of all production' (Minchinton, 1982: 219), the analysis of consumption has been largely neglected in favour of production and distribution. This neglect may have resulted from the assumption that consumption was unproblematic because it was based upon the concept of rational individuals buying goods to maximize their satisfaction. That rational choice might be modified by social pressures such as the customs and habits of the people was given only minor acknowledgement. In the late nineteenth century we find some interest in external effects on utility, such as conspicuous consumption, the snob effect, and the bandwagon effect as found in particular in the writings of Veblen (1953) (see also Minchinton, 1982: 221). In general, sociological interest in the move to mass consumption in the second half of the nineteenth century was restricted to indicating the limitations of strictly economic or market explanations of human behaviour. This sociological critique of economics has sometimes been coupled with a concern that mass consumption brought about social deregulation and a threat to the social bond. The move to intensified mass production, mass consumption, and the extension of the market into more areas of life is thus generally seen as harmful to culture. The new culture produced for mass consumption, then, was often viewed negatively, especially by neo-Marxist critics, who regarded advertising, the mass media and the entertainment industries as logical extensions of commodity production in which markets were monopolized to produce mass deception and a debased consumer culture. The tendency has been to deduce the effects on consumption of culture from the production of culture and, within the neo-Marxist framework, to follow variants of the base–superstructure model. From this perspective it is possible to regard the logic of capitalist mass production as leading to a more extensive mass society.

One of the clearest statements on the power of the productive forces in society to harness consumption to fit with its designs is the Frankfurt School's theory of the culture industry. Non-work activities in general become subsumed under the same instrumental rationality and commodity logic of the workplace, and artistic and cultural goods become subjected to the same standardization and pseudo-individualization used in the production of other goods. Hence Horkheimer and Adorno (1972: 137) state that 'Amusement under late capitalism is the prolongation of work.' Art, which formerly supplied the *promesse de bonheur*, the yearning for the otherness that transcends the existing reality, now openly becomes a commodity. As Horkheimer and Adorno remark, 'What is new is not that it is a commodity, but that today it deliberately admits it is one; that art renounces its own autonomy and proudly takes its place among consumption goods constitutes the charm of novelty' (1972: 157). The culture industry offered the prospect of a manufactured culture in which discrimination and knowledge of culture (the high culture of the literati) was swamped and replaced by a mass culture (the prestige seeker replacing the connoisseur) in which reception was dictated by exchange value. For Adorno the increasing dominance of exchange value obliterated the original use value (in the case of art, the *promesse de bonheur*, the enjoyment, pleasure, or 'purposiveness without purpose' with which the object was to be approached) and replaced it with exchange value (its instrumental market value or 'currency'). This freed the commodity to take on a wide range of secondary or artificial associations, and advertising, in particular, took advantage of this capacity.

From this perspective advertising not only used, transformed or replaced traditional high culture to promote the consumption of commodities and further mass deception but also drew attention to the symbolic aspect of commodities. The triumph of economic exchange need not just entail the eclipse of traditional culture and high culture, but a new 'artificial' culture was generated from 'below', via the logic of commodity production, to replace them. Hence, a number of commentators have focused upon the centrality of advertising in the genesis of a consumer culture (Ewen, 1976; Ewen and Ewen, 1982; Leiss *et al.*, 1986).

Another example of the interpretation of the culture of consumption in terms of the commodification of everyday life is found in the work of Fredric Jameson. Following the capital logic approach, which points to the profusion of a new artificial culture with the extension of commodity production, Jameson (1979: 139) emphasizes that 'culture is the very element of consumer society itself; no society has ever been saturated with signs and messages like this one . . . the omnipresence of the image in consumer capitalism [means that] the priorities of the real become reversed, and everything is mediated by culture'. This perspective is central to his influential paper 'Postmodernism or the cultural logic of late capitalism', in which he outlines the contours of postmodern culture (Jameson, 1984a: 87).

A similar emphasis upon cultural profusion and disorder, which threatens to obliterate the last vestiges of traditional popular culture or high culture, is found in the work of Jean Baudrillard, on which Jameson draws. Baudrillard (1970) builds on the commodification theory of Lukács and Lefebvre, arguing that consumption involves the active manipulation of signs and that what is consumed is not objects but the system of objects, the sign system that makes up the code. Baudrillard draws on semiology to develop the cultural implications of commodity analysis and argues that in late capitalist society sign and commodity have fused to produce the commodity-sign. The logic of political economy for Baudrillard has therefore involved a semiological revolution entailing not just the replacement of use value by exchange value, but eventually the replacement of both by sign value. This leads to the autonomization of the signifier, which can be manipulated (for example through advertising) to float free from a stable relationship to objects and establish its own associative chains of meaning.

In Baudrillard's later writings (1983a, 1983b), reference to economics, class and mode of production disappear. Indeed at one point in *Symbolic Exchange and Death* Baudrillard (1993) tilts at Bourdieu when he argues that social analysis in terms of normativity or class is doomed to failure because it belongs to a stage of the system that we have now superseded. The new stage of the system is the postmodern simulational world in which television, the machine of simulation *par excellence*, endlessly reduplicates the world. This switch to the production and reproduction of copies for which there is no original, the simulacrum, effaces the distinction between the real and the imaginary. According to Baudrillard (1993: 148), we now live 'in an "aesthetic" hallucination of reality'. The ultimate terminus of the expansion of the commodity production system is the triumph of signifying culture and the death of the social: a 'post-society' configuration that escapes sociological classification and explanation, an endless cycle of the reduplication and overproduction of signs, images and simulations that leads to an implosion of meaning. We are now in the increasingly familiar territory of the alleged transformation of reality into images in the postmodern, schizoid, depthless culture. All that remains on the human level is the masses, the silent majority, which acts as a 'black hole' (Baudrillard, 1983b: 9), absorbing the overproduction of energy and information from the media and cynically watching the fascinating endless play of signs. Baudrillard's conception of mass has taken us a long way from mass culture theory, in which the manipulation of the masses through the popular media plays a central role. For him the logic of commodity development has seen the triumph of culture, a new post-modern phase of cultural disorder in which the distinctions between levels of culture – high, folk, popular, or class – give way to a glutinous mass that simulates and plays with the overproduction of signs.

Today the high culture/mass culture debate arouses little passion in academic life. Since the mid-1970s the attacks on the distinction between high culture and mass culture have proceeded apace. Particularly influential in the British context has been the work of the Birmingham Centre for Contemporary Cultural Studies (see Hall *et al.*, 1980) and the Open University (see Bennett *et al.*, 1977; Bennett *et al.*, 1981). One finds a wide range of criticisms revolving around the alleged elitism of the Frankfurt School's pro-high-culture distinction between individuality and pseudo-individuality, which condemns the masses to manipulation (Bennett *et al.*, 1977; Swingewood, 1977). Other criticisms include the outmoded puritanism and prudery of those arguments that favour notions of creative production against the right of the masses to enjoy its consumption and pleasures (Leiss, 1983; *New Formations*, 1983); the invalidity of the distinction between true and false needs found in the critiques of consumer society and its culture in the work of Marcuse (1964), Debord (1970) and Ewen (1976) (see Sahlins, 1976; Leiss, 1983; Springborg, 1981); and the neglect of the egalitarian and democratic currents in mass culture, the process of levelling up and not down, that finds one of its strongest statements in Shils (1960) (see also Swingewood, 1977; Kellner, 1983). There have also been criticisms that the foundation of the critique of mass culture is to be found in an essentially nostalgic *Kulturpressimismus* perspective on the part of intellectuals who were entrapped in a myth of premodern stability, coherence and community (Stauth and Turner, 1988a), or a nostalgia for a presimulational social world such as we find in Baudrillard's work. The critics of mass culture theories have also neglected complex social differentiations (Wilensky, 1964), the ways in which mass-produced commodities can be customized, or signs can be reversed with their meanings renegotiated critically or oppositionally (see the work on youth subcultures by the Birmingham Centre for Contemporary Cultural Studies, especially Hebdige, 1979 on punk; also de Certeau, 1981). In addition there is Raymond Williams's (1961) pronouncement that 'there are no masses, only other people'. Such critiques point to the importance of transcending the view that uniformity of consumption is dictated by production and emphasize the need to investigate the actual use and reception of goods in various practices. Such critiques also entail a revaluation of popular practices, which are no longer to be seen as debased and vulgar. Rather, the integrity of the culture of the common people is defended and suspicion is cast upon the whole enterprise of the construction of an autonomous cultural sphere with its rigid symbolic hierarchies, exclusive canons, and classifications.

Symbolic goods and social order

Focusing on the consumption of culture rather than on production points us toward the differential reception and use of mass-produced cultural goods and experiences and the ways in which popular culture has failed to be eclipsed by mass culture. Indeed, if we take a long-term process approach to cultural formation it is clear that cultural objects are continually redesignated and move from popular to high to mass, and vice versa. In this sense, popular and folk culture cannot provide a pristine baseline for culture because they have a long history of being packaged and commodified. Hence, the emphasis should switch from more abstract views of cultural production to the actual practices of cultural production on the part of particular groups of cultural specialists and the ways in which they relate to the actual practices of consumption on the part of different groups.

Considerable insight into this process is gained by analysing anthropological research on consumption that focuses on the symbolic aspect of goods and their role as communicators. From this perspective, goods are used to mark boundaries between groups, to create and demarcate differences or communality between figurations of people (see Douglas and Isherwood, 1980; Sahlins, 1976; Leiss, 1983; Appadurai, 1986). Leiss (1978: 19), for example, argues that, while utilities in all cultures are symbolic, goods are in effect *doubly* symbolic in contemporary Western societies: symbolism is consciously employed in the design and imagery attached to goods in the production and marketing process, and symbolic associations are used by consumers in using goods to construct differentiated lifestyle models.

The work of Douglas and Isherwood (1980) is particularly important in this respect because of their emphasis on how goods are used to draw the lines of social relationships. Our enjoyment of goods, they argue, is only partly related to physical consumption. It is also crucially linked to their role as *markers*; we enjoy, for example, sharing the names of goods with others (the sports fan or the wine connoisseur). In addition, the mastery of the cultural person entails a seemingly 'natural' mastery, not only of information (the autodidact 'memory man') but also of how to use and consume appropriately and with natural ease in every situation. In this sense the consumption of high cultural goods (art, novels, opera, philosophy) must be related to the ways in which other, more mundane, cultural goods (clothing, food, drink, leisure pursuits) are handled and consumed, and high culture must be inscribed into the same social space as everyday cultural consumption. In Douglas and Isherwood's (1980: 176ff.) discussion, consumption classes are defined in relation to the consumption of three sets of goods: a staple set (for example food), a technology set (travel and capital equipment), and an information set (information goods, education, arts, and cultural and leisure pursuits). At the lower end of the social structure the poor are restricted to the staple set and have more time on their hands, but those in the top consumption class require not only a higher level of earnings but also a competence in judging information goods and services. This entails a considerable investment in time, both as a lifelong investment in cultural and symbolic capital and as an investment in maintaining consumption activities (it is in this sense that we refer to the title of Linder's [1970] book, *The Harried Leisure Class*, another play on the work of Veblen [1953] on conspicuous consumption). Hence the competition to acquire goods in the information class generates high admission barriers and effective techniques of exclusion.

The phasing, duration and intensity of time invested in acquiring competences for handling information, goods and services, as well as the day-to-day practice, conservation and maintenance of these competences, are, as Halbwachs reminds us, useful criteria of social class. Our use of time in consumption practices conforms to our class habitus and, there-fore, conveys an accurate idea of our class status (see the discussion of Halbwachs in Preteceille and Terrail, 1985: 23). This points us towards the importance of research on the different long-term investments in infor-mational acquisition and cultural capital of particular groups. Such research has been carried out in detail by Bourdieu and his associates (Bourdieu *et al.*, 1965; Bourdieu and Darbel, 1966; Bourdieu and Passeron, 1971; Bourdieu, 1984). For Bourdieu (1984) particular constel-lations of taste, consumption preferences and lifestyle practices are associ-ated with specific occupation and class fractions, making it possible to map the universe of taste and lifestyles with all its structured oppositions and finely graded distinctions that operate at a particular point in history. Yet within capitalist societies the volume of production of new goods results in an endless struggle to obtain what Hirsch (1976) calls 'positional goods', goods that define social status. The constant supply of new, fashionably desirable goods, or the usurpation of existing marker goods by lower groups, produces a paperchase effect in which those above have to invest in new (informational) goods to re-establish the original social distance.

It is therefore possible to refer both to societies in which the tendency is for the progressive breakdown of the barriers that restrict the production of new goods and the capacity of commodities to travel, and to societies with the counter-tendency to restrict, control and channel exchange in order to establish enclaved commodities. In some societies, status systems are guarded and reproduced by restricting equivalences and exchange in a *stable* universe of commodities. In other societies with a fashion system, *taste* in an ever-changing universe of commodities is restricted and controlled, and at the same time there is the illusion of individual choice and unrestricted access. Sumptuary laws are an intermediate consumption-regulating device for societies with stable status displays which face the deregulation of the flow of commodities, for example premodern Europe (Appadurai, 1986: 25). The tendencies noted by Jameson, Baudrillard and others towards the overproduction of symbolic goods in contemporary societies suggest that the bewildering flow of signs, images, information, fashions and styles would be impossible to subject to a final or coherent reading (see Featherstone, 1991a).

Examples of this alleged cultural disorder are often taken from the media (Baudrillard, for example, does this), yet apart from grand statements such as 'television is the world', we are given little understanding of how this disorder affects the everyday practices of different figurations of people. It can be argued that as long as face-to-face encounters continue between embodied persons, attempts will be made to read a person's demeanour for clues as to his or her social standing. The different styles and labels of fashionable clothing and goods, however much subject to change, imitation and copying, are one such set of clues. Yet as Bourdieu (1984) reminds us with his concept of symbolic capital, the signs of the dispositions and classificatory schemes that betray a person's origins and trajectory through life are manifest in body shape, size, weight, stance, walk, demeanour, tone of voice, style of speaking, sense of bodily ease or discomfort, and so on. Hence culture is incorporated, and it is not just a question of what clothes are worn but of how they are worn. Advice books on manners, taste and etiquette – from Erasmus to Nancy Mitford's 'U' and 'Non-U' – impress on their subjects the need to naturalize dispositions and manners, to be completely at home with them. At the same time the newly arrived may display signs of the burden of attainment and the incompleteness of their cultural competence. Hence the new rich, who often adopt conspicuous consumption strategies, are recognizable and assigned their place in the social space. Their cultural practices are always in danger of being dismissed as vulgar and tasteless by the established upper class, the aristocracy, and those 'rich in cultural goods' – the intellectuals and artists.

From one perspective, artistic and intellectual goods are enclaved commodities whose capacity to move around in the social space is limited by their ascribed sacred qualities. In this sense the specialists in symbolic production will seek to increase the autonomy of the cultural sphere and to restrict the supply and access to such goods, in effect creating and preserving an enclosure of high culture. This can take the form of rejecting the market and any economic use of the goods and adopting a lifestyle that is the opposite of the successful economic specialist (disorder versus order, the cultivation of transgressions strategies, the veneration of natural talent and genius against systematic achievement and work, and so on). Yet as Bourdieu (1979, 1984) indicates, there is an interest in disinterestedness, and it is possible to chart the hidden and misrecognized economy in cultural goods with its own forms of currency, rates of conversion to economic capital, and so on. The problem of the intellectuals in market situations is that they must achieve and retain this degree of closure and control that enables artistic and intellectual goods to remain enclaved commodities. Indeed, as many commentators have pointed out, this is the paradox of intellectuals and artists: their necessary dependence on, yet distaste for and desire for independence from, the market. Within situations of an overproduction of symbolic goods, there may be intensified competition from new cultural intermediaries (the expanding design, advertising, marketing, commercial art, graphics, journalistic, media, and fashion occupations) and other 'outsider' intellectuals that have emerged from the postwar expansion of higher education in Western societies. This competition may lead to the inability of established intellectuals to maintain the stability of symbolic hierarchies, and the resultant phase of cultural declassification opens a space for the generation of interest in popular culture on what is proclaimed to be a more egalitarian and democratic basis.

We have therefore moved from considering the production of culture from a mode of production perspective to one that, following Preteceille and Terrail's (1985: 36) depiction of Bourdieu's work, we can call a *mode of consumption* approach. From this point of view, demand and cultural consumption are not merely dictated by supply, but they must be understood within a social framework, that is, as sociogenetically induced: a perspective which emphasizes that 'consumption is eminently social, relational, and active rather than private, atomic, or passive' (Appadurai, 1986: 31).

Romanticism, desire and middle-class consumption

The mode of consumption perspective emphasizes the continuities in the socially structured handling and use of goods between contemporary capitalist and other types of societies. The 'psychogenetic' perspective, like the production of consumption approach, focuses on explaining the proliferation of new goods. In contrast to the latter's emphasis on *supply*, the psychogenetic approach concentrates on the problem of the *demand* for new goods. This entails a move from economic-centred analysis to questions of desire – to the puzzle of the genesis of the propensity to consume anew, the motivational complex that develops a thirst for pleasure, poverty, self-expression and self-realization through goods. In a manner reminiscent of Weber's *Protestant Ethic*, Campbell (1987) argues that the rise of consumption, like that of capitalist production, requires an ethic, and in this case it is romanticism, with its focus on imagination, fantasy, mysticism, creativity and emotional exploration, and not Protestantism, that supplies the impetus.[1] He writes: 'The essential activity of consumption is thus not actual selection, purchase or use of products, but the imaginative pleasure-seeking to which the product image lends itself, "real" consumption being largely a result of this "mentalistic" hedonism' (Campbell, 1987: 89). From this perspective, the pleasure derived from novels, paintings, plays, records, films, radio, television and fashion is not the result of manipulation by the advertisers or an 'obsession with social status', but it is the illusory enjoyment stimulated by daydreaming. The disposition to live out desires, fantasies and daydreams, or the capacity to spend a good deal of time in pursuit of them, may vary among different social groups. Campbell locates its origins in relation to consumerism within the eighteenth-century English middle class. Groups that have achieved a high degree of literacy are likely to be more disposed to take ideas and character ideals seriously and, as Weber pointed out, to seek to achieve consistency in conduct. Yet how far can we understand mass consumption by focusing solely upon the development of a romantic ethic in the middle class? To understand the consumption habits of the middle class in the eighteenth century we need to locate the habits of this group in relation to those of the lower and the upper classes.

We have already referred to the contrast between societies that restrict the exchange of commodities in order to reproduce a stable status system and societies that have an ever-changing universe of commodities and a fashion system with the appearance of complete interchangeability, which actually can be considered in terms of socially structured taste. Consumption in the upper class or aristocracy tends more towards the reproduction of a stable status system, which also includes phases of liminal excess and transgression (carnivals, fairs, and so on). Mennell (1987) reminds us that the aristocracy in court society became 'specialists in the arts of consumption entrapped in a system of fine distinctions, status battles, and competitive expenditure from which they could not escape because their whole society depended upon it'. Here the fashion code was restricted rather than elaborated and the courtier had to conform to strict rules of dress, manners and deportment (Elias, 1983: 232). In court societies such as Versailles during the reign of Louis XIV, consumption was highly structured in terms of the regulation of etiquette, ceremony, taste, dress, manners and conversation. Every detail was perceived as an instrument in the struggle for prestige. The ability to read appearance and gestures for slight giveaway clues and the time spent in decoding the demeanour and conversation of others indicate how a courtier's very existence depended on calculation.

These tight restrictions on behaviour in court society produced a number of countermovements that sought to compensate for the suppression of feeling and court rationality by the emancipation of feeling. We are generally inclined to perceive these contrasting positions as involving class differences between the aristocracy (the dissimulating, artful, false courtier) and the middle class (the virtuous, sincere, honest citizen) and to formulate them in terms of other-directed and inner-directed qualities. Elias (1978: 19), in the early part of *The Civilizing Process*, shows how the German middle class venerated *Kultur* with romantic ideals of love of nature, solitude, and surrender to the excitement of one's own heart. Here the middle-class outsiders, spatially dispersed and isolated, can be contrasted to the established court with its ideals drawn from French *civilisation*. From this a further series of contrasts can be made between the middle-class intelligentsia and the aristocratic courtier: inwardness and depth of feeling versus superficiality and ceremony; immersion in books and education and the development of personal identity versus formal conversation and courtly manners; and virtue versus honour (see Vowinckel, 1987).

Yet there are also links between the middle-class romantic emphasis upon sincerity and the development of romantic tendencies within the aristocracy. Elias (1983: 214ff.), in 'The sociogenesis of aristocratic romanticism', argues that one of the influential forerunners of bourgeois romanticism, Rousseau, owed some of his success to the ways in which his ideas were perceived as a reaction to court rationality and the suppression of 'feeling' in court life. The idealization of nature and the melancholic longing of country life is found in the early eighteenth-century nobility at the court of Louis XIV. The sharp contrast between court and country, the complexity of court life, and the incessant self-control and necessary calculation contributed to a nostalgia for the idealized rural existence described in the romantic utopias filled with shepherds and shepherdesses in novels such as *L'Astrée* by Honoré d'Urfé. Elias can detect both clear discontinuities and similar processes in the sociogenesis of bourgeois and aristocratic romanticism. He refers (1983: 262) to the middle classes as 'dual-front classes' that are exposed to social pressures from groups above who possess greater power, authority and prestige and from groups below who are inferior in these qualities. The pressures for self-control in relation to the codes of professional life, coupled with pressures of being in a dual-front class, may help to generate an ambivalence towards the system of rules and self-constraints that nourish a dream-image of a more direct, spontaneous expression of emotion.

The implications of the role of the romantic ethic in the genesis of consumerism should now be clearer. Romanticism cannot be assumed just to work as a set of ideas that induced more direct emotional expression through fantasies and daydreaming and that translated into the desire for new commodities to nourish this longing. Rather, we need to understand the sociogenesis of romantic tendencies that were generated in the rivalries and interdependencies of the aristocracy and the middle classes. These pressures may have nourished a romantic longing for the unconstrained, expressive and spontaneous life that was projected on to commodities and manifest in fashion, novel reading, and other popular entertainments catered for in the burgeoning public sphere. Yet the practicalities of everyday life, the social demands of sustaining one's acceptability, were also important forces. Social constraints demanded from middle-class professionals careful attention to etiquette, dress, demeanour, and an ordered, measured consumption. Unlike the courtier class, the middle classes enjoyed a private life in which they could be 'off stage'. Yet it is easy to overestimate the freedom and independence of the private sphere. The pressures to maintain a style of social life concomitant with one's status led to increasing pressures to codify and regulate domestic consumption, artistic taste, food and festivities (see Elias, 1983: 116).

When we look more specifically at the middle class, we need to consider the different situations in particular nations in the eighteenth century. The situation of the English middle class was very different from that of the French and the German. England provided a middling case in which closer links existed between court life and country life and between a more differentiated aristocracy, the gentry, and the middle class (Elias and Dunning, 1987: 35; Mennell, 1985: 119). In the eighteenth and early nineteenth centuries, landed London society was a reference group for those in the rising middle-class strata who emulated its tastes, manners and fashions (Mennell, 1985: 212). Davidoff (1973: 13) has noted how, in early nineteenth-century housekeeping manuals, etiquette books and magazines, increased expenditures on ceremonial displays to maintain an expected lifestyle became requisite (and see Mennell, 1985: 209).

Evidence suggests that the middle class in eighteenth-century England encountered increasing pressure for consumption from below. What has been referred to as the 'consumer revolution' in the eighteenth century involved increased consumption of luxury goods, fashion, household goods, popular novels, magazines, newspapers and entertainment and the means of marketing them through advertising to an enlarged buying public (see McKendrick et al., 1982). The lower classes were drawn into this expansion of consumption by adopting fashions that emulated the upper classes, and fashion diffused down the social scale much more widely in England than in other European countries (McKendrick et al., 1982: 34ff.).

One important reason why emulation was possible and new fashion was transmitted so rapidly was that they took place within an urban milieu. London was the largest city in Europe in the eighteenth century and it exercised a considerable dominance over other European countries. Changing fashions, the display of new goods in shops, and conspicuous consumption were clearly visible and were topics of everyday conversation. The narrowing of social distances and the swing towards informal relations between the classes also became manifest in a new use of public space within London, which has come to be called the *public sphere*. The public sphere was comprised of social institutions: periodicals, journals, clubs, and coffee-houses in which individuals could gather for unconstrained discussion (see Habermas, 1974; Eagleton, 1984; Stallybrass and White, 1986: 80ff.). The emergence of the public sphere is closely tied to the development of the cultural sphere. The profession of literary criticism and the independent specialists in cultural production who wrote for newspapers and magazines and produced novels for their newly enlarged audiences developed dramatically by mid-eighteenth century (Williams, 1961; Hohendahl, 1982). The city coffee-houses became centres where people gathered to read or to hear newspapers and magazines read aloud and to discuss them (Lowenthal, 1961: 56). Not only were the coffee-houses democratic domains for free cultural discussion (cf. Mannheim, 1956), they were also spaces of civility, a cleansed discursive environment freed from the low-others, the 'grotesque bodies', of the alehouse (Stallybrass and White, 1986: 95). The coffee-houses replaced 'idle' and festive consumption with productive leisure. They were *decent*, ordered places that demanded a withdrawal from popular culture, which was increasingly viewed from a negative perspective.

While there was therefore a movement towards a democratization of cultural interchange *and* a differentiation of culture between the respectable, decent and civil and the ill-controlled lower orders in the eighteenth century, this was a part of a long-term process. Burke (1978: 24) argues that in the sixteenth century there were two traditions in culture: the classical tradition of philosophy and theology learned in schools and universities and the popular tradition contained in folksongs, folktales, devotional images, mystery plays, chapbooks, fairs and festivals. Yet the upper levels directly participated in popular culture, and even in the early eighteenth century not all were disengaged from the culture of the common people. Burke (1978: 286) suggests that in 1500 the educated strata despised the common people although they shared their culture. Yet by 1800 their descendants had ceased to join spontaneously in popular culture and were rediscovering it as something exotic and interesting. The culture of the lower orders remained a source of fascination, and the symbolism of this tradition remained important as a strand within the high culture of the middle classes (Stallybrass and White, 1986: 107). The carnivalesque, with its hybridization, mixing of codes, grotesque bodies and transgressions, remained a fascinating spectacle for eighteenth-century writers, including Pope, Rousseau and Wordsworth. While one part of this tradition emerged in the artistic bohemias of the mid-nineteenth century, with their deliberate transgressions of bourgeois culture and invocation of liminoid grotesque body symbolism associated with the carnivalesque, another developed into romanticism. When Frederick the Great published his *De la littérature allemande* in 1780, he protested against the social mixing and transgression and manifest lack of taste in 'the abominable works of Shakespeare' over which 'the whole audience goes into raptures when it listens to these ridiculous farces worthy of the savages in Canada' (quoted in Elias, 1978: 14). For the bourgeois intellectuals and their public against whom Frederick directed his remarks, the actual savages of North America (Voltaire's *L'Ingénu*) and of Tahiti (Bougainville's *Voyage*) held a growing fascination as 'exotic otherness'.

At the same time, then, that traditional popular culture was beginning to disappear, European intellectuals were discovering, recording and formulating the culture of the people (see Burke, 1978). In part this was a reaction against the enlightened gentility of the 'civilized' classical culture of the court and the aristocracy (Lunn, 1986) and the uniform rationalism and universalism of the Enlightenment. Herder, for example, was sensitive to cultural diversity, the particularity of each cultural community, and wanted the different cultures to be considered on an equal basis. This strand developed into a critique of the French sociocentric identification of their own culture, designated as 'civilization' and 'high culture', as *the* universal metaculture of mankind (Dumont, 1986).

Concluding remarks: the development of the cultural sphere

The development of the cultural sphere must be seen as part of a long-term process that involved the growth in the power potential of the specialists in symbolic production which produced two contradictory consequences. There was a greater autonomy in the nature of the knowledge produced and the monopolization of production and consumption in specialist enclaves with the development of strong ritual classifications to exclude outsiders. There was also a greater expansion of knowledge and cultural goods produced for new audiences and markets in which existing hier-archical classifications were dismantled and specialist cultural goods were sold in similar ways to other 'symbolic' commodities. It is these processes that point to the autonomy and heteronomy of the cultural sphere.

It would be useful to take Norbert Elias's observations (1971: 15) and examine the process of formation of the 'autonomization' of particular spheres, which should be understood in terms of the changing power balances and the functional interdependencies of different social groups. To understand, therefore, the development of the economic sphere, we need to link the term *economic* to the rise of particular social strata and the theorization of the growing autonomous nexus of the relations generated by this group and other groups. Elias (1984) focuses on Quesney and the Physiocrats (who were soon followed by Adam Smith and others) as the first groups to synthesize empirical data in the belief that they could detect the effects of the laws of nature in society that would serve the welfare and prosperity of humankind. The ideas of the Physiocrats, according to Elias (1984: 22), were positioned halfway between a social religion and a scientific hypothesis. They were able to fuse two, until then largely independent, streams of tradition: the large-scale philosophical concepts of book writers and the practical knowledge accumulated by administrators and merchants.

As the power of middle-class groups of economic specialists in com-merce, trade, and industry increased, the object of enquiry changed in structure and formed the basis for a more autonomous scientific approach. Therefore the growing autonomy of social phenomena such as markets found expression in the gradual and growing autonomy of theory about these phenomena and in the formation of the science of economics that carved out a separate sphere with immanent, autonomous laws of its own. The claim of middle-class entrepreneurs that the economy ought to be autonomous and free from state intervention became actualized. (For an interesting account of the attempts to create a 'market culture' and to persuade people that the theory was in line with actuality, see Reddy, 1984.) The idea developed that the economy was a separate sphere and was, in fact, autonomous within society. Elias (1984: 29) suggests this claim for autonomy had at least three strands:

> It was a claim asserting the autonomy of the nexus of functions which formed the subject-matter of the science of economics – of the autonomy in relation to other functions, the subject-matter of other disciplines. It was a claim to

autonomy of the science whose subject-matter this nexus was – of its theories and methods in relation to those of other disciplines. And it was also a claim to autonomy of the class of people who were specialists in the performance of these functions in relation to other social groups and particularly in relation to governments.

We can therefore attempt to understand the processes whereby the economy became posited as an independent social sphere and the relative autonomous science of economics was developed. We have already noted some ways in which the cultural sphere may also have moved in the direction of autonomy, and this trend of course merits a much fuller treatment. There are, however, important differences between the spheres, not only in the level of autonomy achieved but also in the deficit in the power potential of the specialists in symbolic production (artists, intellectuals, academics) compared with economic specialists and other groups and in the nature of the form, content and social effectivity of the symbols and cultural goods produced. As Bendix (1970) points out, following Weber's reasoning, the religious specialists who monopolized magical-mythical knowledge supplied beliefs that had a mundane meaning and a practical usefulness as a means of orientation for ordinary people. The knowledge of artists and intellectuals did not offer similar practical benefits, despite the convictions of their advocates. Although artists, by virtue of their skills, possessed mysteries that made them formidable, these skills did not provide power in the religious sense, and arcane knowledge without apparent purpose may even have made the cultural elites suspect to the populace (Bendix, 1970: 145). Nevertheless, the demand for such goods may increase with the shift toward a consumer and credential based society, with its wider market for cultural goods and associated expansion of higher education.

The endeavour to establish an autonomous sphere of high culture may conceal a series of tensions and interdependencies within the production of culture in general. Pierre Bourdieu (1984, 1985), for example, has suggested that the major organizing principle in cultural production is whether symbolic considerations (which generate what he calls the 'field of restricted cultural production') or economic considerations (the 'field of large-scale cultural production') come first. As mentioned, artists and intellectuals tend to emphasize their autonomy from the market and economic life. For Bourdieu, however, a relational dynamic operates here, because the denial of the market and the relevance of economic capital is based on 'interests in disinterestedness', an interest in the enhancement of the prestige and relevance of their cultural goods – of cultural capital over economic capital. The picture is further complicated by the fact that the subfield of artistic and intellectual production itself can be seen as part of a continuum. This continuum consists of four parts: (1) the tiny mutual admiration societies of avant-gardes and bohemians who follow myths of charismatic creation and distinction and who are highly autonomous from the market; (2) cultural institutions such as academies and museums that are relatively autonomous from the market and that establish and maintain their own symbolic hierarchies and canons; (3) the cultural producers who achieve 'high-society' and upper-class endorsement and success and whose cultural success is closely tied to economic profit and market success; and (4) the cultural producers who achieve mass audience or 'popular' success and whose production is closely tied to the dictates of the market (see Bourdieu, 1983a: 329).

A number of points can be made about the interrelationships of the subfields and the notion of cultural production as a whole.

First, such a model, which emphasizes the relative heteronomy and autonomy of the various subfields from the market, points to the relational determinism of the various parts of the cultural sphere as a whole. It suggests that the valuation of high culture, and the devaluation of popular culture, will vary with the extent to which cultural avant-gardes and cultural institutions develop and maintain autonomy and legitimacy. We therefore need to examine the interdependencies and shifting power balances between symbolic specialists and economic specialists in a manner that accounts for the differentiation of the various subfields of the cultural sphere.

Second, we should not focus exclusively on these groups. The processes that gave rise to the cultural sphere and mass market culture took place within different state formation processes and national traditions. Maravall (1986), for example, disputes that the development of a mass culture in seventeenth century Spain should be understood solely in terms of economic factors. Rather, he conceives of the development of baroque culture as a conservative cultural reaction to the crisis faced by the Spanish state (in particular the monarchical and seignorial sectors), which manipulated culture production to generate a new culture of spectacles for the growing urban masses.

Another example is directly relevant to the potential autonomy of culture. The peculiarities of the French state formation process, which attained a high degree of centralization and integration, also promoted the view that French culture represented universal civilization and the meta-culture of humankind. This view not only facilitated a serious attitude towards culture through the development of cultural institutions but also favoured the development of culture as a prestigious specialism and lifestyle. This was particularly true for those fractions within the middle class that were attracted to the cultural ideals of the Enlightenment and the lifestyle of the independent writer in the eighteenth century (Darnton, 1983). It also provided the basis for the development of autonomous artistic and literary bohemians and avant-gardes in Paris from the 1830s onward (Seigel, 1986). Hence, to understand different societal evaluations of 'high culture' or the transcultural applicability of Bourdieu's notion of 'cultural capital', we need to be aware that the acceptance and the social efficacy of recognizable forms of cultural capital vary in relation to the society's degree of social and cultural integration. Outside specific metropolitan centres in the United States, cultural capital, that is, knowledge of high culture and acquired dispositions and tastes that manifest such knowledge, is accorded less legitimacy and investment potential than in France (Lamont and Lareau, 1988).

Third, although certain subfields of the cultural sphere attain relative autonomy, their cultural practices may still affect everyday culture and the formation of habitus and dispositions within broader groups outside the cultural sphere, as our French example indicates. It would be useful to investigate the place of cultural ideals such as 'the artist as hero' and the veneration of the artist's and intellectual's lifestyle within different groups, education processes and mass cultural media (some tentative steps in this direction are provided in the following two chapters). For some commentators the cultural sphere is credited with a considerable influence on everyday culture. Bell (1976) asserts that artistic modernism, with its transgressive strategies, has strongly influenced consumer culture and threatens the basis of the social bond. Martin (1981) has also considered the effects of cultural modernism and the counterculture on mainstream British culture. We also need more systematic studies on the role of the cultural sphere in the formation of dispositions, habitus and means of orientation for different groups. Such studies would help to explore the connections between sociogenetic and psychogenetic perspectives in that the formation of the cultured or cultivated person entails tendencies that parallel the way civilizing processes ensure the control of affects and the internalization of external controls. In addition we need to focus on the long-term processes that form larger audiences and publics for the particular types of cultural goods produced within the various subfields of the cultural sphere.

Our discussion of the cultural sphere therefore suggests the need for a more differentiated notion of the cultural sphere in which the relative autonomy of the various subfields is investigated. This would better enable us to understand the relationship between those sectors that seek to achieve greater autonomy (high culture) and those sectors that are more directly tied to production for the popular markets in cultural goods (mass consumer culture). As we have emphasized, the relationship between these sectors is not fixed or static but is best conceived of as a process. It is important to consider various phases that entail spurts toward autonomy (which, as mentioned, was particularly marked in nineteenth-century France) and towards heteronomy (phases of cultural declassification in which cultural enclaves are pulled into wider economic markets for cultural goods such as postmodernism). We need to focus upon certain phases in the history of particular societies to understand the processes that lead to the formation and deformation of the cultural sphere. This entails examining the particular intergroup and class fractional power struggles and interdependencies that increase or diminish the power potential of cultural specialists and the societal valuation of their cultural goods and theories.

Here it would be useful to investigate the relationship between particular theoretical conceptions of the nature, scope and purpose of culture produced by cultural specialists and the differential pulls towards autonomy and heteronomy. The intention is this chapter has been to argue for a long-term process perspective on culture in which the focus is on neither cultural production nor cultural consumption *per se*. Rather, we need to examine both their necessary interrelationship and the swings towards theorizations that emphasize the exclusivity of the explanatory value of either approach given the rise and fall of particular figurations of people involved in interdependencies and power struggles. In effect we need to focus on the long-term process of cultural production within Western societies that has enabled the development of a massive capacity for producing, circulating and consuming symbolic goods.

Notes

An earlier version of this chapter was presented at the German-American Theory Group Conference held in Bremen in July 1988 and was printed in R. Munch and N. Smelser (eds) *Theory of Culture* (California University Press, 1992). I would like to thank Peter Bailey, Josef Bleicher, David Chaney, Mike Hepworth, Stephen Kalberg and Stephen Mennell for commenting on this earlier version.

1. The relationship between values and action is complex, as the secondary literature on Weber's *Protestant Ethic* thesis attests (see Marshall, 1982: 64ff.). Bendix's (1970: 146ff.) discussion of the *Protestant Ethic* is a useful clarification of the different ways in which cultural values are transmitted to the populace under contrasting conditions of intense religiosity and secularization. Campbell's study does not direct sufficient attention to the interpersonal nexus of conduct and the key role that cultural specialists play in attempting to promote, transmit and sustain beliefs under conditions of increased secularization in which one can presume a greater hiatus between high culture and everyday experience. Although we do know that the middle classes have a greater capacity to take beliefs seriously, we need more evidence of the effects of beliefs on actual conduct.

3

PERSONALITY, UNITY AND THE ORDERED LIFE

'The painter takes his body with him,' remarks Valéry (quoted in Merleau-Ponty, 1964a: 162). So too does the sociologist, not only in the sense that he wrestles with the problem of the imposition of his embodied and situated gaze on the social relationships he seeks to decipher, but also in the communication of the results of his efforts to others. Yet in theorizing it is quite easy to lose sight of the body: the act of reading or writing all too easily occludes the fact that these are embodied practices which depend on a complex set of social relationships and interdependencies to sustain the necessary solitude (Bourdieu, 1983b). It is evident when we go to a lecture that we not only have the text but the embodied perform-ance, the inflections of the spoken words, the tone of voice, gestures, body language, stance, and so on, which provide additional resources which serve to clarify and give intelligibility and persuasiveness to the message.

I can still vividly recall attending John Rex's first series of lectures after he was appointed professor at Durham University. He opened the lecture on Durkheim's *Elementary Forms of the Religious Life* with the striking biographical remark that he first read the book while studying divinity in South Africa and that the impact of the book was so momentous that he took out his bicycle and pedalled down to the ministry to hand in his resignation. Statements like this have an impact not only through the dramatic nature of the event recounted, but through the way they are told. The mode and style of communication are assumed not only to throw light on the veracity of the statement, but also to provide an indication of the character of the speaker.

There is, then, a sense in which a lecture has the quality of an exhibition or show (Bourdieu, 1992). Hence those who enjoy intellectual or academic success are in demand to speak around the world.[1] We go along to see them not only to attain the clarification and immediacy of understanding that co-presence seems to deliver, but also to observe the *person*. Here, we are influenced by the assumption that seeing the person, capturing a fragment of his life, will somehow enable us to gain some significant angle not only on his writings, but also on his more fundamental basic problematic or life-purpose. It is not only the working out of the possible traces of rhetoric and charisma, the potential for identification and heroicization that is of interest, but the assumption that there is a *unity* to a life and work, some style, motif or underlying structure which gives them coherence.

It is in this sense that Elias (1987a) disputed Hildersheimer's assertion that although Mozart was a brilliant musician he was a failure as a person. For Elias the life and the work form an integrated whole. Elias is, of course, far from being alone in making this assumption. Peter Gay (1973: 439), for example, tells us that 'Cassirer's *The Question of Jean-Jacques Rousseau* seeks to make sense of the whole man and to relate him to his writings – to discover, as Cassirer usually tried to do, an inner unity behind superficial contradictions.' Ray Monk (1990), in discussing his book on Ludwig Wittgenstein remarks, 'When one considers his life and work as a unity – which is, above all, what I tried to do – this striving for *Anständingkeit* [decency, honesty] is central, for he considered it a prerequisite, not only to be a good person, but also to be a good philosopher.' Yet the assumption that we should see a person's life and work as framed from the outside by the commentator, or constructed from within by the subject through the lens of unity, is by no means undisputed. David Frisby (1981) focuses upon the alleged fragmented nature of Simmel's *oeuvre*, only to be taken to task by Roland Robertson (1982: 97) who argues that we should endeavour to seek the unity in Simmel's lifework. But within sociology it is perhaps Max Weber's life and work which provides the most vivid example of the struggles over whether his work should be conceptualized through the frame of unity. Such struggles have been heightened by the current wave of postmodern theorizing with its emphasis upon discontinuity, fragmentation, syncretism and otherness. Before examining such theories it would first be useful, however, to turn to a discussion of Max Weber.

Personality and the life orders

A good deal has been written in recent years about the 'thematic unity' (Tenbruck, 1980) and 'central question' (Hennis, 1988) of Weber's life and work. Arguing against the 'fragmented appreciation' of Max Weber, which has made Weber appear for some as the archetypal *'post-modern* writer', Albrow (1990: 3) has argued that Weber's work has an inner logic and coherence. He quotes with approval the task which Ralf Dahrendorf (1987: 580) has identified as the prime requirement for Weber scholars: 'to weld his works and times together in the best tradition of *Verstehen*'. This echoes a long tradition of Weber scholarship in which Karl Jaspers's (1989: 145) assumption that 'Max Weber's life and thought were insolubly entwined' is characteristic. Jaspers's admiration for Max Weber was of course unrestrained and he made the life and personality of Weber the model for his existential philosophy. For Jaspers Weber showed a remarkable consistency, which revealed itself not only in actions, but in his lack of artifice which became effectively written into his body:[2]

Physiognomy and gestures were original with him. No affectation and pretence surrounded him, he merely took his stand without the protection of conventions and masks. He placed no importance on himself. His naturalness automatically put aside all illusion and surrendered itself to every possible attack. He was the phenomenon of a human being who was entirely a human being, who thought what was, and became experiential. (Jaspers, 1989: 154)

This lack of guile, artifice and stylization was for Jaspers manifest in the uniformity of the form within which Weber lived his life, a form in which we could say the ethic of responsibility (*Verantwortungsethik*) was lived with the relentless commitment of an ethic of ultimate ends (*Gesinnungsethik*). To become a personality one could not pursue a myriad of new sensations and value commitments, rather one had to impose one's stamp on life, to form it and subject it to a specific purpose.[3] This entailed commitment, consistency and a sense of duty, the patience and strength, 'the strong slow boring of hard boards' which takes both 'passion and perspective' (Weber, 1948a: 128). At the same time, the sense of duty should not be understood as dull and cautious; it was animated by a demonic intellectual passion to surpass and surmount all fixity in pursuit of the end he has grasped. For Weber we could all meet the demands of the day in our vocation and interpersonal relations if each of us 'finds and obeys the demon who holds the fibers of his very life' (Weber, 1948b: 156). This type of commitment and consistency is not to be confused with an attempt to manufacture charisma. As Manasse (1957: 384) remarks, 'The demonic person does not attract but repel others who desire to devote and to subject their individualism to his own. Instead of passing out the slogans to a flock of idolisers he is suspicious of every fixed formula.'[4] While an irrational commitment to ultimate values is given its affective charge by some demonic emotional impulse which drives the person and can give life a fatefulness, the means to realize the given end entail the suppression of desires and emotions through systematic devotion to the task.

It is this tension which has led Weber's life to be understood via the concepts of heroic ethics, heroic stoicism and heroic defiance: this feeds interpretations such as Jaspers's, which claims that Weber's life formed a new type of personality which could be the inspirational model for the modern age.[5] Individuals who organized their lives around an ultimate value to follow 'hero ethics' or 'genuine idealism' were the only ones who could be regarded as establishing distinctive personalities according to Weber (Portis, 1973: 118). Weber, like Simmel, considered the selection of ultimate values to entail a wager, a commitment which could not be substantiated amid the plurality of conflicting values and the differentiation of the value spheres which was characteristic of the modern age. Yet despite this uncertainty and the suspicion it cast on all manifestations of totality and an ethics of ultimate ends, as cultural beings it was our responsibility to pursue our ideals relentlessly. As Portis (1973: 116) remarks:

An individual who devotes himself to the realization of his ideals not only has a greater sense of personal identity and a higher degree of self-esteem than one whose direct goal is to establish an identity, he actually is a more substantial 'person' because he 'is more than his mere appearances.'

Hence for Weber while we may encourage others to develop the desire for self-clarification and a sense of responsibility, we should avoid the desire to impose our own standards upon others and accept that for those who follow science as a vocation there is no answer to the vital question Tolstoy posed, 'What shall we do? How shall we arrange our lives?' (Weber, 1948b: 152–3).

Yet there is a sense in which this commitment to an ethic of responsibility can itself become an ultimate end, especially if we take into account the heroic and vital language in which it was expressed – the language which so captivated the audience which first heard 'Science as a vocation', and continues to captivate subsequent generations of readers. Hence Lassman and Velody (1989: 172) argue that 'what we are presented with is the construction of an "epical" denial of the possibility of an "epical" theory for the modern age'. While, as they point out, this anti-foundational stance of Weber has meant that he has been rediscovered in the debates over postmodernism – in that Weber's account of the modern world is not dissimilar to that of Lyotard (1984) and others who point to the delegitimation of 'grand narratives' – it is important to stress that this is not the whole story. Where Weber differs from Lyotard is that for him science is a vocation, a will to truth based on 'an inner need for truth which makes science a form of faith' (C. Turner, 1990: 114).

As mentioned earlier, to become a personality requires a firm commitment to one's convictions within a context of value pluralism and uncertainty. It involves a 'Here I stand and can do no other' wager, which by its very commitment and steadfastness implies an ethical judgement of the lack of worth of other standpoints. As Charles Turner (1990: 115) remarks: 'This Weberian move away from an (ironic) "totalizing perspective" refuses to substitute for an ethical "totality" a series of postmodern partial standpoints.' Two points can be made here which direct the discussion towards postmodernism: first, the centrality of aesthetics within postmodern theories and the scepticism with which Weber addressed aesthetics as a mode of theorizing and a way of life suggests that the relationship between ethics and aesthetics needs to be explored; and, second, related to this, we need to discuss the relationship between 'hero ethics' and 'average ethics' which Weber formulated, and which can also be formulated in terms of masculinity and femininity (Bologh, 1990: 102). This chapter will focus on the first question; the second, though equally deserving of attention, we will leave to a future occasion.

Ethics and aesthetics

In the final chapter of *The Religion of China* Weber (1951) contrasts Confucianism with Puritanism. The Puritan viewed the world as material to be fashioned ethically whereas Confucianism asked for adjustment to the world. There was no attempt in the latter to order conduct into a systematic unity. The Confucian ideal was that the 'cultivated man' showed propriety, he was 'harmoniously attuned and poised in all social situations' (Weber, 1951: 156), he displayed a 'watchful self-control, self-observation and reserve', and an 'aesthetically cool temper' which caused all duties to be 'frozen into a symbolic ceremonial' (Weber, 1951: 234).[6] His life was therefore a 'complex of useful and particular traits', it did not constitute a 'systematic unity'. As Weber comments:

> Such a way of life could not allow a man an inward aspiration towards a 'unified personality', a striving which we associate with the idea of personality. Life remained a series of recurrences. It did not become a whole placed methodically under a transcendental goal. (Weber, 1951: 235)

For Weber, this wholeness or systematic unity had emerged most successfully in the Puritan, who was dedicated to a cause through ethical imperatives not through tradition. Yet, as Hennis (1988: 93) argues, the spiritual bond between dedication to one's vocation and the 'innermost ethical core of personality' became broken with the establishment of capitalism in the West, leaving problematic the 'human type' which would replace the Puritan. In the modern world the loss of an ethical totality proved difficult to repair. The problems of grafting a comprehensive ethic for the totality of life-conduct on to the separate aesthetic, erotic and intellectual life-orders within a differentiated cultural sphere proved demanding. The prospect of this being achieved via an ethic of responsibility, or its alleged twentieth-century existentialist replacement which Jaspers had formulated, which was so clearly based upon the hero ethics of the life and work of Max Weber, was also problematic as it needed social conditions which would support independent *rentiers* – a solution which along with other intellectual and mystical attempts at salvation 'was not accessible to everybody' and hence entailed some form of aristocracy (Weber, 1948c: 357). Yet why were not the aesthetic, erotic and intellectual spheres viable alternatives to the Puritan ethic and its paler vocational twentieth-century shadow, the ethic of responsibility? Why could one not speak of an ethic of aesthetics, or even an ethic of eroticism as viable life-orders which could produce unified personalities?

The simplest answer would be to presume a prejudice on Weber's part against aesthetics and eroticism arising from his Protestant and Kantian background. In effect, both the preoccupation with forms and the immersion in 'the greatest irrational force of life: sexual love' (Weber, 1948c: 343) drew attention away from the ethic of brotherhood and responsible commitment to a lifelong cause; ethics could be reduced to a matter of taste and style. Furthermore, for Weber these inner-worldly, anti-rational life forces were in his time not merely content to remain confined within their respective spheres, but through their opposition to the 'iron cage' routinization, rationalization and meaninglessness of modern life were being offered up as solutions, as effective ways of life which were surrogate forms of salvation (Scaff, 1989: 104).

There is evidence that Weber softened his attitude towards the erotic and aesthetic spheres in the last decade of his life, and this is manifest in his increased sympathy to these modalities of experience in each progressive revision of the 'Zwischenbetrachtung' (Green, 1976: 171). This may have derived from Weber's encounter with the particular blend of eroticism, psychoanalysis, romanticism, bohemianism and *Lebensphiloso-phie* which was manifest in Otto Gross and his followers. It is true that Weber was very critical of Gross's beliefs, and this was apparent in his unsympathetic response to Gross's article submitted to the *Archiv* and his use of the dismissive label 'psychiatric ethic' (Bologh, 1990: 102), yet this is by no means the whole story. Weber's affection for Else Jaffe, who had been closely involved with Gross, and his subsequent passionate love affair with her certainly altered his view of the status of eroticism, and by association aestheticism.[7] Weber's increased contact with Gross and his followers and the visits he made in 1913 and 1914 to the 'alternative lifestyle' communes they set up at Ascona, also helped to give Weber a more nuanced appreciatlon of eroticism. According to Marianne Weber this led to a more differentiated view of the contrast Weber had developed between 'hero ethics' and 'average ethics'. Now the idealist 'hero ethics' was accompanied by a new insight which allowed the followers of an erotic-emotional lifestyle to be admitted:

> There is a gradation of the ethical. If the ethically highest step is unattainable in a concrete case, one must try to achieve the second or third best. What that is cannot be derived from a theory, only from the concrete situation. (Weber, 1975: 388; translation adapted and quoted in Schwentker, 1987: 490)

The sexual life, for Weber (1948c: 346–7), represented the only tie linking man to animality and with its 'boundless giving of oneself' provided an 'inner worldly salvation from rationalization', especially for 'the vocational specialist type of man'. While eroticism represented an escape from both the supra-personal ethical values and the routines of everyday life, with its 'indifference to everything sacred and good', its very worth could be said to 'derive just from this hostility and indifference' (Weber, 1949: 17; see Green, 1976: 171). Hence what was an irrational passion could become a value.[8]

With regard to the aesthetic sphere, Weber (1948c: 342) tells us that modern men tend to transform moral judgements into judgements of taste, and that 'this shift from the moral to the aesthetic evaluation of conduct is a common characteristic of intellectualist epochs'. Yet while Weber sought to map out the problems with which this confronted the individual – an individual who sought to order his life and develop his personality in a critical manner, while leaving room for ethical consistency and responsi-bility – he also shared a good deal with Simmel. As Scaff (1989: 127) tells us, for Weber 'Simmel was above all the modern *Kulturmensch*, or cultural being, who figures so prominently in key passages of Weber's writings, the essentially *new* human self fully absorbed into the life-order of aesthetic modernism, the ahistorical self actualized in a world of limitless possibilities.' For Simmel human beings tear themselves away from the natural world through a process of 'cultivation', and the formation of life through the development of personality offers the prospect of a solution to the subject–object dualism (Scaff, 1989: 196). Simmel states that we cannot become cultivated into a unified person 'by having developed this or that individual bit of knowledge or skill; we become cultivated only when all of them serve a psychic unity which depends on but does not coincide with them.' He adds:

> The development of every human being, which is examined in terms of identifiable items, appears as a bundle of developmental lines which expand on different directions and quite different lengths. But man does not cultivate himself through their isolated perfections, but only insofar as they help to develop his indefinable personal unity. In other words: Culture is the way that leads from the closed unity through the unfolded multiplicity to the unfolded unity. (Simmel, 1968: 29)

For Simmel (1971c: 230, 232), then, 'culture is a perfection of man' and 'the development of our inner totality'. The tragedy is that for this development to take place (subjective culture) man depends upon externally created objects (objective culture) which are capable of possessing a conceptual unity, an ideal structure which lives only in the work itself and which cannot be replicated in a person's life. Hence, as Weingartner (1962: 168) remarks, for Simmel 'the personality of the individual understood to be a unified, integrated whole' is in Simmel's (1986: 14) words

> always a goal of development that is attained only imperfectly. Every great philosophy, however, is an anticipation of this unity of form which is unattainable in any real psyche. The image of the world has the roundness of the ideal of personality.

The great works of culture (art, religion, and so on) are so measured by their own criteria that they resist harmonious assimilation with other elements necessary for the development of a spiritual wholeness. The consequent hiatus between objective and subjective culture in which things become more autonomous leads to an impoverishment and fragmentation of subjective culture, which becomes particularly marked in modern life (Simmel, 1971c: 232, 234).

Weber (1948c: 356) also captures this in his 'Zwischenbetrachtung' essay where he tells us that 'the "cultivated" man who strives for self perfection' may become '"weary of life" but cannot become "satiated with life" in the sense of completing a cycle'. This is because the perfectibility of the cultural man can in principle progress indefinitely, hence the amount the individual, as recipient or 'builder of cultural values', can handle in the course of his life 'becomes the more trifling the more differentiated and multiplied the cultural values and goals of self-perfection become'. It becomes impossible for us to conceive of absorbing the 'whole' of culture or defining the criteria on which we could make an 'essential' selection. He continues:

> The 'culture' of the individual certainly does not consist of the *quantity* of 'cultural values' which he amasses; it consists of an articulated *selection* of culture values. But there is no guarantee that this selection has reached an end that would be meaningful to him precisely at the 'accidental' time of his death.

This passage resonates strongly with Simmel's diagnosis of the problems of modern culture in a world in which the delusion of unitary meaning had been lost while 'a longing for synthesis and wholeness' remained (Scaff, 1990: 289).[9]

Simmel did, however, discuss a number of responses to the contradictions of modern culture (see Scaff, 1989: 199ff.). First, he refers to the various organizations, interactions and modes of sociability, which attempt to provide a meaningful order for life. Yet such attempts as joining a political party or social movement cannot provide an overarching sense of certainty and cultural unity in the differentiated modern world. Second, there is the aesthetic response which seeks to provide salvation through art, or the living of one's life as a work of art. Art can provide particular momentary glimpses of unity in which the world is viewed as a delimited whole, the mystical unity in which the world is viewed *sub specie aeternitatis*. Third, there is the 'cool reflection' of intellectual detachment. Here there is the tragic acceptance that conflicts and problems cannot all be solved and that 'the present is too full of contradictions to stand still' and while we 'gaze into an abyss of unformed life beneath our feet' we have to recognize that 'perhaps this very formlessness is itself the appropriate form for contemporary life' (Simmel, 1968: 25; Scaff, 1989: 201). The uncertainty in the face of the conflicting and competing forms of the world may then lead to the affirmation of life itself as the only surety (Whimster, 1987: 276); an acceptance of 'the paradoxical idea of form's absence as itself a form' (Scaff, 1990: 293). It might be possible to conceive of some fusion of the second and the third perspectives, as for example in the work of specific artists who sought not to flee from life into another totality of objective culture, but to capture the sense of the formlessness of life itself in a form. In his last essay on Rodin, Simmel concluded that the goal of art should not be merely salvation from 'the confusion and turmoil of life' but could entail a movement in the opposite direction via 'the most perfect stylization and enhanced refinements of life's own contents'; hence Rodin 'redeems us from just that which we experience in the sphere of actuality, because he allows us to experience our deepest sense of life once again in the sphere of art' (Simmel, 1983: 153; Scaff, 1989: 103).

Simmel's depiction of Rodin's project can also be used to point to the way in which he too sought to develop forms of expression capable of doing justice to the fleeting impressions, the fragmentation and formlessness which made up the experience of modern life and the various ways in which this experience itself was subjected to rapid formation and deformation. It is in this sense that Simmel's contribution to the understanding of the cultural dimension of modernity, particularly in the large cities which were the heart of modern culture, has been highlighted to the extent that he has been proclaimed as 'the first sociologist of modernity' (Frisby, 1985a, 1985b). Simmel sought to explore the experience of the everyday world of modernity in the sense which Baudelaire had invoked in his depiction of the essence of the experience of *modernité* as being the problem of how to live amidst the endless parading of the new. Here the focus was on the new experiences of life in the big cities, the constant parade of new fashions and styles, the generation of defences against overstimulation and neurasthenia in the blasé attitude and playful modes of sociability. The emphasis is upon the overwhelming flow of life, the genesis of new forms, some of which celebrated and prolonged the tension between life and form by their temporary and transitory nature – what Maffesoli (1988) has referred to as '*formisme*', the playful development of temporary affectual identifications (*Einfühlung*) and modes of sociability which in the modern city offer new forms of individuation and collectivities. To refer to processes of formation and deformation, swings between immersion in, and distantiation from, experiences and sensations is to draw attention not only to the salience of culture, but to a more general aestheticization of everyday life. Here the emphasis is not just upon the massive increase in the production of aestheticized objects as part of the development of a mass consumer culture, which changes the nature of the urban landscape, but also to point to the changes in the mode of perceiving, living and acting within this new consumer culture which heighten aesthetic sensibilities (see Featherstone, 1991a). Some of these tendencies have been labelled postmodernism, which raises the question of whether they are genuinely new and distinctive to the late twentieth century, or whether there are continuities with the modes of experience which Simmel sought to comprehend in the turn-of-the-century modernity. In addition we need to enquire into their implication for the development of personality and a unified or ordered life-course. Do they point to the viability of an 'ethics of aesthetics' as an alternative mode of ordering life within the contemporary world? Or does this represent a further attenuation and dissipation of the elements of personality formation we have spoken of?

The centrality of aesthetics within Simmel's whole work has often been remarked on. Goldscheid (1904: 411–12; quoted in Frisby, 1981: 86) for example writes that

> behind Simmel's whole work there stands not the ethical but the aesthetic ideal. And it is this aesthetic ideal which determines his whole interpretation of life and thus his whole scientific activity. What holds him back from all democracy is the

feeling . . . that he denotes with the category of distinction [*Vornehmheit*] . . . for him this distinction is always only expressed as aesthetics and not as an ethical distinction.

Frisby (1981: 85) tells us that Simmel substituted an aesthetic for an ethical stance on reality which Kurt Lamprecht referred to as 'an aesthetic ethics'. The question is not whether this mode of orientation is a legitimate or illegitimate frame of reference with which to understand the social world in some timeless categorical sense, but whether Simmel's specific mode of perception was both formed by and a response to particular sets of changes which were restructuring the nature of everyday experience. If this is the case then his choice can in no way be dismissed as capricious; rather it needs to be fully investigated, not least because what we refer to as 'postmodernism' may either be understood as continuous with these developments, or as representing a new and distinctive set of breaks with it – which points to the need to investigate these alleged linkages and 'conditions of possibility' within a new historical context.

Postmodernism

A good deal of confusion and justified scepticism exists about the terms 'postmodern', 'postmodernism', 'postmodernity' and 'postmodernization' and their relationship to the family of terms associated with the modern (for a discussion of these terms see Featherstone, 1991a). The history of the terms suggests that postmodernism was first used to point to a movement beyond artistic modernism centred in New York in the 1960s. It was then picked up by philosophers and literary critics who detected homologies between the artworks and practices of postmodern artists and poststructuralism and deconstructionism. The rapid transmission of information between Europe (particularly France) and North America helped to draw in other critics, intellectuals and social scientists, which resulted in the stretching of the concept towards an epochal shift: postmodernity understood as something we are on the threshold of detecting, which points to the decay and dissolution of modernity. It may well be that the concept has little lasting utility for the social sciences (at least if the emphasis is placed on the term 'science'), being itself a product of de-monopolization processes in academic life which are breaking down some of the barriers between subjects and subject-based establishments – tendencies which are themselves inimical to the maintenance of science. Where the term may, however, have some utility is in the way it directs our attention to cultural change.

The main features associated with postmodernism can be briefly summarized. First, a movement away from the universalistic ambitions of master-narratives where the emphasis is upon totality, system and unity towards an emphasis upon local knowledge, fragmentation, syncretism, 'otherness' and 'difference'. Second, a dissolution of symbolic hierarchies which entail canonical judgements of taste and value, towards a populist collapse of the distinction between high and popular culture. Third, a tendency towards the aestheticization of everyday life which gained momentum both from efforts within the arts to collapse the boundary between art and life (pop art, Dada, surrealism, and so on) and the alleged movement towards a simulational consumer culture in which an endlessly reduplicated hallucinatory veil of images effaces the distinction between appearance and reality. Fourth, a decentring of the subject, whose sense of identity and biographical continuity give way to fragmentation and superficial play with images, sensations and 'multi-phrenic intensities'.

Of particular interest here are the third and fourth features. Let us take as an example one of the most influential writers on postmodernism, Fredric Jameson. The phrase 'multi-phrenic intensities' is his and is used to indicate what he regards as an effect of the postmodern tendencies which have emerged in the postwar culture of the consumer society (Jameson, 1984a, 1984b; see also Featherstone, 1991a). It refers to a breakdown of individuals' sense of identity through the bombardment of fragmented signs and images which erode all sense of continuity between past, present and future, all teleological belief that life is a meaningful project. In opposition to the notion that life is a meaningful project, here we have the view that the individual's primary mode of orientation is an aesthetic one, and like the schizophrenic she/he is unable to chain together the signifiers and instead must focus on particular disconnected experiences or images which provide a sense of intense immersion and immediacy to the exclusion of all wider teleological concerns. Jameson's views have been influenced by the writings of Baudrillard, although in contrast to the latter's nihilistic conclusions, he has sought to retain a Marxist framework to conceptualize these postmodern tendencies as the cultural logic of late capitalism. For Baudrillard (1983a, 1993) we live in a depthless culture of floating signs and images in which 'TV is the world', and all we can do is watch the endless flow of images with an aestheticized fascination and without possible recourse to moral judgements. Some have argued that evidence of these tendencies is to be found within everyday life and modes of signification: in the sign-play of youth cultures, the styles and fashions of the *flâneurs* who move through the new postmodern urban spaces, and in the particular fusions of art and rock which produced contemporary popular music (Hebdige, 1988; Chambers, 1987; Frith and Horne, 1987; Harvey, 1989).

The implications for the theory of personality, character formation, and the project of a unified and ordered life which we discussed in terms of the writings and lives of Weber and Simmel in the previous section, would seem to be clear. A new version of the ethic of aesthetics seems to be in the offing, one which lacks the underpinning sense of the unified life-order which is to be found in Weber and Simmel's deliberations. Yet troubling questions remain: how far are the formulations referred to as postmodern genuinely new – are there, for example, clear historical antecedents which would suggest that they should be reconceived as *transmodern*? How far are such decentred identities actually possible and is it possible to conceive them not as actually disordered lives, but as lives which still retain some sense of teleology and life-order, albeit within a more flexible generative structure which allows for a greater play of differences?

It would be useful to approach these questions via a discussion of Rorty's work. Rorty follows the postmodern emphasis upon a decentred self by arguing that there is no underlying coherent human essence behind our various social roles. Rather than being something unified and consistent, the self should be conceived as a bundle of conflicting 'quasi-selves', a random and contingent assemblage of experiences (Rorty, 1986; Shusterman, 1988: 341–2). Once the old essentialist self has been discarded as impossible to found, the thirst for new experiences and constant self-enlargement can become the ethical justification for life: aesthetics becomes the ethical criterion for the good life. For Shusterman, Rorty's position represents a rehash of *fin-de-siècle* aestheticism. G.E. Moore, who was influential in the Bloomsbury Group, argued for an aesthetic life structured around the search for, and appreciation of, beautiful things, people and experiences.

Wilde and Pater shared a similar ethic, with the latter anticipating Rorty's Freudian-Faustian aesthetic life by advocating a 'quickened, multiplied consciousness' and thirst for enriching our experience via the intense excitement of novelty (Shusterman, 1988: 354). Wilde's advocacy of an aesthetic life entailed: (1) a life of pleasure in aesthetic consumption; (2) the need for life to form an aesthetically pleasing whole; and (3) occasionally, the assumption that such unity could be found in constant change (Shusterman, 1988: 354). But in contrast to Rorty's denial of any coherent structuring to the bundle of quasi-selves, in Wilde's case we have the injunction to turn life into a work of art; and here 'the idea is not so much a life of aesthetic consumption, but a life which is itself a product worthy of aesthetic appreciation for its structure and design as organic unity' (Shusterman, 1988: 347). Hence while Wilde maintained a subversive and critical attitude towards culture, and saw the artist as the true revolutionary figure because 'he expresses everything', he saw the great artist as inventing a type 'which life tries to copy' (Rieff, 1990: 276–7). There are clear parallels here with the life of Stefan George, whose aestheticism and blurring of the boundaries between life and art was one of the modern secular ethics with which Weber was concerned. In addition, there are echoes of the Ancient Greeks' reluctance to separate the good and the beautiful. In this context it is evident that one source of the current preoccupation of theorists of postmodernism with repairing the relationship between ethics and aesthetics, which were so long held separate in the Western tradition, has been the later writings of Michel Foucault.

Foucault argues that Baudelaire's description of the new sense of the fleeting, ephemeral nature of time, which comes into being with modernity, emphasizes that to be modern is not merely to lose oneself in 'presentness', the flux of the passing moments (cf. Simmel's notion of the formless flow of experienced life); it also entails an ascetic attitude in taking oneself as an object of formation and elaboration. Dandyism entailed the art of inventing oneself, of making life into a work of art (Foucault, 1986: 40–2). There would seem to be a strong Nietzschean element here in the assumption that the aim of life is to give style to one's character via some form of self-fashioning. It also raises again the question of the reconciliation of the goal of character formation with a modernist cultivation of a protean, dispersed, transgressive self, which we shall shortly return to. In his final writings Foucault examined the Greek ethic that we have to aspire to be the type of person who builds his or her existence into a beautiful life, an aesthetic ideal of self-nobility. This did not entail conformity to a moral code, whether religious or juridical; rather, Foucault wished to shift the focus to the analysis of the ways in which the individual is meant to constitute him- or herself as an ethical subject. This notion of ethics emphasized both asceticism and teleology in the subjection of the self through the obligation to 'give your existence the most beautiful form possible' (Foucault, 1986: 353). This stylization of life and aesthetics of existence did not entail a restless hermeneutics of desire, but a moderate and prudent ordering of the conduct of life in terms of formal principles in the use of pleasures (Foucault, 1987: 89–90), a conception of the achievement of a structured and unified life which, like dandyism, entailed the pursuit of the goal of distinction which was not open to all.'[10]

Given that both the Greek aesthetics of existence and nineteenth-century dandyism were exclusive ethics not open to all, how far can we assume that a similar ethics of aesthetics is possible outside the realms of postmodern theory and should be understood as a sign of an epochal shift, a movement towards postmodernity? Foucault (1987: 362), for his part, is keen to distinguish the Greek ethic from 'the Californian cult of the self' and indeed regards them as 'diametrically opposed'. Neither new consciousness movements nor consumer culture would therefore seem to offer a basis for an ethics of aesthetics. Yet there are clear tendencies within consumer culture and youth movements which emphasize the stylization of life, albeit on a less grand scale, and it would only be through the analysis of self-help books, manners books and how-to-live manuals and their companions in newspapers, magazines and television – a contemporary effort to follow the methodology devised by Norbert Elias (1978, 1982) – that a preliminary answer could be arrived at. There also remains the question of how unified and life extensive such postmodern attempts to create an ethics of aesthetics are.

Maffesoli (1988, 1991, 1995), for example, emphasizes the emergence of new forms of collective solidarity which are found especially in the metropolis. These transitory affective collectivities, which Maffesoli refers to as 'neo-tribalism', emerge within complex societies which have given way to a polytheistic 'swarming multiplicity of heterogeneous values'. This draws attention to features of the contemporary world which more rationalistically orientated sociologists are apt to neglect: the persistence of strong affectual bonds through which people come together in constellations with fluid boundaries to experience the multiple attractions, sensations, sensibilities and vitalism of an extra-logical community, the embodied sense of being together, the common feeling generated by a common emotional adherence to a sign which is recognizable by others. The whole post-1960s movement of rock festivals and the 1980s 'Feed the World' and Band-Aid-style concerts provide good examples. Emphasizing the temporary, transitory and fickle nature of these 'neo-tribes', Bauman (1990: 434) has argued that they fit well the Kantian concept of 'aesthetic community'. Such communities hold out the promise of unanimity, temporary republics of united taste in which each fragile consensus is constantly doing and undoing itself. It would seem that such temporary communities draw on neo-Durkheimian notions of the emotional charge and sense of the sacred which the group immersion and excitement generates. It is argued that this is clearly a collective sense of the ethic of the aesthetic in which the mass, which was formerly so negatively evaluated in terms of the efforts which the individual was required to make to distinguish himself through the Greek or dandyist 'aristocratic' individualistic modes, now becomes positively evaluated. The individual does not seek Apollonian distinction but immerses himself in the Dionysian collective. Maffesoli's (1991: 16) particular definition of the ethic of aesthetics, unlike Foucault's, is one with 'neither obligation nor sanction': there is 'no obligation other than coming together and being a member *of* the collective body'. The movement from considerations *of* personality, character, individuation and identity towards collective identification leaves behind notions of duty, obligation, asceticism, unity and teleology which are central to the theories of the aesthetic life-order as formulated by Foucault, Weber and Simmel.

This movement could also be understood in terms of the more general shift in the attitude of some academics, artists and intellectuals towards a positive evaluation of the mass, in terms of embracing the 'tactility' and embodied presence of groups in 'lower' social orders whose proximity, manners and lifestyles were once held to be so threatening and enervating – the fear of engulfment by the 'herd' which is a dominant motif in mass culture theory from Nietzsche to Eliot and Adorno. On a global level it also means an increased interaction and visibility of images and information about other cultures and traditions which could formerly be placed in a strict hierarchical and evolutionary order (for example the extent to which they are civilized within the Western mode) which are now accepted not as inferior, but as having the right to be different (see Featherstone, 1990).

The acceptance of syncretism, polytheism and tolerance of difference and otherness – which is a feature highlighted in postmodern theories, undermining the particular conjunction of a politics and aesthetics which attempts to sustain universal judgements, which we find, for example, in critical theory – is itself both advocated on a theoretical level and a response to changes in the relative situation of cultural specialists, on both an inter- and intra-societal level. Postmodernism has been associated with both the end of the avant-garde (Burger, 1984; Crane, 1987) and the end of the intellectuals (Jacoby, 1987). This is largely to be conceived in terms of the cohesiveness of their project, which entailed explicit and implicit judgements about the worth of art and intellectual knowledge for humankind. It is in this sense that Bauman (1988b) has detected a post-modern shift in intellectuals from the acceptance of their self-proclaimed Enlightenment role as *legislators* to the lesser role of *interpreters*. The loss of confidence in their ability to manufacture plausible, coherent or rational world-views which offered the prospect of some form of inner-worldly salvation, has meant that we should not just speak of the secularization of religion, but of the secularization of science, art and intellectual knowledge too. Along with a decline in the charismatic authority of the artist and intellectual, manifest in notions such as the artist or intellectual as hero or genius, we have had a decline in the specialist countercultural communities and lifestyles, such as bohemias, which helped to sustain them.

Postmodernism, with its emphasis on the repetitive nature of all art, its already-seen quality, which makes it at best only a copy (to the extent that the artist should only simulate what is already there in everyday life and consumer culture), manifests a distance from any attempt to conceive these changes in terms of any tragic reduction of subjective culture, such as we find in Simmel, or alternative Weberian conceptions of heroic stoicism. This also amounts to the denial of creativity, the capacity of human beings to create their culture ever anew in many varied ways, which was so central to the German cultural science tradition especially as found in the works of Weber, Simmel and Dilthey. Instead of the possibility of living out the life of an active *Kulturmensch*, all that remains is the attraction of the aesthetic play with fragments of already-formed culture, which we survey with passive fascination in a manner akin to the player of Herman Hesse's glass-bead game. Yet we should beware of taking at face value the claim that this fragmentation is absolute. While deconstruction and, by association, postmodernism manifest a hostility to what de Man refers to as 'the organic unity' and 'the intent at totality of the interpretive process' of works of art in favour of a celebration of heterogeneity, multivocality and intertextuality – the variety of incompatible arguments which inhabit a text – unity cannot be dispensed with altogether (see Culler, 1983: 199–200). Rather, deconstruction and postmodernism problematize unity in favour of more complex notions of syncretic unity and unicity. To banish the frame altogether is to move from culture into life, and this surrender to formlessness is not a viable option for cultural specialists, in terms of either their works or their lives.

Concluding remarks

So we have a wide range of positions on the question of whether it is possible to develop a unified personality in the contemporary world. Before we summarize the various positions in terms of a typology, it would be useful to briefly recap Max Weber's view. Goldman (1988: 165) provides a useful assemblage of what he takes to be the four fundamental conditions for the generation of personality which are scattered throughout Weber's work

> First, there must be the creation or existence of a transcendental-like ultimate goal or value that gives leverage over the world through the tension it creates between the believer and the world. Second, there must be a 'witness' to action that is not social, seeing the 'outer' person, but transcendent, regarding the 'inner'. Third, there must be the possibility of salvation or redemption from death or from the meaninglessness of the world and the attainment of a sense of certainty about it. And fourth, there must be no ritual, magic or external means for relieving one's burden of guilt, or despair. Together these four conditions anchor the sense of meaning and may later provide possibilities that life in an age without religion has otherwise lost.

It may be possible, following Weber's invocation of a gradation in his discussion of hero ethics, to conceive of a similar gradation of personality formation, with the above set of characteristics taken as summarizing the conditions of possibility for the full development of personality. The Puritan and Old Testament prophet clearly falls at this end of the continuum. Next we might place the aesthetics of existence of the Greeks. The artist, cultural specialist, intellectual or scientist in the modern world might come next, bearing in mind that, with whatever heroic stoicism they might attempt to order their lives, for Weber modern culture could not provide a viable replacement for the solutions proposed by religious theodicy. For Weber these secular ethics merely fuelled desire and inflated the sense of the possible without providing an ordered cosmology which would fulfil the psychic need for a meaningfully ordered life (Whimster, 1987: 289). It can be suggested that the plea Weber made for the maintenance of the separation of the various life-orders in the modern world has gone unheeded and we have seen not only partial signs of the collision of the spheres he referred to in 'Politics as a vocation', but a heightened dedifferentiation, the changes which some want to label as the end of art, the end of the avant-garde and the end of the intellectuals, which some would place under the sign of postmodernism. In effect the deformation of the cultural sphere has collapsed the authority and prestige which maintained the distance between the cultural specialist and the ordinary person. While we are currently entering a more exacerbated phase of the demonopolization of the power of cultural establishments vis-à-vis outsider groups, there is no reason to believe that in the future new global conditions might come into being which would reverse this trend.

If, however, we consider some of the cultural tendencies which are
associated with the term postmodernism, it is clear that we would have to
move further along the continuum, with the possibility of a unified ordered
life in terms of some ethic of aesthetics as conceived by, for example Rorty
or Maffesoli, giving way to a looser agglomeration of experiences and
sensations which may become syncretized into a less coherent form of
unity, or unicity. Something which may provide the excitement of role
change and mask-wearing, as Hennis (1988) reminds us, cannot provide
the ordered life. Weber, too, had his misgivings about the possible
emergence in the West of similar tendencies to that found in the Confucian
ethic, being scathing about this Eastern case of utilitarianism, the
Mandarin blend of the cautious, calculating pursuit of earthly pleasures
and pragmatic, bureaucratic conformism (see Liebersohn, 1988). As we
move further along the gradation we encounter some of the intensities,
immersions and immediacies of the vivid disconnected experiences that
some associate with the shift towards a postmodern culture. Jameson's
'multi-phrenic' intensities point to the complete breakdown of form into
life. Yet however frightening this prospect may be for those whom this is
thrust upon (and it is hard to conceive of schizophrenia as otherwise), for
those who plunge into the stream of life in a controlled way, the artists,
intellectuals, critics and the cultural intermediaries and audiences who
empathize with them, there is the comforting possibility of a different
return, this time a return from life to form. However attractive and
transgressive the dissolution of established forms, the collaging and
reordering of existing ones and the immersion into life may seem, this
process gives rise to new objectifications. These are not only the new forms
of art and intellectual life, but also the piling-up of forms with which to
interpret this process, some of which are pedagogies to help the uninitiated
learn how to make sense of the new experiences and modes of *formisme*. In
effect, how to decontrol their emotions, to play with a variety of new and
potentially threatening images and sensations without the fear of a total
loss of control must also be considered. The process of formation and
deformation of culture continues apace.

In this sense the fears expressed by Daniel Bell (1980) about the transgressive and antinomian characteristics of modernism and postmodernism
need not be so strong, nor his nostalgia for the Puritan so marked, for the
modern artist and intellectual necessarily plays with and shapes life in
ways which, however much they may seem to stretch our intellects and
sensibilities, necessarily aim at some eventual, albeit more complex, multi-
readable, recovery of form into life – but a form more flexible and less
elevated: a form on the side of life and against form itself. The turn-of-the-
century publics and audiences may have found the transgressions of the
followers of the artist and erotic life-orders threatening, disturbing and
troubling, yet today we have larger audiences who can attune themselves
to a wider range of more complex sensations and forms, who can rapidly
switch between aesthetic distantiation and the heady immediacy of

temporary immersion. Rather than this being interpreted nostalgically as signalling the end of morality, perhaps it points to a more complex range of unities, syncretic blends and differentiations between both the ethical and the aesthetic, and an involvement and detachment which entail varying degrees of mutual respect, restraint and tolerance within a new cultural context. This could be a context in which some of the old communalities (the 'common culture' as a goal of both the state's national self-formation process and oppositional countercultural movements of artists and intellectuals) will wither away, or find themselves uncomfortably juxtaposed alongside other traditions and value-complexes, which are difficult to discredit or ignore within a wider, more complex cultural form of global compression.

It may seem a massive and unwarranted step to speak about personality formation in the same sentence as the global cultural order, especially in today's specialized world; yet the tradition of sociology associated with Weber, Simmel and those such as Elias and Rex who have sought to carry on the scope of their efforts is one which had little time for the boundary-maintainers who kept to their own territories and identified sociology with the narrowly conceived study of society – society which was generally regarded as the leftover bits after the economy, the nation-state, international and transnational relations, cultural values and personality formation had been taken out. It is this more widely conceived trans-disciplinary sociology which would seem to be best suited to attempt to answer the vital questions of our time, questions which demand perspective and detachment, the capacity to range far away to understand something which is very near to our hearts.

Notes

The original version of this chapter was written for a collection of essays in honour of John Rex (*Knowledge and Passion: Essays in Sociology and Social Theory in Honour of John Rex*, ed. H. Martins, I.B. Tauris, 1993). John Rex was my first teacher in sociology when he was appointed to the chair at the University of Durham in 1965. Incidentally the patronizing myopia, and even contempt and hostility towards the 'non-subject' of sociology found in much of British academic life was still evident in the unwillingness to accept the subject's name (a bastard mixture of Latin and Greek) as a valid title for either courses or a department in the university. Rex's department was therefore called . Social Theory and Institutions (something which remains inscribed on my BA certificate). Needless to say he managed to reverse the title and change the name to sociology some years later.

1. Georg Simmel's capacity to attract a varied audience to his lectures, which became public events, is well known. His mode of delivery was remarkable, as a contemporary noted:

One could observe how the process of thought took possession of the whole man, how the haggard figure on the lecture platform became the medium of an intellectual process the passion of which was expressed not in words only, but also in gestures, movements, actions. When Simmel wanted to convey to the audience the core of an idea, he not only formulated it, he so-to-speak picked it up with his hands, his fingers opening and closing; his whole body turned and vibrated under the raised hand. . . . His intensity of speech indicated a supreme tension of thought; he talked abstractly, but this abstract thought sprang from live concern, so that it came to life in the listener. (Fechter, 1948: 52–6, quoted in Coser, 1977: 211)

Yet in fact Simmel's lectures were also a show in the sense that he gave the same lecture on several occasions with virtually no changes, and his ability to give the impression that he was struggling to work out his ideas in front of the audience shows that he was a master of impression management (see Staude, 1990).

2. Apart from such descriptions by Weber's contemporaries, we can only see the embodied Weber in photographs. It is worth recording that in John Rex's study at Durham University a framed photograph of Max Weber was prominently displayed on the mantelpiece. This was the steadfast leonine portrait of Weber which is the frontispiece of Gerth and Mills's *From Max Weber* (1948).

3. This should not be taken to mean that Weber strove to become a personality; far from it – see his attack on the idols of 'personality' and 'personal experience' in 'Science as a vocation' (Weber, 1948b: 137). He despised the cult of personality, and the romantic search for experience and emotional fulfilment. This was manifest in his attitude towards the idols of the cult of youth such as Stefan George. Only the person who showed inner devotion to a specialist task could become a genuine personality (Albrow, 1990: 44).

4. For a discussion of the derivation of Weber's sense of the demonic from Goethe, as well as the Protestant and Kantian sources of Weber's commitment to the ordering and unifying of life via the free action of the person, see Albrow (1990).

5. Jaspers was not alone in his admiration for Weber. Theodor Heuss, the future President of West Germany, began his obituary of Weber:

> For us young people meeting him meant the experience of a daemonic personality. He had power over men, the power of destructive anger, of objective clarity, attractive grace; all his utterances were suggestive, endowed with 'charisma', with the grace of inborn leadership. (Green, 1976: 278)

6. Weber (1951: 131–2) tells us that the 'gentleman ideal' was 'the man who had attained all-around self-perfection, who had become a "work of art" in the sense of a classical canon of psychical beauty, which literary tradition implemented in the souls of disciples'. This was accumulated through education in the classics, which was subjected to certified examinations so that 'canonical and beautiful achievements' could be displayed in a 'salon' culture.

7. The main account of the relationship is in Green (1976). It is also referred to in Roth's (1988: xlii) new introduction to Marianne Weber's biography of Max and Whimster's (1989: 463) review article. The love letters from Max Weber to Else as yet remain unpublished and there is considerable controversy as to their actual contents. In the German edition of Marianne Weber's (1988) *Lebensbild* Roth adds to the controversy by arguing that Marianne knew about the affair and hence there was never a time when Max fell short of his obligation to be totally honest with his wife about the situation (see Liebersohn, 1988–9: 126). It is worth adding that the discovery came as a tremendous blow to Karl Jaspers, for here was the person he had built up to be a paragon of consistency, honesty and responsibility, who had gone to great lengths to conceal his affair from his wife (see Whimster, 1989; Henrich, 1987).

8. Well before the 'Ethical neutrality' essay (1917) was written, Weber is reported as having asked Else Jaffe in 1908: 'But wouldn't you say that any *value* could be embodied in eroticism?' To which she replied 'But certainly – beauty!' (Green, 1976: 171).

9. See, for example, his discussion in *The Philosophy of Money* (Simmel, 1978) and the essay 'On the concept of the tragedy of culture' (Simmel, 1968) where he tells us that the 'voracious accumulation' of objective culture is 'deeply incompatible with the forms of personal life'. He adds:

> The receptive capacity of the self is limited not only by the force and length of life, but also through a certain unity and relative compactness of its form. The individual might pass by what his self-development cannot assimilate, but this does not always succeed so easily. The infinite growing supply of objectified spirit places demands before the subject, creates desires in him, hits him with a feeling of individual inadequacy and helplessness, throws him into total relationships

from whose impact he cannot withdraw, although he cannot master their particular contents. Thus, the typically problematic situation of modern man comes into being: his sense of being surrounded by an innumerable number of cultural elements which are neither meaningless to him, nor in the final analysis, meaningful. In their mass, they depress him, since he is not capable of assimilating them all, nor can he simply reject them, since after all, they do belong *potentially* within the sphere of his cultural development. (Simmel, 1968: 44)

10. Foucault (1987: 341) writes:

it was reserved for a few people of the population, it was not a question of giving a pattern of behaviour for everybody. It was a personal choice for a small elite. The reason for making this choice was the will to live a beautiful life, and to leave to others memories of a beautiful existence. I don't think that we can say that this kind of ethics was an attempt to normalize the population.

4

THE HEROIC LIFE AND EVERYDAY LIFE

The modern hero is no hero; he acts heroes.

(Benjamin, 1973: 97)

Perhaps it is precisely the petit-bourgeois who has the presentiment of the dawn of a new heroism, a heroism both enormous and collective, on the model of arts.

(Musil, *The Man without Qualities*, quoted in de Certeau, 1984: 1)

I do not like heroes, they make too much noise in the world.

(Voltaire, quoted in Gouldner, 1975: 420)

To speak of the heroic life is to risk sounding a little dated. Intellectual and academic life have long sustained strong countercultural traditions which have favoured an anti-heroic ethos. Periodically these traditions have gained greater prominence, for example in the 1960s. The most recent manifestation of this antinomian spirit, postmodernism, has little time for elevating artistic, intellectual and other cultural pursuits to the status of coherent lifestyles capable of making grand statements which will be generally illuminating and instructive. Conceptions such as the artist as hero with their associated notions of genius and a life-ordering sense of calling and mission have given way to a less elevated valuation of the popular and the detritus of everyday mass and consumer cultures. Postmodernism has also been associated with the positive evaluation of local and popular cultures, the minor traditions and the 'otherness' excluded by the universalistic pretension of the modern. This suggests an increasing sensitivity to the more complex levels of unity, to the syncretism, heterogeneity, and the common taken-for-granted, 'seen but unnoticed' aspects of everyday life. Of course, the sociology of everyday life cannot be reduced to an effect of postmodernism. Rather we should regard postmodernism as enhancing tendencies to transform the cultural sphere which gained a strong impetus from the 1960s. The rise of new social movements, feminism, ecology and the increasing significance of leisure and the quest for self-expression and self-realization not only pointed to the capacity to transform the institutions of public life, but also raised the profile of the life left behind. Everyday life, with its focus upon reproduction, maintenance, common routines, the sphere of women, receptivity and sociability has gained impetus with the problematization of the dominant legitimacy of the world of production with its emphasis upon instrumental rationality, transformation and sacrifice.

If everyday life is usually associated with the mundane, taken-for-granted, commonsense routines which sustain and maintain the fabric of our daily lives, then the heroic life points to the opposite qualities. Here we think of extraordinary deeds, virtuosity, courage, endurance and the capacity to attain distinction. If the very taken-for-grantedness of everyday life means the necessity of subjecting one's activities to practical knowledge and routines whose heterogeneity and lack of systemicity is rarely theorized, then the heroic life cuts a swathe through this dense facticity. It points to an ordered life fashioned by fate or will, in which the everyday is viewed as something to be tamed, resisted or denied, something to be subjugated in the pursuit of a higher purpose.

Everyday life

More than most sociological concepts 'everyday life' has proved exceedingly difficult to define. This would seem to be because everyday life is the life-world which provides the ultimate ground from which spring all our conceptualizations, definitions and narratives. At the same time, from the perspective of constituted specialist forms of knowledge which have forgotten this, it appears to be a residual category into which can be jettisoned all the irritating bits and pieces which do not fit into orderly thought. Indeed, as commentators are quick to point out, to venture into this field is to explore an aspect of life whose central features apparently lack methodicalness and are particularly resistant to rational categorization (see Geertz, 1983; Heller, 1984; Sharrock and Anderson, 1986; Bovone, 1989; Maffesoli, 1989). Bearing in mind this inherent ambiguity and lack of consensus, we can outline the characteristics most frequently associated with everyday life. First, there is an emphasis upon what happens every day, the routine, repetitive taken-for-granted experiences, beliefs and practices; the mundane ordinary world, untouched by great events and the extraordinary. Second, the everyday is regarded as the sphere of reproduction and maintenance, a pre-institutional zone in which the basic activities which sustain other worlds are performed, largely by women. Third, there is an emphasis upon the present which provides a non-reflexive sense of immersion in the immediacy of current experiences and activities. Fourth, there is a focus on the non-individual embodied sense of being together in spontaneous common activities outside, or in the interstices, of the institutional domains; an emphasis upon common sensuality, being with others in frivolous, playful sociability. Fifth, there is an emphasis upon heterogeneous knowledge, the disorderly babble of many tongues; speech and 'the magic world of voices' are valued over the linearity of writing.

This aspect can be developed by referring to Agnes Heller's discussion of Plato's contrast between *doxa* (general opinion grounded in daily routines) and *episteme* (scientific knowledge which aims to provide more lasting truths). This can lead us to a relational view of everyday thought with its meaning defined in terms of its opposite modes of thought. Whereas everyday thought is heterogeneous and syncretic, scientific, philosophical and other formalized modes of thought are more systemic, reflexive and de-anthropomorphizing (Heller, 1984: 49ff.). Such more formalized modes of thought themselves can be seen as striving for systemicity, which increasingly separates them from their dependence on the prime symbolic media in which they are grounded.

Alfred Schutz (1962) has referred to the everyday commonsense world as the 'paramount reality' which can be distinguished from a series of 'multiple realities' or 'finite provinces of meaning'. There are the 'worlds' of dreams, fantasies, daydreams, play, fiction and the theatre as well as the more formalized worlds of science, philosophy and art. Each demands a different 'natural attitude', time sense and structure of relevance, and there are problems for individuals who do not observe them. Here it is possible to recall Schutz's (1964) description of the difficulties encountered by Cervantes's Don Quixote in mixing together fantasy and everyday life. There are, of course, some socially sanctioned occasions in which such intermixing is encouraged, where the world of fantasy becomes lived out in the midst of everyday life, such as festivals and the carnivalesque. Such liminal moments are usually well circumscribed, yet it can be argued that the syncretic and heterogeneous nature of everyday life means that the perceptions of the doubly-coded, the playful, desires and fantasies lurk within the interstices of everyday life and threaten to irrupt into it.

As Schutz, Garfinkel and the ethnomethodologists remind us, it takes considerable taken-for-granted practical skill to negotiate these various worlds and the transitions between them. It can be added that the capacity to mobilize such a flexible generative structure capable of handling a wide variety and high degree of complexity of finite provinces of meaning cannot be understood as a historical constant. Indeed the nature and number of finite provinces of meaning and their relative separation or embeddedness in everyday life will vary historically. Hence it can be argued that a precise definition of everyday life cannot be given, rather we should seek to understand it as a process – and, as Nietzsche reminds us, that which has a history cannot be defined.

A number of theorists have sought to comprehend the historical processes which have led to the increasing differentiation and colonization of everyday life. The Frankfurt School (Held, 1980) and Lefebvre (1971) have, for example, focused on the commodification and instrumental rationalization of everyday life. Habermas (1981) has elaborated a distinction between system and life-world in which the instrumental rational action employed by the political-administrative and economic systems are seen to invade and erode the emancipatory communicative potential of the everyday life-world. Heller (1984), following Lukács, has drawn attention to the ways in which the heterogeneity of everyday life has been subjected to processes of homogenization. It is therefore possible to refer to an initial process of differentiation in which science, art, philosophy and other forms of theoretical knowledge originally embedded within everyday life become progressively separated and subjected to specialist development, followed by a further phase whereby this knowledge is fed back in order to rationalize, colonize and homogenize everyday life.

The danger is to assume that this process has a self-propelling momentum and universalizing force which turns it into a logic of history beyond human intervention. Rather, it might be more useful to conceive of it in terms of the changing struggles and interdependencies between figurations of people bound together in particular historical situations in which they seek to mobilize various power resources, than to refer to a logic of history.[1] Elias (1987a) has discussed the process of differentiation whereby specialist functions previously carried out by the group as a whole become separated. Hence there is the emergence of specialists in violence control (warriors), knowledge specialists (priests) and eventually economic and political specialists. It is also possible to trace the emergence of other groups of specialists, such as cultural specialists who participate in the formation of a relatively autonomous cultural sphere in which scientific, philosophical and artistic symbolic media are developed. In addition in modern societies there is the whole array of experts such as those in the helping professions and mass media occupations which supply a variety of means of orientation and practical knowledge for everyday life. This should not be understood as an automatic and orderly process: the particular conditions of a society's state formation, and its relation to the other nation-states in which it is bound in a figuration, determine the actual type and degree of differentiation which may propel and maintain certain groups of specialists in positions of power. Under certain conditions priests may attain a dominant position within society and in other circumstances warriors may become dominant. The nature, extent and duration of their dominance will clearly have an impact upon everyday life.

With the rise of Western modernity cultural specialists such as scientists, artists, intellectuals and academics have gained in relative power and have sought in various ways to advocate the transformation, domestication, civilization, repair and healing of what are considered the shortcomings of everyday life. Yet other cultural specialists have sought to promote and defend the intrinsic qualities of everyday life through the celebration of the integrity of popular cultures and traditions. For them everyday life is less regarded as raw material and 'otherness' ripe for formation and cultivation; rather they can be seen to advocate a reversal of the process of differentiation and a greater awareness of the equal validity, and in some cases even superior wisdom, of everyday knowledge and practices. Hence under certain conditions popular cultures are celebrated and the ordinary person's mundane life, the life of 'the man without qualities' heroicized. Such processes of de-differentiation, of re-heterogenization and re-immersion into the everyday have featured prominently in countercultural movements such as romanticism and postmodernism. This is also evident in the critique of the heroic image of the cultural specialist, the scientist, artist or intellectual as hero, in favour of an emphasis upon everyday mundane practices which are regarded as equally capable of producing what some want to regard as extraordinary or elevated insights or objectifications.[2]

In this sense the positive or negative evaluation of everyday life can be seen to relate to the way in which its counterconcept is evaluated. For Habermas (1981) the system is the danger to the life-world and its intrusions must be controlled if the capacity for everyday life to open up its communicative potential is to be realized. Lefebvre (1971) also emphasizes the need to go beyond the commodification of contemporary everyday life in the 'bureaucratic society of controlled consumption' and release the festive aspects of everyday life. The positive evaluation of the qualities of everyday life are highlighted in Maffesoli's (1989) work in which he draws attention to the capacity of everyday life to resist the process of rationalization and preserve and foster sociality, a concern for the present, the frivolous, imaginative and Dionysiac forms of life which provide a sense of collective immersion, of giving up one's own individual being (*Einfühlung*). In a similar way de Certeau (1984) affirms the ordinary practices of everyday life and its capacity to utilize modes of syncretism, the 'non-logical logics' of everyday life to oppose, transgress and subvert official dominant cultures and technical rationality.[3] Likewise Gouldner (1975: 421) seeks to draw attention to the critical potential of everyday life and the way in which it can function as a counterconcept:

> I have suggested repeatedly that EDL [everyday life] is a *counter*concept, that it gives expression to a *critique* of a certain kind of life, specifically, the heroic, achieving, performance-centred existence. The EDL established itself as real by contrasting itself with the heroic life and by reason of the crisis of the heroic life.

As we have suggested, there are a range of counterconcepts against which everyday life can be defined; we will now turn to what can be considered the major one, the heroic life and the ways in which it becomes transformed and transfigured in other modes of life in the cultural sphere.

The heroic life

If everyday life revolves around the mundane, taken for granted and ordinary, then the heroic life points to its rejection of this order for the extraordinary life which not only threatens the possibility of returning to everyday routines, but entails the deliberate risking of life itself. The emphasis in the heroic life is on the courage to struggle and achieve extraordinary goals, the quest for virtue, glory and fame, which contrasts with the lesser everyday pursuit of wealth, property and earthly love. The everyday world is the one which the hero departs from, leaving behind the sphere of care and maintenance (women, children and the old), only to return to its acclaim should his tasks be completed successfully. A basic contrast, then, is that the heroic life is the sphere of danger, violence and the courting of risk whereas everyday life is the sphere of women, reproduction and care. The heroic life is one in which the hero seeks to prove himself by displaying courage. Warriors were amongst the first heroes, and as specialists in violence they experienced the intense excitement of combat, an emotional force which needed to be controlled and subjected to the cunning of instrumental reason to ensure survival.[4] To achieve great deeds requires both luck, a sense of destiny, that one's particular quest and life are driven by forces outside oneself which offer extraordinary protection, and an inner sense of certainty that with circumspection, craft and compulsion one can overcome the greatest dangers and misfortunes: in effect that one can make one's own fate.

In many ways the heroic life shares the quality of an adventure, or series of adventures. Georg Simmel (1971a) in his essay on the adventure tells us that the adventure falls outside the usual continuity of everyday existence which is disregarded on principle. The adventurer has a different time sense which entails a strong sense of the present and disregard for the future. Simmel captures well the mixture of abandoning oneself to fate and making one's own fate we have spoken of. In the adventure we abandon ourselves to the 'powers and accidents of the world, which can delight us, but in the same breath can also destroy us' (Simmel, 1971a: 193). At the same time we forsake the careful calculation and accumulation of the world of work, for the capacity to act decisively in the world. Hence the adventurer 'has the gesture of the conqueror' who is quick to seize the opportunity and also 'treats the incalculable elements in life in the way we ordinarily treat only what we think by definition calculable' (Simmel, 1971a: 193). Furthermore the adventurer is capable of creating a sense of unity, a synthesis of activity and passivity, of chance and necessity. The adventurer makes a system out of his life's lack of system. It is this capacity to form life that points to the affinity between the adventurer and the artist, as well as the attraction of adventure for the artist. As Simmel (1971a: 189) remarks:

> the essence of the work of art is, after all, that it cuts out a piece of the endless continuous sequences of perceived experience, detaching it from all connections with one side or the other, giving it a self-sufficient form as though defined and held together by an inner core. A part of existence, interwoven with the uninterruptedness of that existence, yet nevertheless felt as a whole, as an integrated unit – that is the form common to both the work of art and the adventure.

In some cases life as a whole may be perceived as an adventure and for this to happen 'one must sense above its totality a higher unity, a super-life, as it were' (Simmel, 1971a: 192). This capacity to order and unify life, to form it from within in terms of some higher purpose which gives life a sense of destiny, it can be argued, is central to the heroic life, especially those who are in Simmel's words 'adventurers of the spirit': intellectuals and artists. The way in which the adventure is lived from within like a narrative which has a beginning, middle and end points to the way life may seem to be like a work of art.[5]

In retrospect the adventure may appear to have a particularly compelling dreamlike quality in which accidental elements and inspired acts are woven together to give a strong sense of coherence. This capacity to retrospectively impose a narrative structure on the adventure should not be taken to imply that the original life 'beneath' the narrative was itself formless. Rather it is important to emphasize the potential to deliberately seek to live life as a unity from within and control and shape chance elements into a structure which seemingly serves some higher purpose, be it one's own glory, God's will, the survival of a nation or people. MacIntyre (1981: 191ff.) emphasizes this point when he argues against the existentialism of Sartre and the sociological theories of Goffman and Dahrendorf who present the enactments of an individual life as a series of unconnected episodes. We find, for example, that Sartre's character Antoine Roquentin in *Nausea* argues that to present human life in the form of a narrative is always to falsify it (MacIntyre, 1981: 199). This approach is also evident in Merleau-Ponty's (1964b) statement in the introduction to *Sense and Non-Sense* that at each stage of our lives we are for all intents and purposes separate persons which have happened 'accidentally' to inhabit the same body and whose various distinct selves become retrospectively woven together through a 'false' narrative which gives biographical unity. Indeed this 'liquidation of the self' into a set of separate situational role players also resonates with the emphasis in postmodern theories on the decentring of the self and the presentation of the person as a bundle of loosely connected quasi-selves (see the discussion in the previous chapter).

For MacIntyre (1981: 197) this misses the point that human actions are enacted narratives; narratives are not imposed upon events which have no narrative order by novelists and dramatists. He quotes Barbara Hardy, who remarks that 'we dream in narrative, day-dream in narrative, remember, anticipate, hope, despair, believe, doubt, plan, revise, criticize, construct, gossip, learn, hate and love by narrative'. Yet the extent to which a larger narrative is employed and sustained to structure and unify a person's life as a whole can vary a great deal. We describe a person as displaying character or personality who achieves a high degree of consistency of conduct; in effect he seeks to impose a form on his life by seeking to follow some higher purpose rather than merely letting his life drift capriciously.

At this stage it might be useful to clarify the distinction between the hero, the heroic life and the heroic society. It is of course possible for anyone to become a hero, to perform a heroic deed without being a member of a heroic society or having a commitment to the heroic life. Hence in the popular media there is a constant celebration of ordinary heroes, those individuals who are thrust into a situation of extreme physical danger in which they show extraordinary courage such as risking or sacrificing their lives to save other people. It is this chance element – that fate might intervene and shatter the everyday order of the happy life and thrust any individual into a situation beyond his or her control – which demands a response, which is fascinating to the public, who cannot but help wonder, 'How would we respond to the test?' This can also be related to hero worship: the ways in which heroes are used as role models for people to identify with (see Klapp, 1969). In this case it is usually some strong person, politician, sportsman, explorer, adventurer, or those who increasingly represent these ways of life, the celebrities and stars of film, television and popular music, who becomes the object of various blends of fantasy and realistic identification.

This can be contrasted with heroic societies such as those described in the Homeric epics or the Icelandic and Irish sagas. Whatever the actual conditions of production of these heroic narratives and their relationship to particular social realities, they provide a picture of social orders in which a person's role and status and associated duties and privileges were well defined within kinship and household structures. Such societies do not admit the possibility of a disjunction between motive and action, as MacIntyre comments (1981: 115): 'A man in heroic society is what he does.' Courage was a central quality necessary to sustain a household and a community, for the courageous person was one who could be relied upon, something which was an important element in friendship. For the Greeks the hero not only displayed courage, but sought to live up to the ideal of *areté*,[6] a term which is often mistakenly translated as 'virtue', but is better rendered as 'excellence' (Kitto, 1951: 171ff.). The heroic ideal was to attain excellence in all the ways in which a man can be excellent – physically, morally, intellectually, practically – without any privileging of the mind over the body. The individual who excelled in battle or contest was accorded the recognition of *kudos*, or glory, by his community (MacIntyre, 1981: 115). Yet while the hero is one who lives within a fragile world in which he is vulnerable to fate and death and can display courage in face of his destiny, he is effectively seeking to live up to an ideal of excellence which is a social role. Hence in heroic societies, the heroic person is one who excels at the performance of a necessary social role.

What is interesting is the way in which the image of the hero is taken out of its context, and woven into a heroic life in which the social context becomes played down, or becomes one in which the hero distinguishes himself from and rises above the social. The influential reading of the Greek past in which a particular late nineteenth-century vision of distinction and individuality is blended together with elements from Greek heroic society became a compelling image in the writings of Nietzsche, an image which MacIntyre (1981: 122) finds particularly misleading:

What Nietzsche portrays is aristocratic *self*-assertion: what Homer and the sagas show are forms of assertion proper to and required by a certain *role*. The self becomes what it is in heroic societies only in and through its role; it is a social creation, not an individual one. Hence when Nietzsche projects back on to the archaic past his own nineteenth-century individualism, he reveals that what looked like an historical enquiry was actually an inventive literary construction. Nietzsche replaces the fictions of the Enlightenment individualism, of which he is so contemptuous, with a set of individualist fictions of his own.

MacIntyre's assertion that Nietzsche's version of the heroic life was a projection of nineteenth-century individualism might be more precisely formulated to highlight the tension between the higher person who displays genuine individuality and distinction (*Vornehmheit*) and the narrow *ressentiment* of the mass man. Furthermore Nietzsche's version of the heroic life did not merely remain as a set of individualist fictions: his particular fiction resonated strongly with notions of artistic and intellectual distinction which gained impetus from the life of Goethe and the Romantic Movement, to develop into a powerful cultural image, one which became influential in certain circles of turn of the century Germany and was subjected to sociological investigation and theoretical formulation by Max Weber and Georg Simmel.[7]

Hero ethics, distinction and the cultural sphere

Max Weber's life and work have often been characterized as heroic. Manasse (1957: 287), for example, remarks that he was a 'type of man who was born in the world of Homer and of the Jewish prophets and has not yet disappeared with Nietzsche. Thus far he had his last great representative in Max Weber.' Manasse's statement was made in the context of a discussion of the impact of Weber on Karl Jaspers. For Jaspers, Weber represented an extraordinary man, driven by a restless demonic force animated by a strong ethic of responsibility. This was manifest in Weber's honesty and consistency of purpose which was expressed in his work, the directness and lack of pretence in his life activities and dealings with other people and in his bodily gestures, bearing and demeanour. Jaspers regarded Weber as a representative of a new type of man and made him the model for his existential philosophy. This modern form of heroism is captured not only in the courage, consistency and unity of purpose Weber attained, but in a quality frequently associated with the heroic life: sacrifice. Without seeking immediate death this type of person 'lived as though they were dead' (Manasse, 1957: 389).

Such questions were, of course, addressed by Weber in his writings. In his discussion of charisma he refers to the capacity for sacrifice displayed by the charismatic leader and demanded of his followers. The charismatic hero's power does not lie in a legitimized social role, but in his extraordinary qualities as a person, the 'gift of grace' and the capacity to constantly subject it to demonstration and test. As Weber (1948d: 249) remarks, 'If he wants to be a prophet, he must perform miracles; if he wants to be a war lord, he must perform heroic deeds.'[8] Such individuals intentionally organized their lives around an ultimate value and were therefore less dependent upon conventional modes of social approval and institutional authority. The injunction to follow some ideal or ultimate value, to form life into a deliberate unity whatever the personal cost, is also central to Weber's discussion of 'hero ethics'. He states:

> One can divide all 'ethics', regardless of their material content into two major groups according to whether they make basic demands on a person to which he can generally *not* live up except for the great high points of his life, which point the way as guideposts in his *striving* in infinity ('hero ethics'), or whether they are modest enough to accept his everyday 'nature' as a maximal requirement ('average ethics'). It seems to me that only the first category, the 'hero ethics', can be called 'idealism'. (Weber's comments on an essay by Otto Gross, quoted in Marianne Weber, 1975: 378)

Weber was later to qualify this strict dichotomy between 'hero ethics' and 'average ethics' to admit a more nuanced gradation. As Marianne Weber (1975: 388) tells us, his new insight was that 'there is a scale of the ethical. If the ethically highest is unattainable in a concrete case, an attempt must be made to attain the second or third best.' This can be related to the discussion of the various modern life-orders that had replaced the possibility of an ethical totality and unified personality which were associated with Puritanism. The process of differentiation has resulted in separate economic, political, aesthetic, erotic, intellectual and academic life-orders (Weber, 1948c). Yet despite his heroic defence of science as a vocation and the ethic of responsibility as valid ways of living in the modern world, there is no sense for Weber that, in a cultural context of value pluralism, they could provide a sense of certainty and solutions to the problems of coherent meaning. The same could be said of the ways of life offered by the other life-orders in the cultural sphere: the aesthetic, intellectual and erotic. For Weber the general process of rationalization signified the decline in the possibility of developing into a genuine person, a unified personality who displays consistency of conduct and who can attain distinction which is captured in the Protestant idea of *Persön-lichkeit*, an ideal which Weber sought to uphold throughout his life.[9]

Weber gives qualified acknowledgement to the idea that the artist, intellectual and erotic life-orders could develop personalities, albeit 'lesser' ones, and with progressive difficulty. In this sense it would be legitimate to investigate the artist as hero and examine, for example, the extent to which particular artists in specific social figurations (figures such as Goethe, Beethoven, Berlioz, Flaubert, van Gogh) were sustained by lifestyles and prestige economies which favoured the development of 'hero ethics'. In a similar way one could investigate the notion of the intellectual as hero and examine, for example, figures such as Marx, Zola or Sartre. Further categories suggest themselves in terms of the erotic life in social forms such

as bohemias and countercultures (Otto Gross), and the turning of life
itself into a work of art in dandyism and other modes (Beau Brummell,
Huysmans's des Esseintes, Oscar Wilde, Stefan George, Salvador Dali,
etc.).

From Weber's perspective all these various manifestations of the heroic
life within the cultural sphere tended to create an 'unbrotherly aristocracy'
independent of personal ethical qualities, yet such a cultural aristocracy
would best be sustained within a relatively independent cultural sphere. At
one point Weber speaks of an intellectual aristocracy of independent
rentiers, yet the specific conditions which had developed to favour this
with the formation of the cultural sphere could be equally threatened by
the deformation of the cultural sphere and the loss of the relative
autonomy of cultural producers. On the one hand, this process could
be related to the processes of rationalization, bureaucratization and
commodification which changed the conditions of production and relation
to their various publics of artists, intellectuals, academics and other
cultural vocations. On the other hand, it could be described in terms of a
perceived process of engulfment from below, the rise of the masses and
their culture (Theweleit, 1987).

The latter viewpoint finds one of its clearest expressions in the writings
of Max Scheler, who fretted about the *ressentiment* of the common man,
who is poisoned by the repressed emotions of envy, spite, hatred and
revenge and seeks to dismantle the social hierarchy between him and his
betters and destroy those noble values that he does not possess (see
Staude, 1967). Scheler sought a return to aristocratic values, some new
'spiritual aristocracy' for the modern age to re-establish noble and heroic
models of life through the youth movements. Like Weber, Simmel and
many of the generation which dominated German academic life around
the turn of the century, Scheler was strongly influenced by Nietzsche's
work. Yet of the three, Simmel was the only one who did not take up
some form of nostalgic reaction to modernity and the prospective eclipse
of the heroic life. Simmel's sociology of modernity pointed to the opposite
outcome: it provided a completely new modern ideal of distinction
(*Vornehmheit*) which for our purposes deserves examination for it suggests
the persistence of a form of the heroic life.

It has often been remarked that whereas Simmel favoured the aesthetic
way of being, Weber favoured the ethical (see for example Green, 1988).
Both pointed to the differentiation and fragmentation of modern life, yet
Simmel (1978) developed a more positive appreciation of the possibilities
for an aestheticization of life released by the very capitalist money
economy which many held was destructive of art and culture. While it is
possible to point to a general aestheticization of everyday life in the large
cities of the late nineteenth century (see Featherstone, 1991a: Ch. 5), the
effects of the money economy on the development of personality have
usually been regarded as negative. Simmel refers to the capacity of money
to turn everything which has a specific quality into quantity, prostitution

being a good example of this process of commodification, which points to the deformation of the person.

It is, however, one of the merits of his *Wechselwirkung* interaction approach, which points to the dense network of reciprocal interactions that make up the social world, that it provides unusual insights into how things usually held apart influence each other (e.g. culture on the economy, not just the economy on culture). Hence the processes of the levelling of distinct differences and the quantification of everyday life through the expansion of the money economy is presented as capable of provoking an opposite reaction: the determination to preserve and develop one's essential quality as a person which Simmel (1978: 389ff.) referred to as *Vornehmheitsideal*, the ideal of distinction. Liebersohn (1988: 141) remarks that 'Simmel argued that the modern ideal of distinction was an absolutely new value brought into existence by the challenge to personal values of the money economy.' According to Liebersohn, Simmel took the ideal of distinction from Nietzsche's *Beyond Good and Evil*. Here Nietzsche argues that the distinctive type of man has developed in aristocratic societies with their rigid social hierarchy and well-defined differences which can supply the 'pathos of distance' whereby the ruling caste can look down on, and keep its distance from the rest.[10] For Simmel (1986: 168–9) this 'social aristocraticism' and 'morality of nobility' advocated by Nietzsche meant the employment of discipline and a sense of duty, a severity and 'selfishness in the preservation of the highest personal values'. Yet self-responsibility should not be confused with egoism and hedonism, for in the ideal of distinction or personalism: 'Egoism aspires to have something, personalism to be something.'

Liebersohn (1988: 143) captures well the characteristics of the modern form of distinction when he states that

> The person of distinction was possessed by a sense of the absolute worth of his soul without regard for the world and was ready to sacrifice everything to remain true to himself. His distinction supposedly asserts his independence from society. Yet paradoxically it shared modern society's impersonality. If impersonality signified the shifting effects or institutions and conventions on individual idiosyncrasies, *Vornehmheit's* inner law, too, eradicated every spontaneous impulse in the name of an artificial order. Absolute personal autonomy offset the social order only by internalizing its logic, creating, to be sure, a style setting the bearer apart, but doing so only through a pattern or radical repression. This was the price one paid for turning the modern fate into a personal destiny.

There are clear resemblances here with Weber's Protestant and Kantian ideal of *Persönlichkeit*, which suggest that the ethical and aesthetic ideals are not so easily separated as some would like. Yet Weber held that *Persönlichkeit*, which had its origins in traditional Christianity, was increasingly becoming less tenable in the modern age, whereas Simmel's concept of *Vornehmheit*, which depended upon social differentiation, could never have existed in a traditional community.[11]

Women, consumer culture and the critique of the heroic life

The critique of everyday life is not a new phenomenon. As Gouldner (1975: 419) informs us, the critique of everyday life was evident in the literature of the Ancient Greeks. Euripides, for example, stood on the side of the common people, the world of women, children, old people and slaves. He called for the rejection of power, fame, ambition, physical courage and virtue, the essential features of the heroic life. The growth in the power potential of outsider groups such as women, the young, the elderly and ethnic and regional minorities has been part of a long-term process within Western modernity – something which some want to refer to as postmodernism and characterize as a significant cultural shift – and has led to an assault on the heroic life.

A key element in the current critique of the viability of the heroic life in the modern age has been provided by feminism, which regards the heroic life as extolling the essentially masculine virtues of sacrifice, distinction, discipline, dignity, self-denial, self-restraint and commitment to a cause. In her extensive critique of Max Weber's commitment to the heroic life, Roslyn Bologh (1990: 17) remarks:

> If I had to encapsulate all of these ideas into an image it would be that of the strong, stoic, resolutely independent, self-disciplined individual who holds himself erect with self-control, proud of his capacity to distance himself from his body, from personal longings, personal possessions and personal relationships, to resist and renounce the temptations of pleasure in order to serve some impersonal cause – a masculine, ascetic image. The image of devotion to some impersonal cause can be interpreted as rationalizing and justifying self-repression while channeling the aggressive, competitive, jealous, angry feelings that accompany such repression.

Against this masculine ideal of manliness and aggressive will to power, Bologh presents a feminine image of passivity and the acceptance of powerlessness. This lack of power is accompanied by a sense of vulnerability and desire for attachment, to be loved by others. The masculine heroic image requires the suppression of vanity: in effect, recognition and glory should only be expected with the ultimate resolution of the quest. Hence the individual who follows the heroic life should be indifferent to hero worship, recognition and the love of others. The feminine ethic operates on the basis of a more prosaic desire for reciprocity in the love of the other, it accepts the emotional bonding with the other, identification and empathy. It assumes that erotic love can be maintained within everyday life, that it is possible to move to and fro from attachment to separation, from communion to differentiation within the same relationship. Bologh (1990: 213ff.) therefore advocates an ethic of sociability against hero ethics which is less elevated, and more open to an egalitarian exploration of playfulness and pleasure with the other, to the immersion and loss of the self rather than the preservation and elevation of the self.

Sociability was, of course, one of the characteristic features of everyday life which we discussed earlier. To speak of sociability is immediately to recall the work of Georg Simmel and his influential essay on the topic. Sociability – *'the play-form of association'* (Simmel, 1971b: 130) – entailed the setting aside of the normal status and objective qualities of the personality and is essentially a form of interaction between equals, without any obvious purpose or set content, in which talk and light playfulness becomes an end in itself. It is a further example of Simmel's *Wechsel-wirkung* approach, with its capacity to tease out unusual insights from seemingly contradictory perceptions, that in discussing the responses to the contradictions of modern culture, he not only pointed to the possibility of *Vornehmheit*, aesthetic responses and the detachment of turning life into a work of art, but pointed to an opposite response through the immersion in playful sociability. A further response which Simmel developed in the face of the tremendous expansion of objective culture and the oppressive weight of cultural forms was the affirmation of life itself. Life, the formless form, provided a sense of immersion and loss of self in the immediacy of experiences; it also proved to be a central preoccupation within cultural modernism with its fascination with the prosaic, the ordinary and the everyday (e.g. surrealism) which favoured an anti-heroic ethos and heroization of the mundane which sharply contrasts with the heroic life (Featherstone, 1991b).

The twentieth-century consumer cultures which developed in Western societies, with their expanded means of technical production of goods and reproduction of images and information, constantly play back these possibilities. Consumer culture does not put forward a unitary message. The heroic life is still an important image in this culture, and as long as there still exists interpersonal violence and warfare between states there is a firm basis for the preservation of this image, as the risking of life, self-sacrifice and commitment to a cause are still important themes sustained within male culture. Here one thinks of the discussion of the heroic military culture of extraordinary men who became involved in the development of the space programme of the United States described by Tom Wolfe in *The Right Stuff* (1989). At the same time consumer culture puts out mythical hero images of the Superman and Rambo type, as well as pastiches and parodies of the whole heroic tradition such as the film, *Monty Python and the Holy Grail* (1975) and various blends of both such as are found in the Indiana Jones films.

The twentieth century, however, has also seen the development of a strong anti-heroic ethos fostered by cultural modernism's antinomian movement away from notions of artistic and intellectual genius[12] and the retreat from life into art, to favour a blurring of the boundaries between art and everyday life which has been enhanced by surrealism, Dada and postmodernism.[13] Consumer culture has enhanced this aestheticization of everyday life through the development of advertising, imagery and publicity which saturate the fabric of the lived environment and everyday encounters.

The decline of hero ethics also suggests a feminization of culture. Not that patriarchy and male supremacy have been eclipsed – far from it. But there has been a long-term swing of the balance of power between the sexes (Elias, 1987b) which has become more marked over the last century and has seen a rise in the power potential of women, one symptom of which has been their increased prominence and ability to raise questions in the public sphere about male domination, domestic violence and child abuse, issues which formerly could not be admitted.

In the cultural sphere one manifestation of this relative shift in the balance of power has been the movement to accord greater legitimacy to everyday culture, the cultural pursuits of women such as popular romance and soap operas. These areas of popular and mass culture and the whole area of women's everyday culture which revolves around the production and management of consumption, areas which were previously seen as peripheral in contrast to the perceived centrality of production and stratification, are being subjected to more intense study by social scientists and students of the humanities, and hence are gaining in legitimacy. Yet if this provides an alternative set of mass cultural images to those of the heroic life, to what extent does it suggest possibilities for new heroes and heroines? How far do Hollywood and media stars and celebrities provide extensions of Simmel's model of distinction or Weber's notions of *Persönlichkeit* and charisma? Is it possible to discuss these issues in a relatively detached way without making the judgement that they can only achieve the status of regressions, pale imitations of the heroic life?

It has been remarked that mass culture has often been associated with women and real authentic culture with men (Huyssen, 1986: 47). Certainly in Nietzsche's view the masses, the herd, are perceived as feminine, in contrast to the artist or philosopher as hero who displays masculine characteristics. As Huyssen (1986: 52) remarks, an examination of European magazines and newspapers of the late nineteenth century would show that

> the proletarian and petit-bourgeois were persistently described in terms of a feminine threat. Images of the raving mob as hysterical, of the engulfing floods of revolt and revolution, of the swamp of big city life, of the spreading ooze of massification, of the figure of the red whore at the barricades – all of these pervade the writings of the mainstream of the media.[14]

Nietzsche provides a further indication of the association of femininity and mass culture in his hostility towards theatricality, shown, for example, in his writings on the Wagner cult. In *The Gay Science* he also writes that 'It is impossible to dissociate the questions of art, style and truth from the question of women' (quoted in Sayre, 1989: 145). For Nietzsche and, following him, for Weber and Simmel the genuine heroic person was characterized not by what they do, but by what they are – the qualities are within the person and hence genuine personality is a matter of fate. Weber, for example, held in contempt the development of the modern notion of personality which is associated with mask-wearing and celebrity.

Yet within the consumer culture which developed in the twentieth century, the new popular heroes were less likely to be warriors, statesmen, explorers, inventors or scientists and more likely to be celebrities, albeit that some of the celebrities would be film stars who would play the role of these former heroes. Lowenthal (1961: 116) reminds us that whereas in the past heroes were 'idols of production', now they are 'idols of consumption'. The characteristic demanded of celebrities is to have *personality*, to possess the actor's skills of presenting a colourful self, to maintain allure, fascination and mystery. These are seen to replace the more traditional virtues of *character*, which emphasized moral consistency, sincerity and unity of purpose. Kasson (1990) has detected a shift in etiquette books in late nineteenth-century America from proclaiming the virtues of moral character to acting as guides for individuals who must learn to read and portray techniques of self-presentation in a complex urban environment with the ever present possibility of deception. The perception of the self as a series of dramatic effects, of learned techniques as opposed to inherent good moral characteristics, leads to a problematization and fragmentation of the self.

Today's stars in the motion picture, television and popular music industries (Dyer, 1979; Frith and Horne, 1987; Gledhill, 1991) would therefore appear to be a long way from the heroic life. But need this be the whole story? Does not this judgement show a nostalgia for a particular formulation of the heroic life, one which penalizes women and mass culture in allowing men to achieve heroism through high cultural pursuits? To answer this question we would need to investigate more closely the formation of consumer culture stars and celebrities in particular contexts. It might be, for example, that the position of monopolization achieved by the Hollywood studio system in the 1930s was able to support lifestyles akin to those of the artist as hero, or artists of life. Moreover, the major contemporary 'superstar' Madonna has been instrumental in developing a different type of femininity which is more self-confident and assertive as well as attempting to redefine her performances as art rather than popular music. Such crossovers (Walker, 1987) may suggest that while the end of art, the end of the intellectuals and the avant-garde have been proclaimed interesting new possibilities could have been developing in the twentieth century which present new variations on the heroic life – that is, if one still accepts that we do not yet live in a postmodern 'retro' or playback culture and that the long-term processes of cultural formation, deformation and reformation can still be sustained.

Notes

Earlier versions of this chapter were presented at the Nordplan Conference on Everyday Life, Stockholm, January 1991 and the Center for Twentieth Century Studies, University of Wisconsin at Milwaukee in November 1991. I would like to thank all who attended for their helpful comments. I have also benefited from discussions and suggestions for revision from

Zygmunt Bauman, Eric Corijn, Mike Hepworth, Harry McL. Currie, Hans Mommaas, Roland Robertson, John Staude, Bryan S. Turner, Kathleen Woodward and Cas Wouters. An earlier version of the chapter appeared in *Theory, Culture & Society*, 9(1), 1992.

1. Here we think for example of Heller's (1978) study of the ways in which art, philosophy and science were separated from everyday life and used to criticize it. At the same time she points to the ways in which science percolated down into everybody's daily life and the way in which there were moves to humanize and aestheticize everyday life. Elias's (1978, 1982) investigation of the 'civilizing process' in Western Europe points to the complex interplay between the production of expert knowledge (e.g. manners books) and its utilization and dissemination by various groups of people bound together through the dynamic of state formation processes, to alter the nature of everyday practices.

2. For discussion of the everyday routines of science and the way they operate to produce various notions of 'truth' and 'results' see Knorr-Cetina (1981) and Latour (1987).

3. Traces of this positive evaluation of everyday life by Maffesoli and de Certeau can be found in the writings of Baudrillard. In particular there is his affirmation of the cynical and 'mirror-like' capacity of the masses to resist absorption and manipulation by the mass media (see Baudrillard, 1983b).

4. See on this Horkheimer and Adorno's (1972) discussion of the development of enlightened reason in Homer's Odysseus, the Greek hero who risks his life in the pursuit of glory and who eventually survives to return home to the little pleasures of the settled and ordered everyday life. Odysseus is presented as the prototype of the bourgeois individual.

5. Those individuals who deliberately seek to make of their own life and persona a work of art and aestheticize life (e.g. the dandy) will be discussed below.

6. The assumption that *aretê* was a quality of the body and bodily activities as well as those of the mind implied a unity of the aesthetic, the moral and the practical. For the Greeks *aretê* entailed an aesthetic dimension: activities or lives which displayed excellence were assumed to be beautiful and as a corollary those which were base or disgraceful were ugly (Kitto, 1951: 170; see also Bauman, 1973: 10–17, for an illuminating discussion of the Greek notion of culture). Despite the much remarked upon Western mind–body dualism, the sense of the way they are practically conjoined and the beautiful body goes along with a beautiful soul is an important aspect of our tradition as well. Wittgenstein for example, remarks: 'The human body is the best picture of the human soul', an assumption of unity which has a dynamic life-course aspect as Orwell's statement that 'At 50 everyone has the face he deserves' reminds us (quoted in MacIntyre, 1981: 176).

7. The impact of the First World War is particularly interesting in this context with the interplay of technology, traditional military heroics and various artistic impulses and movements. In addition there was the overall tension between the heroic public imagery and the 'everyday' experience of trench warfare as filth, degradation and terror (see Wohl, 1980; Fussell, 1982; Eckstein, 1990). The various shifts in Simmel's attitude towards the war are discussed in Watier (1991).

8. There is not the space here to go into the relationship between the emotional basis of charisma and the heroic life. For discussions see Wasielewski (1985) and Lindholm (1990). Needless to say there has been a good deal of controversy about the extent to which Weber himself admired the charismatic hero (in some cases with the qualifier 'despite himself'). Hence Lindholm's (1990: 27) statement that 'Thus Weber, the most sophisticated and disenchanted of rational thinkers, fell prey in the last analysis, and very much despite himself, to a desperate worship of the charismatic hero' is hardly uncontentious.

9. Weber's pessimism about the fate of *Persönlichkeit* in the modern age and concern about the newly emerging human type to replace the Protestant type was by no means unqualified. This is apparent in his discussions of the working class. At some points he argues that with the decline of religion, non-elites will find meaning through identification with their communities, through the multiplicity of communal groups with bonds of varying intensity, the most important of which is the nation. Hence 'ethnic honour' with its exclusivity and egalitarianism could provide a sense of identity for the masses, while elites strive adequately

to follow a professional vocation or some diluted notion of *Persönlichkeit* (see Portis, 1973: 117). On the other hand he was intrigued by the results of Gohre's study of the working class which suggested that they had discovered a primitive *Persönlichkeit* manifest in a longing for freedom from residual feudal bonds. This provided a motivation for Weber's proposed study of the press and the question of the effect of the mass media on habitus formation (see Liebersohn, 1988).

10. This is not of course the only ideal Nietzsche presents and in recent years, under the influence of poststructuralism and postmodernism, the Dionysian loss of self and immersion in life as mentioned in *The Birth of Tragedy* has gained favour (see Stauth and Turner, 1988b).

11. For Simmel, Stefan George embodied the modern ideal of attaining distinction. Max Weber, on the other hand, was concerned about the folly of trying to reintroduce charisma in modern societies. Liebersohn (1988: 151) tells us that George was one of the first cultural heroes of the twentieth century and was accorded the adulation later to be experienced by film stars and politicians.

12. Postmodern theory has little time for notions such as genius and originality. Rosalind Krauss (1984), for example, argues that modernism and the avant-garde work within a 'discourse of originality' which wrongly suppresses the right of the copy and repetition. For a critique arguing that she herself inadvertently reiterates the discourse of originality see Gooding-Williams (1987). Scheff (1990) has developed an acute sociological theory of the development of genius. For a discussion of the various historical forms of the idea of genius see P. Moore (1989) and Battersby (1989). The latter provides an important discussion of the ways in which women have been excluded from the idea of genius.

13. This is not to say that the anti-hero cannot himself be sustained by and develop within a form of the heroic life which is particularly compelling and exemplary for a wide following. Jean-Paul Sartre's life is a major example of this (see Brombert, 1960; Bourdieu, 1980).

14. Huyssen (1986: 59) regards the positive evaluation of the masses and the popular and everyday life by postmodernism as associated with the emergence of feminism and women as a major power in the arts which has led to the admittance and re-evaluation of formerly excluded genres (soap operas, popular romance, the decorative arts and crafts, etc.).

5
GLOBALIZING THE POSTMODERN

In the Enlightenment vision which developed within Western modernity the assumption was that the structures of the natural and social worlds could be discovered by reason and science. This would yield techno-logically useful knowledge with which to tame nature, but it would also lead to a parallel social technology designed to improve social life and usher in 'the good society.' Along with the development of science and technology, the expansion of industrial capitalism, state administration, and the development of citizenship rights were seen as convincing evidence of the fundamental superiority and universal applicability of the project of modernity. It was assumed that the Western nations which had first developed and applied this knowledge were well ahead in the process of social development and could confidently maintain their lead as people in other parts of the world eagerly sought, or if need be were instructed, to follow and reap the benefits of modernization. It was assumed that the project had an inherent and demonstrable superiority, in terms of the potential means of empowerment it provided for various types of social groupings, collectivities, institutions and ultimately nascent, or proto nation-states. In the last analysis this meant that everyone throughout the world would have to acknowledge the superiority and universality of the project of modernity. Such was the dream of (Western) reason.

In the cultural sphere reason provided the grounds for a thoroughgoing critique of tradition. Guided by reason and science the Enlightenment sought to order, map and classify the world; the commitment to this fundamental ideal meant the rejection of all previous bodies of knowledge as dogmatic and irrational. Modernity was held to entail a relentless detraditionalism in which collective orientations would give way to indi-vidualism, religious belief to secularization and the accumulated sediment of mores and everyday practices would surrender to progressive rationaliz-ation and the quest for 'the new'. This comforting narrative in which culture necessarily follows the unfolding 'logic' of scientific, technological and economic change is however complicated by the development of countercultural artistic and intellectual movements, as well as the per-sistence, transformation and renewal of religion and the sacred in many aspects of life (not least being nationalism) which will be discussed below.

Let us take the cultural movements which became known as modernism. If the culture of modernity entailed the development of regimes of knowledge which sought the progressive ordering, control and unification

of nature and social life, through capitalist enterprises and state administration, then modernism worked off the principles of disorder and
ambivalence (Bradbury and McFarlane, 1976; Berman, 1982). Baudelaire,
who is often credited with the foundation of modernism, rejected romanticism and traditionalism in favour of a celebration of the new which
refused scientific and technological utopian visions of the good life, and
focused instead on the detritus of modern life (Benjamin, 1973). The
modern city in particular threw up a series of new social types (e.g. the
flâneur), new sites (bohemias, arcades, department stores) and imagery
(consumer culture goods and advertising) which pointed to fragmentation,
boredom and the vitality and resilience of the dark side of modernity.
Modernism, which also drew upon the Nietzschean transvaluation of
values, sought a reversal of the optimistic official culture of modernity with
its ordering unifying and integrative ambitions. It drew upon antinomian
and transgressive impulses and sought to dissemble the established
symbolic hierarchies of order and progress. It sympathized with 'the
other': the gypsy, the bohemian, the mad, the homosexual, the native and
other minority positions which were to be cured, reconstituted and
eliminated by modern institutions in the name of social order and
progress. These became particularly powerful themes within the countercultural bohemias and avant-gardes which engaged in a critical dialogue
with the culture of modernity as well as relentlessly exploring the formal
logic of the various artistic genres (Burger, 1984).

Daniel Bell (1976, 1980) has explored a version of this thesis, arguing
that modernism's celebration of transgression and the erosion of all values
has worked its way into the mainstream of contemporary culture through
its alliance with consumerism. In contrast to the value placed upon the
ordered life, productivity and frugality, which were regarded as essential
elements of the Protestant ethic which laid the foundations for capitalist
modernity, Bell argues for a shift in the twentieth century towards consumption, play and hedonism. In effect the work ethic became replaced by
a consumption ethic. Modernism's iconoclastic and critical impulses not
only threatened traditional values, religious morality and the sacred, but
filtered through to endanger the economic and political spheres. For Bell
postmodernism represents a further heightening of the destructive elements
in modernism with the instincts and inchoate life now turned against art,
or merged with art to produce an aestheticization of everyday life which he
depicts as a further triumph of the irrational.

For some theorists, then, the project of modernity has become threatened
or exhausted by developments within the cultural sphere which have seen
an alliance develop between consumer culture and modernism. The
confident belief in an ordered social life, coupled with ever-extending
progress, has been seen to have reached its limits and a reversal has set in.
Hence postmodern theorists have emphasized fragmentation against unity,
disorder against order, particularism against universalism, syncretism
again holism, popular culture against high culture and localism against

globalism. It is in this context that we find references to Nietzsche's 'last men', as well as 'the end of history' (Vattimo, 1988). Postmodernism and consumer culture are both often taken as signs that we are going through dramatic changes which are altering the nature of the social fabric as a result of a double relativization: of both tradition, and the 'tradition of the new' (modernism), with the latter resulting in a questioning of all modes of fundamental values – a transvaluation of values which has not only moved humankind beyond the possibility of constructing a moral consensus and the good society, but which has caused some to see the only solution as being the rejection of all forms of subjective identity construction in favour of immersion in the libidinal flows of the 'body without organs' (Deleuze and Guattari, 1983). Yet when faced by such sweeping generalizations and speculative assertions, we need to ask the question of how widespread these changes are, and whether the alleged crises extend beyond the crises of artists and intellectuals into the everyday culture of ordinary people. In short we need to raise the question of the relationship of the carriers of values (fundamental or critical) to their respective audiences and publics and the various means of transmission and media which are used in this process.

It is difficult to disentangle such discussions of the nature of the social changes which postmodernism points to, from the recognition of the changes. From this perspective could it not be the case that the emergence of new terms, such as postmodernism, actually provides a new concept which not only directs our gaze to hitherto seen but unnoticed aspects of reality, but helps to form that reality at the same time? Here we can refer to form in a double sense. First, in terms of directing our gaze to the reformation and discrediting of the existing conceptual apparatus which is dominant within a discipline and the substitution of a new concept, model or image, which will allegedly more accurately grasp or form reality. Second, by drawing to attention the fact that the academic or intellectual observer participates in the society which he or she researches, and that social science and other types of academic knowledge are rapidly circulated and fed back through the media to wider audiences and publics, especially in the sectors of the middles classes which have received higher education. Hence there is the possibility of a bandwagon effect, a thirst for new and fashionable concepts with which to make sense of experience, which may actually be used to re-form and reinterpret existing experiences and develop new sensibilities.

So it is important when we seek to examine the quest for fundamental values not to err too much on the side of abstraction and assume a plurality of different value positions as coexisting in some ideal value sphere which confronts the individual with an agonizing choice between potentially meaningful (or meaningless) alternatives. Values only effectively exist if they are used practically and mobilized by various groups of people. Rather than talk about the individual and his or her crisis of belief we need to ask how particular discourses, theories and images are used by specific groups and in particular the means of transmission of beliefs and practical knowledge between people. Without an understanding of the production of culture by academics, intellectuals and artists and the way cultural goods are packaged and transmitted by cultural intermediaries to various audiences and publics, we cannot assume that the crises detected by cultural specialists necessarily are the general social and cultural crises claimed.

It is in this sense that postmodernism cannot be successfully understood if it is detached from the analysis of the practices, interdependencies and interests of cultural specialists, intellectuals, academics, artists, critics and cultural intermediaries, who struggle to provide interpretations and explanations of the social world. This is not to suggest that they are the cynical and self-seeking peddlers of inflated and dubious ideas that some claim; rather it is to acknowledge their dual role. They are sensitized interpreters of the social world who are professionally involved in detecting changes in that world and in theorizing them. At the same time they are involved in all sorts of power struggles and interdependencies which can be regarded as being, on the one hand, of an *internal* nature – they can restrict or increase the demand for new theories; and, on the other hand, of an *external* nature, in that they govern the relations to wider audiences and publics which may, under certain circumstances, seek to translate these ideas into reality. I would argue that a sociology of postmodernism should be sensitive to both these aspects.

Postmodernism and consumer culture

A number of commentators have linked the rise of postmodernism to consumer culture (Bell, 1976; Jameson, 1984b; Featherstone, 1991a). Both terms give a central emphasis to culture. Here there seems to have been two displacements. The term *consumer society* marked a shift from considering consumption as a mere reflex of production, to conceiving consumption as central to social reproduction. The term *consumer culture* points not only to the increasing production and salience of cultural goods as commodities, but also to the way in which the majority of cultural activities and signifying practices become mediated through consumption, and consumption progressively involves the consumption of signs and images. Hence the term consumer culture points to the ways in which consumption ceases to be a simple appropriation of utilities, or use values, to become a consumption of signs and images in which the emphasis upon the capacity to endlessly reshape the cultural or symbolic aspect of the commodity makes it more appropriate to speak of *commodity-signs*. The culture of the consumer society is therefore held to be a vast floating complex of fragmentary signs and images, which produces an endless sign-play which destabilize long-held symbolic meanings and cultural order (Baudrillard, 1983a, 1993; and Jameson, 1984a, develop this argument).

This key feature of consumer culture – the fragmentation and over-production of culture – is often regarded as the central feature of postmodernism, something which was taken up by artists, intellectuals and academics in various ways as a problem to be expressed and theorized. Hence we often get references to the fragmentation of time into a series of perpetual presents and the loss or end of a sense of history (Vattimo, 1988). The inability to order the fragmented culture is also held to lead to an aestheticization of everyday life through the inability to chain together signs and images into a meaningful narrative. Instead, the constant flow and bizarre juxtapositions of images and signs, as found for example in MTV, is regarded as producing isolated, intense affect-charged experiences (Jameson, 1984a). The thematization of this fragmented, depthless culture in the 1960s within art and intellectual life underwent a further shift away from the high cultural stance of distanced moral indignation and con-demnation of the impoverished mass culture towards embracing and celebrating the popular and mass culture aesthetic. Not only do we find that the mass cultural techniques of advertising and the media were copied and celebrated, as in pop art, but that the long-held doctrines of artistic originality and genius were rejected. In addition, this artistic movement criticized the high modernism system of artistic production and reproduc-tion in which key artefacts and texts were canonized and institutionalized in the gallery, museum and the academy. Now art was seen and proclaimed to be everywhere: in the city street, in the detritus of mass culture. Art was in advertising, advertising was in art.

We can make a number of points about the relationship between postmodernism and consumer culture which suggest that many of the modes of signification and experiences labelled as postmodern cannot simply be regarded as the product of a new epoch: 'postmodernity', or the cultural changes accompanying the postwar shift to a 'late capitalist' economy.

It is common in depictions of postmodern experiences to find references to: the disorientating mêlée of signs and images, stylistic eclecticism, sign-play, the mixing of codes, depthlessness, pastiche, simulations, hyper-reality, immediacy, a *mélange* of fiction and strange values, intense affect-charged experiences, the collapse of the boundaries between art and everyday life, an emphasis upon images over words, the playful immersion in unconscious processes as opposed to detached conscious appreciation, the loss of a sense of the reality of history and tradition; the decentring of the subject (see Jameson, 1984a; Chambers, 1987; Lash, 1988; Baudrillard, 1983a, 1993; Hebdige, 1988). The first point to note is that these experiences are generally held to take place within the context of consumer culture leisure. The locations most frequently mentioned are theme parks and tourist sites (Disneyland being the exemplar), shopping centres, out-of-town malls, contemporary museums, gentrified inner city areas and docklands. Television is often referred to, with the emphasis given to the fragmented distracted mode of viewing with the channel-hopper or MTV viewer being the paradigmatic form. The most influential figure cited here is Baudrillard (1983a, 1993) who suggests that television has produced the end of the social to the extent that social encounters become simulations with an 'as if it has already happened' hyperrreal quality; at the same time television provides an overload of information which leads to an implosion of meaning (for examples of those who have sought to build on Baudrillard's work see Kroker and Cook, 1988; Kaplan, 1987; Mellencamp, 1990).

The first thing we can note is that, with the exception of television, these experiences seem confined to specific locations and practices which are themselves not new in the sense that there is a long history within consumer culture of shopping centres, department stores, tourist sites which have produced simulations, sign-play and amazing spaces which encourage a childlike sense of wonder and controlled *decontrol* of the emotions. We find references to this in the depictions of the nineteenth-century modern city in the writings of Benjamin (1973) and Simmel (1990, 1991). Indeed it can be argued that this experience can be traced back to the carnivals and fairs of the Middle Ages (see Featherstone, 1991a: Ch. 5). Yet the techniques for producing consumer culture illusion and spectacles have become more refined. There is a good deal of difference in technical capacity between the simulation of a trans-Siberian railway journey in which one sits in a carriage and looks through the window at a canvas of the landscape unfolding at the 1990 Paris Exposition and the latest Disney World simulator 'rides' in the sophistication of the detail achieved (through animatronics, sound, film, holograms, smell, etc.) and the capacity to achieve a complete sense of immersion in the experience. Virtual reality is the latest stage in this process (see Featherstone, 1995; Featherstone and Burrows, 1995). Yet it is hard to argue that for the respective audiences we can necessarily assume that there is a greater suspension of disbelief today when one considers the sense of wonder on the faces of participants at earlier spectacles. What there may be is a greater capacity within consumer culture to be able rapidly to switch codes and participate in an 'as if' manner, to participate in the experience and then to switch to the exami-nation of the techniques whereby the illusion is achieved, with little sense of nostalgic loss. The 'as if' *world* is of course heightened by the experience of television and the ways in which it can collapse time and space. The experiences, people, places and emotional tone captured on television and film give a particularly strong sense of instanciation and immediacy which can help to de-realize reality. Yet it is all too easy to assume that there is a complete socio-semantic loss through these postmodern tendencies in television. The meaning of television programmes and advertisements is neither a programmed manipulated one in line with the intentions of the programme-makers, nor is it completely an open postmodern sign-play.

At the same time Disney World is not yet the world and the postmodern experiences usually take place in carefully circumscribed settings within consumer culture and leisure activities. When people leave these enclaved moments they have to return to the routinized everyday and work worlds in which they are enmeshed in a dense network of interdependencies and power balances. Here the dominant practical orientation makes it necessary to read other people's appearance and presentation of self with care, for clues of intentionality, albeit in commonsense taken-for-granted ways. It may be possible to switch codes to forms of play and parody, yet the imperatives of adhering to practical routines and getting the business done obviates too much sign-play, emotional decontrol and swings between aesthetic detachment and immersion.

The collapse of the distinction between high and mass culture, the breaking down of academic categories, chimes closely with the perceived breaking down of the categories in everyday consumer culture. The various blends of poststructuralism, deconstructionism and anti-foundationalism evident in the writings of Baudrillard, Lyotard, Derrida and Foucault were often lumped together (not without resistance from those so labelled) as postmodern theory. In their different ways they criticized the universalist claims of the metanarratives of the Western Enlightenment and argued for a greater appreciation of local knowledge, 'otherness', and the syncretism and multicoding of culture. In particular these theories offered a sharp critique of attempts to provide a unitary general explanation of society and history, be they founded on sociological, economic or Marxist premises. Yet it is a paradox that some of those who have been most centrally concerned in the popularization of the term postmodernism in the academic sphere have attempted to do just this: to neutralize the anti-foundational critical potential of postmodern theories by explaining them from the security of a meta-site.

Explaining the postmodern

Fredric Jameson (1984a) has perhaps done more than any other academic to popularize the term postmodernism, yet he has remained one of its sharpest critics. For Jameson postmodernism is to be regarded as the cultural logic of late, or consumer, capitalism. Here Jameson builds on the Marxist scheme of Mandel (1975) in regarding postmodernism as the new cultural formation which has accompanied the transition to late or multinational capitalism in the post-Second World War era, which has replaced the earlier phase of monopoly capitalism with its cultural modernism. Jameson's (1984b) depiction of postmodern consumer culture draws a good deal from Baudrillard in highlighting the surfeit of signs and images, the oversaturation of culture which has given rise to a depthless hallucinatory simulational world which has effaced the distinction between the real and the imaginary. Yet while Baudrillard is content to pursue this nihilistic logic at the heart of the commodity-sign to its extreme, Jameson draws back to the safe house of neo-Marxism from which to explain and criticize it.

We also find a similar reductionism in seeking to explain cultural changes as derivative of economic changes in David Harvey's influential *The Condition of Postmodernity* (1989), in which he presents postmodernism as the set of cultural changes which have accompanied the move from Fordism to flexible accumulation. Like Jameson, Harvey sees postmodernism as a negative cultural development with its fragmentation and replacement of ethics by aesthetics leading to a loss of the critical edge and political involvement which he regards as characteristic of the works of artistic modernism.

Yet from the point of view of those who take the implications of postmodernism seriously, analyses such as those by Jameson and Harvey rely on a totalizing logic which assumes that the universal structural principles of human development have been discovered and that culture is still caused by, and is a reflection of, economic changes (for a critique of Jameson in this respect see Featherstone, 1991a: Ch. 4). They rely upon a neo-Marxist metanarrative and metatheory which insufficiently analyses its own conditions and status as a discourse and practice. As one critic remarks, Harvey's metatheory is 'a fantasy projected by a subject who imagines his own discourse position can be external to historical and geographical truths' (Morris, 1992). This leads to an inability to see culture and aesthetic forms as practices in which their meanings are negotiated by users. It also displays an inability to see that economics should itself be regarded as practices which depend upon representations and need to be seen as constituted in and through culture too. In addition, while Harvey pays lip-service to the attention postmodernism draws to various modes of 'otherness' and localisms (such as women, gays, blacks, ecologists, regional autonomists) he is worried that by acknowledging the pluralism and autonomy of other voices we lose the capacity to grasp the whole, and that without such a representation or explanatory model, we will lose the capacity to act to change the world. The consequence of this indifference to the particularity and difference of various modes of otherness is that they are lumped together and dismissed as place-bound traditionalisms. As Morris (1992) remarks: 'Harvey can only understand postmodernism by first rewriting as "the same" all the differences that constitute it for him as a topic for debate in the first place.'[1]

Hence there is the danger that many of those who wish to explain the rise of postmodernism will do so in a way which suggests that the old master explanatory models still function unproblematically, that postmodernism is merely a cultural reflection of a new phase of capitalism. For Jameson and Harvey it is still the logic of capitalism which inexorably grinds away in the background.[2] Neither Jameson nor Harvey is willing to treat seriously the import of postmodern theory: that models of such a high level of generality, which label vast expanses of time and space as capitalism or modernity, themselves may be flawed, or of limited value. On the one hand there is a tendency to take postmodernism too seriously, to assume it can be equated with the whole of contemporary culture or that it is even a sign that we are entering a new age. Yet, on the other hand, there is a tendency not to treat the implications of postmodernism seriously enough, to dismiss it as merely a surface cultural phenomenon which leaves the old mechanisms of social reproduction untouched, which by implication assumes that culture is a bounded entity which continues to remain passively in its own domain.

Globalization and postmodern theory

It cannot be denied that it is essential for social theory to develop theories which have both an analytical and synthetic thrust. Yet the confidence in the old synthetic master models such as Marxism is on the decline and the current mood is to favour middle-range models and smaller-scale generalizations on the one hand, and the analytical deconstruction of large-scale theories on the other, such as we find in postmodern theory. It is therefore interesting to enquire into why the current postmodern mood in theory argues for the abandonment of the longstanding ambitions within modernity to develop foundations for knowledge: in effect the abandonment of the quest for unity, generality and synthesis. The first thing we can note about postmodernism is that it assumes it has discovered a greater degree of cultural complexity than can be accounted for by other modes of theorizing. Hence we find an emphasis upon the way in which master narratives occlude more complex combinations of differences, local diversities and otherness, the voices which were ignored or suppressed in the unified models. This would account for the demands for deconstruction and deconceptualization, for a greater appreciation of detail, of the multicoded nature of cultural texts and images.[3]

At its most excessive it seems to ask for rejection of all attempts at generalization and the construction of unities as misguided and false. A stance which challenges the attempt to give form to life as ill-conceived. This would seem to be part of a process, which has been manifest since the rise of artistic modernism, of putting into question established cultural forms and focusing on the raw material of unformed life and experience, raising the question of the nature and justification for the forming process. Yet, unless we are prepared to jettison the concept of form altogether and sink back into the flux of life, any attempt at theorizing entails the construction of forms and modes of representation.

The problem arises when it is assumed that the repertoire of forms used in everyday life, the commonsense routines and typifications, become destabilized and more fluid. Hence it is often assumed that there became established new modes of time-space compression which altered the nature of everyday experience in the large cities of the late nineteenth and early twentieth centuries (see Kern, 1983; Frisby, 1985b). Artistic modernism can be regarded as series of attempts to represent this in art, music, theatre, literature (James Joyce's *Ulysses* is often quoted in this context:

see Bradbury and McFarlane, 1976). At the same time various countercultural movements followed the emphasis on life over form which one
finds in *Lebensphilosophie* such as that developed by Otto Gross and his
followers (see Green, 1976, and the discussion in Chapter 3 in this book,
'Personality, Unity and the Ordered Life'), which attempted to practically
live out the return to the immediacy and vitality of life. The problem was
to give the impression of a return to life in reaction to more rigid classical
forms. Hence artistic modernism and such countercultural movements
represented an attempt to discover some more flexible temporary formal
mode of representing the alleged formlessness of life. This is a conceptual
problem which we find addressed in the work of Georg Simmel and which
has led to him being regarded as not only the first sociologist of
modernity, but as the first sociologist of postmodernity too, by those such
as the Weinsteins (1991) who wish to blur the boundaries between these
two concepts (see Featherstone, 1991b: 11).[4]

Furthermore, it is not just the problem of experience, of rediscovering
life beneath form, which renders the notion of cultural unity problematic,
but also the nature of the everyday practical cultural forms and the modes
of articulating, representing and shaping them both within popular culture
and by cultural specialists which is important. Within certain phases of
nation-state formation processes, such as occurred within Europe in the
nineteenth and early twentieth centuries, the primacy of creating a national
culture led to the formation of unitary conceptions of culture in which
integration became the expressed aim. Yet it is possible to find counter-
examples of more syncretic and polyglot cultures which lacked a
centralizing unifying impulse.[5] Ancient Rome, for example, according to
Serres (1991), remained syncretic and open to multiplicity and was
therefore able to resist the strong insider/outsider divisions which are often
used to create social and cultural unity. A number of historical examples
suggest that the conceptualization of ordered disorder and complex
syncretisms in which wholes are seen as looser agglomerations and
polymers of parts, which we find celebrated in postmodernism, are by no
means unique.

Globalization and the postmodern

The international and trans-societal processes which are taking place in the
late twentieth century are speeding up the process of globalization (see
Robertson, 1990a, 1992b as well as the following chapters in this book).
This term refers to the sense of global compression in which the world is
increasingly regarded as 'one place' and it becomes much more difficult for
nation-states to opt out of, or avoid the consequences of being drawn
together into a progressively tighter figuration through the increasing
volume and rapidity of the flows of money, goods, people, information,
technology and images. Part of the problem of conceptualization which is

highlighted by postmodernism may well have something to do with the attempts to comprehend this resultant rise in global complexity. A global condition in which we in the West find it more difficult to view 'the other' through the long-distance lens implicit in terms such as 'the savage', 'the native' and 'the oriental'. These images are becoming challenged as fantasy projections and illusions, as 'the other' seeks to speak back to us and to challenge our particular depiction of his or her world (Said, 1978). 'The other', via the global flows we have spoken of, is now an interlocutor and part of our figuration. The resultant move to a higher level of complexity in terms of dealing with a multiplicity of images of others, and the need to modify and change our own identifying apparatus and repertoire of self-images, produces difficulties. It would seem to be easier to interact with others who share our own taken-for-granted stock of knowledge at hand, with whom we can slide into familiar typifications and routinized practices. This might be cited as just one of the reasons whereby the process of globalization does not merely produce new varieties of cosmopolitanism, but sets off a series of deglobalizing reactions, the retreat to various localisms, regionalisms and nationalisms.

Part of the perception of fragmentation within the nation-state, the fragmented image of culture we have referred to as the postmodern tendencies within consumer culture, then, may be a result of broader global processes. This suggests that the concept 'society', so closely associated with the nation-state, can no longer be considered as the sole subject-matter for sociology (see the more elaborate discussion in the final chapter of this book 'Travel, Migration and Images of Social Life').

Two observations are in order here. The first relates to a point we have already mentioned: the walls which separate nation-states are increasingly becoming regarded as permeable as a consequence of some of the trans-societal and global processes. Consumer culture's fragmented sign-play is made more complex still by the ease of introduction of images, goods and signs extracted from other cultures, which, as the flows of interchange intensify, cannot merely be regarded as distant, strange and exotic. We have, therefore, to get used to increasing our own flexibility and generative capacity to switch codes, to try different frames and models if we are to make sense of the images, experiences and practices we encounter. In addition new transnational third cultures are emerging which are less directly concerned with the interests of particular nation-states, and represent a level of social life not easily incorporated into the old models.

The second point relates to a more general and longstanding need for the relativization of society as the referent for sociology. The focus upon society necessarily directs attention to social change conceived as internal social development to the neglect of inter- and trans-societal processes such as war, conquest and colonialism (Tenbruck, 1994). Yet nation-states did not just have internal histories; the state-formation process emerged as they were drawn into a figuration which brought them together in power struggles and interdependencies, and the influence of these aspects of social life on the formation of the social relations within state-societies has largely been neglected by sociology, with a number of notable exceptions (e.g. Weber, Elias, Wallerstein, Nelson, Robertson). The various historical trajectories of nation-states, as they become more or less powerful on a regional and then global level, may also influence the status and long-term viability of the types of knowledge they develop.

Theories of modernity strongly reflect the particular experience of successful Western nation-state societies. Rather than regarding globalization as an outcome of modernity (Giddens, 1990, 1991), it may be equally plausible to see modernity as an outcome of globalization (Robertson, 1992a). The West has enjoyed a period of dominance linked to the development of modernity, which now seems to be drawing to a close with the rise of East Asia. Theories which were developed to a large extent in an intra-civilizational dialogue, now become subjected to a global interrogation. What were assumed to be universal theories may well now be regarded as merely those of a dominant particular. The shifting global balance of power which has resulted in the West having to listen to 'the rest' is producing a relativization in which other foundational values and fundamentalism emerge to clash upon the global stage. More players are involved in the game, who not only demand to be heard, but possess the economic and technological power resources to ensure that they are. A good deal has been written about the 'peculiarities of the English' route into modernity as the first industrial nation and we are increasingly aware of the plurality of entry gates into modernity (Therborn, 1995). It may well be that what we consider to be the substantive cultural responses and experiences of modernity likewise can be relativized to the Western particularity. Other nation-states and blocs may discover the particularities of their state-formation process and civilizational traditions which enable them to wrap up and code in different ways economic, technological and administrative institutions. The concept of the 'disembedding' of tradition may be less than adequate here to explain the resilience of tradition and religion, the invention and reinvention of the sacred and the various syncretisms which are emerging around the world. In the humanities and social sciences, theories and models based upon these particular cultural experiences are increasingly being brought on to the global stage as counter-histories to contest those of the West. What was a monologue based upon the authority of an instruction mode with a hierarchical inequality between participants, now becomes turned into a dialogue. Max Weber's (1948c) concept of the clashing of the value spheres in his essay 'Religious rejections of the world and their directions', which ushers in a new polytheistic era, may be nearer the mark.

From this perspective postmodernism can be related to the various ways in which Western intellectuals have detected the symptoms of this shift in the global balance of power, although of course some of them may have read the shift as an internal process taking place within (Western) modernity. The end of modernity, then, would be better referred to as the end of Western modernity. Or, put less dramatically, the end of Western modernity is in sight; the West has 'peaked' with an accompanying sense of exhaustion. But there is no sense of exhaustion in East Asia and other parts of the world which are pursuing their own national and civilizational blend of modernity. Hence it may be more propitious to speak of modern*ities* rather than modernity.

In this context it is germane to mention that very little attention has been given to considering Japan in terms of the postmodernism debates. Here it should now be clear that I do not mean how we place Japan on our continuum of tradition, modernity and postmodernity, but how the Japanese conceptualize Japan in terms of these divisions. Whether they would prefer some other mode of categorization with which to describe their own experience and explain world history is a question we need to address, and we should be aware that there have been a number of affirmative answers.[6] If this is accepted, then the notion of a single *univocal* world history, so long dominant within the West, may have to give way to the acknowledgement of *multivocal* world histories.

To make sense of postmodernism, then, it is insufficient to remain at the level of the nation-state society. This is not merely to suggest that nation-states are plugged into an international financial system, or world system from which they cannot opt out. While this is clearly the case, the continuing political struggles between nations, blocs and civilizations, as well as the cultural aspect of this process, has often been neglected. The resultant problems of intercultural communication, of dealing with others in everyday practices, and in deciphering others' images of us and constructing adequate self-images in a complex figuration, are merely symptoms which increasingly surface in everyday life and become theorized in terms of the difficulties of handling multiplicity and cultural disorder. It is this problem of theorizing complexity within a more complex global figuration with its shifting power balances, which is central to the emergence of postmodernism and the increasing relativization of both the foundations and the value complex of Western modernity.

Notes

This a substantially revised version of earlier papers presented at the American Association of Consumer Research Conference in Chicago in October 1991 and the UNESCO Conference on 'The Search for Fundamentals', Zeist, the Netherlands in November 1991. A version has appeared in L. van Vucht Tyssen (ed.) *Modernization and the Search for Fundamentals*, Kluwer, 1995.

1. The danger of labelling feminism as 'local' is to underestimate the efforts feminists themselves are making to grapple with the problem of universalism and particularism. The notion of 'global feminism' captures this conceptual tension and points to the complexity of the problem (see Enloe, 1989).

2. In a similar way Giddens (1990, 1991), who is also critical of postmodernism, denies its significance and treats it wholly in terms of the assumed claim that we have moved into a new epoch and have left behind modernity. Giddens has no time for a conception of something

beyond modernity, postmodernity, and insists we are still in high modernity (for criticisms of Giddens see Robertson, 1992b; Swanson, 1992). He is also unwilling to consider that postmodernism could exist as an influential movement in artistic, intellectual and academic life which resonates with wider changes taking place in cultural life. This cultural dimension of postmodernism as both a cultural movement and a mode of critique which points to the exhaustion of modes of theorizing associated with 'the modern' is for many the key aspect of the postmodern.

3. On the current passion for detail see Schor, 1987; Liu, 1990.

4. From the perspective of deconstruction the answer to the problem of the dominance of the immediacy of life over form, which we find in artistic modernism, is the reassertion of form. But here it is not the directed form seeking to centre itself within the construction of a metaphysical or logocentric scheme, but the endorsement of the primacy of writing culture, of opting for play against the discipline imposed within formal cultural practices. For Derrida (1973: 135) play entails 'the unity of chance and necessity in an endless calculus'. Life becomes the free play of forms void of any ulterior purpose. Within play-forms the flux of life persists, gathered together into the play of form for its own sake. For Deena and Michael Weinstein (1990), who make this argument from an interesting synthesis of the ideas of Simmel and Derrida, postmodern culture entails this type of deconstructionist play, a privileging of 'deauthorized play', something which occurs when we are watching television (submitting to the flow rather than watching a specific programme). This is, they argue, a general tendency which is to be found within contemporary consumer culture (e.g. the shopping mall, theme park, etc. discussed above).

5. Here it is assumed that entities such as nation-states and empires are themselves involved in a figuration of interdependencies and power balances with the significant others they are drawn into contact with. The density of the figuration and resultant intensity and necessity of contacts will of course vary historically and we can assume there is a great difference between an empire dominating its surrounding area (such as Rome) and nation-states involved in tightly structured bipolar and multi-player elimination contests, as occurred in modern Europe.

6. On Japan and postmodernism see Miyoshi and Harootunian (1989b). An important impetus for arguing that Japanese culture should be understood as having developed within a different culture–society nexus from that which we commonly operate with in the West came from Barthes's (1982) *Empire of Signs*. It is also worth adding that Japan has not relinquished its ambitions to complete some of the grander scientific and technological visions of modernity. Here some of the dreams of reason of the Enlightenment resurface, to be repackaged within the context of a nation-state project which still seeks to maintain its coherence and identity in the face of the recurrent tendencies of globalization to produce a 'borderless economy' – and a borderless culture and society too. This combination of an ultra-modern foundational value project along with the particularities of a resilient national tradition, may well make Japan postmodern in terms of some definitions. But what it does show is that the original coding up of the distinctions which were assumed to be the key differentials necessary in order to make a coherent model, could be suspect and it may be necessary to go back to the drawing-board to reformulate the models and typologies.

6

GLOBAL AND LOCAL CULTURES

Contextualism is heretofore spelled with a capital C; the living world appears only in the plural; ethics has taken the place of morality, the everyday that of theory, the particular that of the general.

(Habermas, 1984b, quoted in Schor, 1987: 3)

The man who finds his country sweet is only a raw beginner; the man for whom each country is as his own is already strong; but only the man for whom the whole world is as a foreign country is perfect.

(Eric Auerbach, quoted in McGrane, 1989: 129)

er lasst sich nicht lesen – 'it does not permit itself to be read'.

(Edgar Allen Poe, 'The Man of the Crowd', 1840)

It has become a cliché that we live in one world. Here we think of a variety of images: the photographs of the planet earth taken in space by the returning Apollo astronauts after setting foot on the moon; the sense of impending global disaster through the greenhouse effect or some other man-made catastrophe; the ecumenical visions of various traditional and new religious movements to unite humanity; or the commercial use of this ecumenical sentiment which we find in the Coca-Cola advertisement which featured images of legions of bright-eyed young people drawn from the various nations of the world singing together 'We are the world'. Such images heighten the sense that we are interdependent; that the flows of information, knowledge, money, commodities, people and images have intensified to the extent that the sense of spatial distance which separated and insulated people from the need to take into account all the other people which make up what has become known as humanity has become eroded. In effect, we are all in each other's backyard. Hence one paradoxical consequence of the process of globalization, the awareness of the finitude and boundedness of the planet and humanity, is not to produce homogeneity but to familiarize us with greater diversity, the extensive range of local cultures.

The globalization of culture

That the process of globalization leads to an increasing sensitivity to differences is by no means preordained. The possibility that we view the world through this particular lens, or form, must be placed alongside other historical possibilities. One perspective on the process of globalization which was accorded a good deal of credibility until recently is that of Americanization. Here a global culture was seen as being formed through the economic and political domination of the United States which thrust its hegemonic culture into all parts of the world. From this perspective the American way of life with its rapacious individualism and confident belief in progress, whether manifest in Hollywood film characters such as Donald Duck, Superman and Rambo or embodied in the lives of stars such as John Wayne, was regarded as a corrosive homogenizing force, as a threat to the integrity of all particularities.[1] The assumption that all particularities, local cultures, would eventually give way under the relentless modernizing force of American cultural imperialism implied that all particularities were linked together in a symbolic hierarchy. Moderniz-ation theory set the model into motion, with the assumption that as each non-Western nation eventually became modernized it would move up the hierarchy and duplicate or absorb American culture, to the extent that ultimately every locality would display the cultural ideals, images and material artefacts of the American way of life. That people in a wide range of countries around the world were watching *Dallas* or *Sesame Street* and that Coca-Cola cans and ring-pulls were to be found all around the world, was taken as evidence of this process.

The separation of cultures in space was seen as reducible to a more fundamental separation in time. The prioritization of time over space has been a central feature of theories of modernity. A central concern of the major figures in social theory from the Enlightenment onwards such as Vico, Condorcet, Saint-Simon, Comte, Spencer, Hegel, Marx, Weber and Durkheim was to seek to understand social relationships and state-society units in developmental terms. The move from traditional to modern societies was seen as accountable in terms of a range of specific processes: industrialization, urbanization, commodification, rationaliz-ation, differentiation, bureaucratization, the expansion of the division of labour, the growth of individualism and state formation processes. It was generally assumed that these processes, which arose within what has increasingly been dubbed Western modernity, had a universalizing force. In effect Western history was universal world history. Incorporated within these theories in varying degrees of explicitness was the assumption that history had an inner logic, or directional impetus, which was understood as progress. The idea of progress implies some direction to history and suggests the finitude of history, the eventual deliverance into, or arrival at, a better or ideal social life or 'good society'.

It is this assumption of a destination for history which has been most strongly challenged by what have become known as postmodern theories. Vattimo (1988), for example, argues that we are taking leave of modernity in abandoning the notion of development. Postmodernity is not to be regarded as a new epoch, a new stage of development on from modernity, but as the awareness of the latter's flawed assumptions. The key assumption of modernity's account of Western history is progress. In fact, this is the secularization of Judaic-Christian notions of salvation and redemption which become transformed into the belief in progress through the development of science and technology to bring about the perfectibility of man and human society. Postmodernism is to be regarded as 'the end of history' in the sense of the end of the belief in the overcoming of the present in pursuit of the 'new'.[2] It does not, of course, refer to the end of the objective process of history, only the end of our awareness of history as a unitary process. This secularization of the notions of progress and the perfectibility of the world entails a greater awareness of the constructed nature of history, of the use of rhetorical devices and the capacity to deconstruct narratives (something that was discussed at great length by Simmel, 1977 over a century ago; for a more recent account see Bann, 1984). It also points to a greater awareness of the plurality of history, the suppressed narratives within history that suggest that there is no unitary privileged history, only different histor*ies*.[3] From this perspective, there clearly are global developments and processes that increasingly bind together the individual histories of particular nation states and blocs, yet the confidence with which they could be incorporated into a single, explanatory, global historical narrative has been lost. In this sense, the attempts to construct a global history become immeasurably complicated as the value perspective from which such a construction takes place becomes contested and effectively relegates theories with universalistic pretensions to the status of local histories.

If one of the characteristics associated with postmodernism is the loss of a sense of a common historical past and the flattening out and spatialization of long-established symbolic hierarchies (see Featherstone, 1991a), then the process of globalization, the emergence of the sense that the world is a single place, may have directly contributed to this perspective through bringing about a greater interchange and clashing of different images of global order and historical narratives. The perception of history as an unending linear process of the unification of the world, with Europe at the centre in the nineteenth century and the United States at the centre in the twentieth century, has become harder to sustain with the beginnings of a shift in the global balance of power away from the West. In the late twentieth century, there is a growing recognition that the peoples of the non-Western world have histories of their own. Particularly important in this process in the post-Second World War era has been the rise of Japan, not only because its economic success seemed to present it as outmodernizing the West, but because the Japanese began to articulate theories of world history that disputed the placing of Japan on the Western-formulated continuum of premodern, modern and postmodern societies (see Miyoshi and Harootunian, 1989a). There has been a growing awareness that history is not only 'temporal or chronological but also spatial and relational' (Sakai, 1989: 106), that our history is generated in relation to other spatially distinct, coexisting temporalities. If nations can maintain isolation from other nations, or possess as a bloc of nations the economic and political power to be able to ignore the challenges of others, there is every possibility that they will be able to sustain fantasy images of their own superiority. This may take a number of forms. One of the best known is the image of the Orient as housing all the exotic differences and otherness which have been repressed and cast out by the West as it sought to construct a coherent identity (Said, 1978). Alternatively, there is the assumption that in the last analysis 'they are just like us', and that the West is consequently granted the moral right and duty to guide and educate the others because of the necessity to civilize the totality.[4] In either case, the West understands itself as the guardian of universal values on behalf of a world formed in its own image. It is only when other nations acquire the power to speak back, to make the West have to listen and notice their resistance, that constructions such as 'the Orient' – which is given some vague sense of unity in terms of it being the construct which objectifies all that is left outside the West when it seeks to constitute its identity as progressive – becomes problematic (Sakai, 1989: 117). It is only then that we begin to discover the complexity and range of oriental and other civilizations' images of the West as the 'other'.

The sense that there are plural histories to the world, that there are diverse cultures and particularities which were excluded from Western modernity's universalistic project, but now surface to the extent that they cast doubts on the viability of the project, is one particular outcome of the current phase of the process of globalization. It points to the more positive evaluation by the West of otherness and differences resulting from the shift in the balance of power between nations which find themselves progressively bound together in a global figuration from which it is increasingly difficult to opt out. This entails the sense that the world is one place, that the globe has been compressed into a locality, that others are neighbours with which we must necessarily interact, relate and listen. Here the assumption is that the density of contacts between nations will itself lead to a global culture. In this case the notion of a global culture must be distinguished from one which is modelled on that of the nation-state.

National cultures have usually emerged alongside state formation processes in which cultural specialists have reinvented traditions and reshaped and refurbished the ethnic core of the people. As nation-states became increasingly drawn together in a tighter figuration of competing nations, they faced strong pressures to develop a coherent cultural identity. The process of the homogenization of culture, the project of creating a common culture, must be understood as a process in the unification of culture of the need to ignore, or at best refine, synthesize and blend, local differences.[5] It is the image of the completion of this process, to the extent that culture oils the wheels of the social relationships and institutions that make up society, which became dominant within sociology: culture regarded as an unproblematic, integrated pattern of common values. Yet the process of formation of such a culture cannot be understood merely as a response to forces within the nation-state, but must also be seen in relation to forces outside of it: the potential for the development of national identity and cultural coherence as relationally determined by the structure of the shifting disequilibriums of power and interdependencies of the figuration of nation-states within which a particular country was embedded.

It is clearly hard to stretch this conception of culture to the global level and in no way can a global culture be conceived as the culture of the nation-state writ large. Not that this is a historical possibility which could automatically be ruled out. It is possible to conceive that one result of the elimination contest of power struggles between nations could have been the dominance of a single nation, which would be in a position to seek to develop a global common culture alongside its extended state formation process. This process of cultural formation would be much easier in the face of some external threat; here one would have to conceive the globe as subjected to some extraterrestrial or intergalactic threat. A further possibility would be the response to a perceived threat to the continued viability of life on the planet through some ecological disaster. In either case, the process of cultural formation and development of a common identity for the world as an 'in-group' is in response to the development of a mission to meet the challenge of an 'out-group'. There is clearly a range of other possibilities (such as a federation of nations, or the triumph of a particular religion or trading company) which could in theory have led to the formation of a global culture (see Robertson, 1990a, 1991).

The ways in which different nations have been drawn together into a tighter figuration through closer financial and trade ties, through the increasing development of technology to produce more efficient and rapid means of communication (mass media, transport, telephone, fax, etc.), and through warfare has produced a higher density of interchanges. There has been a rise in the intensity of a wide variety of cultural flows which make transnational encounters more frequent. Appadurai (1990), for example, refers to the increasing flows of people (immigrants, workers, refugees, tourists, exiles), technology (machinery, plant, electronics), financial information (money, shares), media images and information (from television, film, radio, newspapers, magazines) and ideologies and world-views. While some might wish to see the motor force for these changes as the relentless progress of the capitalist economy towards a world system (Wallerstein, 1974, 1980), or the movement towards a new, disorganized or 'post-Fordist' stage of capitalism (Lash and Urry, 1987), for Appadurai there is a disjunction between the cultural flows. On the practical level, the intensification of flows results in the need to handle problems of inter-cultural communication. In some cases this leads to the development of 'third cultures' which have a mediating function, as in the case of legal disputes between persons from different national cultures (Gessner and Schade, 1990). In addition, there is the further new category of professionals (lawyers, accountants, management consultants, financial advisers, etc.) who have come into prominence with the deregulation and globalization of financial markets with the 24-hour stock market trading, plus the expanding numbers of 'design professionals' (specialists who work in the film, video, television, music, fashion, advertising and consumer culture industries [King, 1990a]). All these specialists have to become familiar with a number of national cultures as well as developing, and in some cases living in, third cultures. The majority of these third cultures will draw upon the culture of the parent country from which the organization originated. It is therefore evident that the cultures which are developing in many of the global financial firms have been dominated by American practices. The same situation applies with regard to many cultural industries, such as television, film and advertising. Yet these third cultures do not simply reflect American values; their relative autonomy and global frame of reference necessitates that they take into account the particularities of local cultures and adopt organizational cultural practices and modes of orientation which are flexible enough to facilitate this. Hence the practical problems of dealing with intensified cultural flows between nations leads to the formation of a variety of third cultures which operate with relative independence of nation-states.

Furthermore, this is not to imply that the increased cultural flows will necessarily produce a greater tolerance and cosmopolitanism. An increasing familiarity with 'the other', be it in face-to-face relations or through images or the representation of the other's world-view or ideology, may equally lead to a disturbing sense of engulfment and immersion. This may result in a retreat from the threat of cultural disorder into the security of ethnicity, traditionalism or fundamentalism, or the active assertion of the integrity of the national culture in global cultural prestige contests (e.g. the Olympic games). To talk about a global culture is equally to include these forms of cultural contestation. The current phase of globalization is one in which nation-states in the West have had to learn to tolerate a greater diversity within their boundaries which manifest themselves in greater multiculturalism and polyethnicity. This is also in part a consequence of their inability to channel and manipulate global cultural flows successfully, especially those of people, information and images, which increases the demand of equal participation, citizenship rights and greater autonomy on the part of regional, ethnic and other minorities. Those who talk about such issues within nation-states are also more aware that they are talking to others outside the nation-state. That there is something akin to the formation of global public opinion was evident in the unfolding of the independence struggles of Lithuania and other nations within the Soviet Union, as well as in the Kuwait Gulf crisis and war in the early 1990s. Such incidents make us aware of the process of the formation and deformation of appropriate norms of behaviour within and between states, which while contested makes people more aware that there is a world stage and that the world is becoming one place. From the point of view of social

science, and sociology in particular, this should make us aware as
Robertson (1992a) argues that the idea of a global culture is in the process
of becoming as meaningful as the idea of national-societal, or local
culture.

Local culture

It is striking that one of the effects of the process of globalization has been
to make us aware that the world itself is a locality, a singular place. This is
apparent not only in the images of the world as an isolated entity in space,
which photographs of the earth from the moon provided, but also in the
sense of its fragility, its finitude and openness to irreparable damage and
destruction. While, as Durkheim argued, the sense of our common
humanity might be expected to grow alongside our awareness of the
sacredness of the human person as the only thing we all have in common
in an increasingly differentiated world in which particularities become
more evident, it is also possible to extend this argument to life, and the
home of our life, the earth. Of course, this perspective is nothing if not
limited and contested, but it does point to the localization of globality, the
perception of the finite and limited nature of our world.

Usually, a local culture is perceived as being a particularity which is the
opposite of the global. It is often taken to refer to the culture of a
relatively small, bounded space in which the individuals who live there
engage in daily, face-to-face relationships. Here the emphasis is upon the
taken-for-granted, habitual and repetitive nature of the everyday culture of
which individuals have a practical mastery (Bourdieu, 1977). The common
stock of knowledge at hand with respect to the group of people who are
the inhabitants and the physical environment (organization of space,
buildings, nature, etc.) is assumed to be relatively fixed; that is, it has
persisted over time and may incorporate rituals, symbols and ceremonies
that link people to a place and a common sense of the past. This sense of
belonging, the common sedimented experiences and cultural forms which
are associated with a place, is crucial to the concept of a local culture. Yet,
as our example of 'planet earth' as a locality shows, the concept of local
culture is a relational concept. The drawing of a boundary around a
particular space is a relational act which depends upon the figuration of
significant other localities within which one seeks to situate it.[6]

For example, if I meet another European in China after spending a
number of years there, it would be expected that we would find sufficient
cultural forms in common from our experience of being European to
revive collective memories which can constitute a temporary sense of
common identity, or community, which demarcates 'us' from the 'them' of
the host people. Alternatively, a similar sense of membership and
belonging may be revived by meeting another Englishman while residing in
France, or a northern Englishman while spending a period of exile in

London (a person who, incidentally, may come from a neighbouring town to mine and with whom I might normally have an intense rivalry). This symbolic aspect of community boundaries (Cohen, 1985) is also evident when one considers relationships within a village in which those who define their localness in terms of length of residence may refuse membership to outsiders. Hence the 'we-images' and 'they-images', which are generated within local struggles to form an identity and exclude outsiders, cannot be detached from the density of the web of interdependencies between people. Such struggles between established and outsider groups (Elias and Scotson, 1994) will therefore become more common with the extent of contact with others, which brings groups of outsiders more frequently into the province of local establishments.

In addition to this face-to-face dimension of direct contact with outsiders, which may under certain circumstances reinforce local cultural identity, there is the perceived threat to this through the integration of the locality into wider regional, national and transnational networks via the development of a variety of media of communication. Here it is possible to point to the development of the various transcultural media of interchange of money, people, goods, information and images of which we have already spoken which have the capacity to compress the time-space geography of the world. This provides contact with other parts of the world, which renders different local cultures more immediate and the need to make them practically intelligible more pressing. For example, given the spatial dispersal of corporations with the flexible specialization of post-Fordist industrial production, local people in Brazil, the north-east of England or Malaysia will have to interpret the strategies of Japanese or American management, and vice versa. It also integrates localities into more impersonal structures in which the dictates of market or administrative rationalities maintained by national elites or transcultural professionals and experts have the capacity to override local decision-making processes and decide the fate of the locality. It is in this sense that the boundaries of local cultures are seen to have become more permeable and difficult to maintain, to the extent that some proclaim that 'everywhere is the same as everywhere else'. It is also often assumed that we live in localities where the flows of information and images have obliterated the sense of collective memory and tradition of the locality to the extent that there is 'no sense of place' (Meyrowitz, 1985).

In terms of our earlier remarks about the deglobalizing reactions to global compression and the intensity of global flows, it would be expected that the generation of such nationalistic, ethnic and fundamentalist reactions to globalization could also entail a strong assertion of local cultures. This might take the form of reviving or simulating local traditions and ceremonies, or inventing new ones. Before proceeding to a discussion of these strategies, it would be useful to focus on the notion of a loss of a sense of place, or homelessness, in more detail. The condition of nostalgia is usually taken to refer to this loss of home in the sense of physical locale (Davis, 1974). But in addition to this 'homesickness', it has also been used to point to a more general loss of a sense of wholeness, moral certainty, genuine social relationship, spontaneity and expressiveness (Turner, 1987). While this sense of loss can motivate some to formulate romantic schemes or art forms to recreate some golden age or deliver some future utopia, it is worth enquiring into how a sense of home is generated.

A sense of home is sustained by collective memory, which itself depends upon ritual performances, bodily practices and commemorative ceremonies (Connerton, 1989). The important point here is that our sense of the past does not primarily depend upon written sources, but rather on enacted ritual performances and the formalism of ritual language. This may entail commemorative rituals such as weddings, funerals, Christmas, New Year, and participation or involved spectatorship at local, regional and national rituals (e.g. royal weddings, nation days, etc.). These can be seen as the batteries which charge up the emotional bonds between people and renew the sense of the sacred. A sacred can only rarely be regarded as operating as an integrating canopy for a nation-state, yet this should not be taken to imply that the sacred has evaporated completely under the assault of the globalizing forces we have mentioned; it would be better to speak of the dissipation of the sacred, that it operates in a variety of ways amongst a wide range of groups of people (see Featherstone, 1991a; Ch. 8; Alexander, 1988).[7]

One of the ways it operates in localities is in the countless little rituals, rites and ceremonies which take place in the embodied practices between friends, neighbours and associates. The little rituals entailed in buying a round of drinks in a particular way, or turning up to occupy the same seats in a pub each week, help formalize relationships which cement the social bonds between people. It is when we leave that place for some time and return that we seek out habits of home in which our body responds with ease as it falls into comforting, taken-for-granted routines – like a dog eager to perform its tricks for a returning master. It is the co-ordination of bodily gestures and movements which have never been verbalized or subject to reflection; the familiar smells and sounds; the ability to touch and look at things which have become charged with symbolism and affect. It is the apparent absence of such affective and symbolic sedimentation into the material fabric of the buildings and environment and the embodied practices of social life which prompts remarks such as Gertrude Stein made with reference to Oakland, California: 'There's no there there.' Of course, for the inhabitants of the town, there may have been a strong sense of place and local culture; what Stein was referring to was recognizable cultural capital.

One of the dangers of the 'no sense of place' type of arguments is that they seem to point to processes that are assumed to be universal in their impact and which do not vary historically. It may, for example, be possible to detect particular phases induced by changes in the process of globalization and relations between states which intensify or decrease the sense of homelessness and nostalgia. It has been argued that the phase of intense globalization which took place between 1880 and 1920, and which drew more nations into a tightly structured, global figuration of interdependencies and power balances, produced an intense nationalism and 'wilful nostalgia' (Robertson, 1990b: 45ff.). The efforts of nation-states to produce homogeneous, integrated common cultures and standardized citizens loyal to the national ideal led to attempts to eliminate local ethnic and regional differences. This was a phase of the establishment of national symbols and ceremonies and the reinvention of traditions which were manifest in royal jubilees, Bastille Day, the Olympic games, the cup final, the Tour de France, etc. Within societies that were rapidly modernizing and eliminating tradition, these rites created a desire to celebrate the past; they instituted forms of imitation and mythical identification which have persisted (Connerton, 1989).

The fact that such rites and ceremonies were invented should not be taken to mean they were invented *ex nihilo*: they drew upon traditions and ethnic cultures which possessed plausibility. The fact that they were spectacles which have become commodified and promoted to wider audiences need not be taken to imply that they have induced passivity amongst citizens who are essentially manipulated. As they became part of the popular culture of modern societies, they were often used by particular groups in ways different from that intended by their originators, groups who effectively renegotiated meanings of symbols and the sacred. Here spectatorship should not be understood as passive, or remote from the bodily enacting of rituals. For those who watch on television major events such as the cup final or a royal wedding, the place of viewing may borrow some of the festive aura of the actual event, with people dressing up, singing, dancing, etc. as they watch together either at home or in public places like bars or hotels.

A second phase of nostalgia can be related to the phase of globalization which has taken place since the 1960s and is associated by many commentators with postmodernism (Robertson, 1990b; see also Heller, 1990). This second phase is in response to some of the globalizing processes we spoke of earlier, which in the current phase can be related to pressures (which for the large part are being successfully met in the West) for nation-states to reconstitute their collective identities along pluralistic and multicultural lines which take into account regional and ethnic differences and diversity. In this present phase, the response to nostalgia in the recreation and invention of local, regional and subnational cultures (in Europe we think of the cultural assertiveness of the Welsh, Scots, Bretons, Basques, etc.) has also to be placed alongside the perceived destruction of locality through the globalization of the world economy, expansion of the mass media and consumer culture, but also can be understood as using these means to reconstitute a sense of locality. Hence the qualities of populism, syncretism, fragmentation and multicoding, the collapse of symbolic hierarchies, the end of the sense of progress and historical 'new', and the positive attitude towards the excluded 'other' which are usually associated with postmodernism, can also be traced back to the emphasis upon these qualities that we find within the development of consumer culture (Featherstone, 1991a). In particular, those developments in architecture and the organization of space which are often referred to as postmodern represent a movement beyond the abstract characterization of space with its emphasis upon pure form which we find in architectural modernism (Cooke, 1990a). With postmodernism, there is a re-emergence of the vernacular, of representational forms, with the use of pastiche and playful collaging of styles and traditions. In short, there is a return to local cultures, and the emphasis should be placed upon local cultures in the plural, the fact that they can be placed alongside each other without hierarchical distinction. The reconstruction of inner city areas and dock-lands in the wake of the 1980s global financial boom produced a spate of such building in the form of new shopping centres, malls, museums, marinas and theme parks. Localization is clearly evident in the processes of gentrification as the new middle class moved back into the city to restore old neighbourhoods or live within purpose-built simulations designed to recreate a certain ambience, whether it be a Mediterranean village in the docklands, or artistic bohemias in a warehouse district.

One characteristic frequently used to describe this type of architecture is 'playful'. Certainly, many of the spaces and façades have been designed to produce a sense of disorientation, wonder and amazement as one steps inside locations which simulate aspects of past traditions and futuristic and childhood fantasies. Theme parks, contemporary museums and the whole heritage industry play to this sense of recreating a home which takes one back to a past experienced in fictional form. Disney World is one of the best examples: there one can ride on Tom Sawyer's riverboat or climb up into the Swiss Family Robinson's tree house in which the combination of realistic film-set scenery, animatronics, sounds and smells are often sufficient to persuade adults to suspend disbelief and relive the fiction. If one is able to journey 'home' to childhood fantasies, then one is also persuaded to relive one's own and others' childhood memories through 'factions' (mixtures of fact and fiction). We find examples in the growing number of open-air and indoor industrial or everyday life museums, such as Beamish in the north-east of England (Urry, 1990). Here the recon-struction of working coal-mines, trams, corner shops and trains can actually take people into the physical reconstruction of past localities where preservation of the real merges with simulations. For old people, this must provide an uncanny sense of the local cultures they lived in, when effectively they can step inside a typical room and handle the tin bathtub or mangle for wringing clothes. Such postmodern spaces could be regarded as commemorative ritual devices which reinforce, or help people regain, a lost sense of place. At the same time, they encourage the performance of rites, the watching of simulated performance or the participation in bodily practices which revive many aspects of the past cultural forms. They encourage a 'controlled decontrol of the emotions', a receptivity to, and experimentation with, emotional experiences and collective memories previously closed off from experience. They encourage the adult to be childlike again, and allow the child to play with simulated ranges of adult experiences.[8] Of course, not everyone experiences these sites in the same ways. It is the new middle class, especially those who have had higher education or who work in the culture industries or the professions, who are most well disposed to experiment with the reconstitution of locality, the controlled decontrol of the emotions, and the construction of temporary aesthetic communities of the type to which Maffesoli (1995) refers. We therefore have a very uneven picture, the possibility of misreadings and misunderstandings as different class fractions, age and regional groupings mingle together in the same urban sites, consume the same television programmes and symbolic goods. Such groups possess different senses of affiliation to localities and the propriety of engaging in the construction of imagined communities. They utilize goods and experiences in a range of different ways, and a careful analysis of their everyday work and liminal practices is necessary if we are to discover the range of affiliations to locality which operate.

Concluding remarks

It should by now be apparent that the notions of global and local cultures are relational. It is possible to refer to a range of different responses to the process of globalism, which could be heightened or diminished depending upon specific historical phases within the globalization process.

First, we can point to the attitude of immersion in a local culture. This could take the form of remaining in a long-established locality by resisting being drawn into wider collectivities and erecting barriers to cultural flows. This, however, is difficult to achieve without military and economic power, which are essential if one is to avoid being drawn into broader regional interdependencies and conflicts. Hence there is the problem of being left alone, of remaining undiscovered, or of controlling and regulating the flow of interchanges even when geographical reasons (e.g. the case of Japan) facilitate isolation. On a more mundane level, from the point of view of some tribes, this may come down to the question of the best strategies which can be used to resist or ignore those tourists who quest after some last authentic, untouched remnant of 'real culture' such as those who go to New Guinea on cannibal tours. This can be related to the problems faced by those in the West who in this context develop a sense of protective responsibility and seek to devise strategies to conserve what they take to be a genuine local culture without placing it in a protective reservation in which it becomes a simulation of itself.

Second, such communities, which are increasingly becoming drawn into the global figuration, will also have to cope periodically with the refugees from modernization, those members of ethnic groups who are romantically attracted to the perceived authenticity of a simpler life and sense of 'home'. Here we think of the disparaging descriptions of them by their host groups which display doubts about these people's capacity to acquire permanent membership with depictions such as 'red apples' (returning first nation North Americans, who are held to be red on the outside and white on the inside), and 'coconuts' (returning Hawaiians seen as brown on the outside and white inside) (Friedman, 1990). While such groups can be seen as searching to live out their version of an 'imagined community', the caution on the part of the locals shows that a crucial dimension of the relationship between them can be understood in terms of established outsider struggles.

Third, variants of the refurbished imagined community also exist in the rediscovery of ethnicity and regional cultures within the current phase of a number of Western nation-states which seek to allow a greater recognition of regional and local diversity and multiculturalism. Within certain contexts it may be appropriate to wear the mask of local affiliation, as when dealing with tourists or confronting local rivals (Scotsmen on meeting Englishmen). This can entail varying degrees of seriousness and playfulness. This capacity to move backwards and forwards between various elements of national cultures, which are manifest in everyday public and work situations and the local affiliation, may take the form of regular ritual re-enactments of the imagined community. This is clearly the case in societies which have been settled by Europeans, such as the United States, Canada, Australia and New Zealand, in which various indigenous local affiliations as well the maintenance of imagined communities on the part of immigrant groups, has pushed the questions of multiculturalism and respect for local cultures firmly onto the agenda.

Fourth, those locals who travel, such as expatriates, usually take their local cultures with them (Hannerz, 1990). This is also the case with many tourists (especially those from the working class) whose expectation from the encounter with another culture is to remain on the level of sun, sea, sand plus 'Viva España' style stereotypes. In effect they seek 'home plus' and will do all they can to take comforting aspects of their local culture with them and limit the dangers of intercultural encounters to 'reservation-style' experiences (Bauman, 1990).

Fifth, there are those whose local affiliation is limited, whose geographical mobility and professional culture is such that they display a cosmopolitan orientation. Here we have those who work and live in 'third cultures' who are happy to move between a variety of local cultures with which they develop a practical, working acquaintance and the bridging third culture which enables them to communicate with like persons from around the world.

Sixth, there are cosmopolitan intellectuals and cultural intermediaries, especially those from the post-Second World War generation, who do not seek to judge local cultures in terms of their progress towards some ideal derived from modernity, but are content to interpret them for growing audiences of those who have been through higher education within the new middle class and wider audiences within consumer culture. They are skilled at packaging and re-presenting the exotica of other cultures and 'amazing places' and different traditions to audiences eager for experience. They are able to work and live within third cultures, as well as seemingly able to present other local cultures from within, and 'tell it from the native's point of view'. This group can be regarded as post-nostalgic, and can relate to growing audiences in the middle classes who wish to experiment with cultural play, who have forgone the pursuit of the ultimate authentic and real, who are content to be 'post-tourists' and enjoy both the reproduction of the effect of the real, the immersion in it in controlled or playful ways, and the examination of the backstage areas on which it draws (Fiefer, 1985).

It should be emphasized that this list of the range of possible affiliations to various forms of local and global cultures should not be understood as exhaustive. One of the tendencies often associated with postmodern theories is to assume that our present stage of development, or particular set of theoretical aporias, is somehow final and eternal. The current fascination with local cultures and the 'other', and the tendency for these to be broken down in a relentless search to discover yet more complex formulations of otherness, may not be sustained. Although this perception may be driven by the populist and egalitarian tendencies associated with postmodernism, the increasing quest to discover particularity and detail, the drive towards deconstruction and deconceptualization, may itself represent a phase in which a partial shift in the balance of power away from the Western nations may be represented as an indication of some present or future final levelling. Hence the discovery of the different voices of a wider and more complex range of localities and modes of otherness may occur at particular phases of a process in which powerful establishments are forced to recognize and acknowledge the claims of outsider groups. This need not mean that a dramatic levelling has taken place; it may point more to a struggle to reconfigure the conceptual apparatus to take account of the implications of this shift: a reconfiguration in which notions of detail, particularity and otherness are used to point to the difficulty of conceptually handling a greater degree of cultural complexity. These struggles, which are often driven by outsider groups within Western cultural establishments, may themselves be regarded as limited and patronizing by those they seek to represent under the blanket concept of otherness. For some others who are denied or granted a very limited access to the global means of communication, there would seem little possibility of compelling those within the dominant cultural centres to take account of their views, in their own terms. In this situation a characteristic response to their self-appointed guardians in the West might be: 'Don't other me!'

This would suggest that our present, so-called postmodern condition is best understood not as a condition, but as a process. The global balance of power may well shift further away from the Western bloc in the future without profoundly benefiting those Third World others who may be the current cause for concern. Certainly, if the rise in the power potential of Japan and other East Asian nations continues, these Third World nations may be confronted by a further source of globalizing and universalizing images which provoke a new range of problems and defensive strategies. Needless to say, such tendencies would also provoke further problems in the reconceptualization of a confident self-image in the West. In addition, if past world history is any guide to the future, while a benevolent world state which tolerates diversity is one possible outcome of the present process, there are alternatives. The intensification of competition between nation-states and blocs cannot be ruled out: this could take the form of elimination contests involving trade wars and various forms of warfare. Under such conditions, one would expect a series of defensive reactions in the form of mobilization of nationalisms and common cultures, with strongly defined stereotyping 'we-images' and 'they-images' which have little time for more nuanced notions of otherness. It is evident that the current global circumstance already incorporates these and other possibilities and we must be careful to avoid perpetuating our own particular conceptions of global and local cultures, however compelling they may seem.

Notes

An earlier version of this chapter was presented at the Netherlands Leisure Studies Association meeting, Utrecht, January 1991. I would like to thank those who attended for their comments. I would also like to thank Hans Mommaas and Donald Levine for helpful suggestions for revising earlier versions of this paper. A further version appeared in J. Bird and G. Robertson (eds) *Mapping the Future*, Routledge, 1993.

1. See the work of Dorfman and Mattelart (1975), especially their *How to Read Donald Duck*, and Schiller (1985). (For critical discussions of cultural imperialist theories see Smith, 1990; Tomlinson, 1991.) Although the notion of Americanization became most explicit in the writings of critics of cultural imperialism, it was also an implicit assumption which could be detected in modernization theories. It is also worth noting that while Americanization was seldom made explicit in the modernization theories which became influential from the 1960s onwards, it was certainly an assumption of a good many American citizens that modernization entailed cultural Americanization.

2. The term 'the end of history' was first used by Cournot in 1861 to refer to the end of the historical dynamic with the perfection of civil society (see Kamper, 1990). Arnold Gehlen adopted it in 1952 and it has been taken up more recently by Heidegger and Vattimo.

3. As we shall shortly see, the impetus for this does not only come from the West in terms of an inward-looking loss of confidence, but arises practically through the encounters with 'the other' who refuses to accept the Western version of history. One example of the construction of global culture is therefore the attempt to construct world histories. For a discussion of the difficulties involved in participating in the UNESCO project to bring together historians from various nations to construct a world history and the resultant conflicts and power struggles, see Burke (1989).

4. Needless to say, this is very different from the assumption that 'we are just like them',

which lacks the assumption that they are subordinates who will eventually become educated to be like us. Rather, to assume that 'we are just like them' is to assume that we can learn from them and are willing to identify with them.

5. It is important to stress that the process of the homogenization of culture is an image which the nation-state represents to itself, which may take numerous forms such as rituals and ceremonies. It is not the actual elimination of differences, the vestiges of regional, ethnic and local affiliations which is crucial, but the perception of the right of the state to do so, that such ties are backward and deviant and must be neutralized through education and civilizing processes.

6. For an interesting discussion of the spatial elasticity of the concept 'homeland' (*agar*) which in Ethiopian culture can mean anything from a local hamlet to the national state, see Levine (1965).

7. That the collective conscience and society-encompassing sense of the sacred might still be generated in modern societies was a preoccupation of Durkheim. Yet little did he and his 'heir', Marcel Mauss, realize that their conception of society would be actualized in the Nuremberg rallies of the Nazis. As Mauss commented, 'We ought to have expected this verification for evil rather than for good' (quoted in Moscovici, 1990: 5).

8. It should also be mentioned that for some of the young people, the newer urban spaces of large cities (such as the Les Halles area of Paris) offer the opportunity to experiment with types of affiliation hitherto often denied. Hence Maffesoli (1995) refers to the emergence of postmodern 'affective tribes' in which young people momentarily come together to generate spontaneously a temporary sense of *Einfühlung*, emotional oneness and intensity. These tribes are not attached to particular locales nor do they have the exclusivity of membership normally associated with tribes, yet they do suggest the capacity to generate collective emotional experiences in terms of the dissipation of the sacred we have spoken of. The same could be said of contemporary rock concerts, which can generate an intense emotional sense of togetherness and an ethical concern for nature, the Third World, etc. This would suggest that the dangers to 'ontological security' which Giddens (1990) associates with our present phase of what he calls 'high modernity' may have been overestimated.

7
LOCALISM, GLOBALISM AND CULTURAL IDENTITY

To live in one land, is captivitie.

(John Donne, 'Change', 1593–8)

There is a third world in every first world and vice-versa.

(Trinh T. Minh-ha, 1989)

To know who you are means to know where you are.

(James Clifford, 1989)

One of the problems in attempting to formulate a theory of globalization is of adopting a totalizing logic and assuming some master process of global integration is under way which is making the world more unified and homogeneous. From this perspective the intensification of global time-space compression through the universalizing processes of the new communications technology, the power of the flows of information, finance and commodities, means that local cultures inevitably give way. Our experiences and means of orientation necessarily become divorced from the physical locations in which we live and work. The fate of our places of residence and work is seen as in the hands of unknown agencies in other parts of the world. Localism and a sense of place gives way to the anonymity of 'no place spaces', or simulated environments in which we are unable to feel an adequate sense of being at home.

There is also the sense that such monological accounts, which equate the success of the globalization process with the extension of modernity, that 'globalization is basically modernity writ large', miss not only the cultural variability of non-Western nation-states and civilizations, but the specificity of the cultural complex of Western modernity. It is insufficient to assume that other non-Western cultures will simply give way to the logic of modernity and adopt Western forms, or to regard their formulations of national particularity as merely reactions to Western modernity.

Rather, the globalization process should be regarded as opening up the sense that now the world is a single place with increased contact becoming unavoidable, we necessarily have greater dialogue between various nation-states, blocs and civilizations: a dialogical space in which we can expect a good deal of disagreement, clashing of perspectives and conflict, not just working together and consensus. Not that participating nation-states and other agents should be regarded as equal partners to the dialogue. They are bound together in increasing webs of interdependencies and power balances, which partly through their complexity and sensitivity to change, and capacity to transmit information about shifts in fortune, means that it is more difficult to retain lasting and oversimplified images of others. The difficulty of handling increasing levels of cultural complexity, and the doubts and anxieties these often engender, are reasons why 'localism', or the desire to remain in a bounded locality or return to some notion of 'home', becomes an important theme. It can also be ventured that this is regardless of whether the home is real or imaginary, or whether it is temporary and syncretized or a simulation, or whether it is manifest in a fascination with the sense of belonging, affiliation and community which are attributed to the homes of others, such as tribal people. What does seem clear is that it is not helpful to regard the global and local as dichotomies separated in space or time; it would seem that the processes of globalization and localization are inextricably bound together in the current phase.

Localism and symbolic communities

Within the sociological tradition the term *local* and its derivatives *locality*, and *localism*, have generally been associated with a the notion of a particular bounded space with its set of close-knit social relationships based upon strong kinship ties and length of residence.[1] There is usually the assumption of a stable homogeneous and integrated cultural identity which is both enduring and unique. In this sense it was often assumed that members of a locality formed a distinctive community with its own unique culture – something which turns the location of their day-to-day inter-actions from a physical space into a 'place'. Much of the research on localities which developed within urban sociology and community studies was influenced by two main assumptions.

The first derived from nineteenth-century models of social change in which the past was regarded as entailing simpler, more direct, strongly bonded social relationships, as we find in the paired oppositions: status and contract (Maine), mechanical and organic solidarity (Durkheim), and community and association (Tönnies). The latter terms, drawn from the ideal types delineated in Tönnies's (1955) influential *Gemeinschaft und Gesellschaft*, have been used to emphasize the historical and spatial continuum between small relatively isolated integrated communities based upon primary relationships and strong emotional bonding and the more anonymous and instrumental secondary associations of the modern metropolis. The work of Tönnies and other German theorists has helped sanction over-romantic and nostalgic depictions of 'the world we have lost' to the relentless march of modernization.

The second, deriving from anthropology, emphasized the need to provide ethnographically rich descriptions of the particularity of relatively isolated small towns or villages. We have, for example, studies of small rural communities in the west of Ireland (Arensberg, 1968; Arensberg and Kimball, 1940) or North Wales (Frankenberg, 1966). Yet here and in other community studies researchers soon became preoccupied with the problems of delineating the boundaries of the locality. It soon became clear that the most isolated community in Britain or the United States was firmly plugged into national societies. The illusion of spatial isolation which drew researchers into focusing upon the rich particularity of local traditions soon gave way to an acceptance that the 'small town was *in* mass society', to paraphrase the title of one of the American studies of the 1950s (Vidich and Bensman, 1958). The intention here, and in earlier influential studies such as those of Middletown (Lynd and Lynd, 1929, 1937) and Yankee City (Warner and Lunt, 1941), was to examine the ways in which local communities were being transformed by industrialization, urbanization and bureaucratization. These modernizing processes were perceived to be all-pervasive and heralded 'the eclipse of community', to use the title of a book by Maurice Stein (1960) which discussed this literature.

In Britain there were also a number of studies of localities, some of which provided rich descriptions of the particularities of working-class life. In studies such as *Coal is Our Life* (Dennis *et al.*, 1956), *Working Class Community* (Jackson, 1968) and *Class, Culture and Community* (Williamson, 1982) we get a strong sense of a distinctive working-class way of life with its occupational homogeneity and strictly segregated gender roles, with male group ties and the 'mateship' code of loyalty predominant in both work and leisure (drinking, gambling, sport) – women were largely confined to the separate home sphere. The classic account of this culture which captures the fullness of everyday working-class life was provided by Richard Hoggart's account of his Leeds childhood in *The Uses of Literacy* (1957). Hoggart (1957: esp. Ch. 5 'The Full Rich Life') documented the sayings, songs, the sentimentality and generous indulgences of working-class life (the Sunday afternoon big meat tea, the Saturday night 'knees-up' and singing in the pub, the charabanc seaside outings at which all the saved-up money had to be squandered, the belly-laugh survival humour and vulgarity, the larger-than-life characters and general emotional warmth and group support, the gossip and knowledge of family histories and local institutions).

As has been pointed out, there is a danger of taking this picture of working-class life as the definitive one, the real working-class community, and missing its particular location in time and space – the northern working-class towns of the 1930s (Critcher, 1979). The same era produced working-class film star heroes, Gracie Fields and George Formby, who epitomized the working-class sense of fun and capacity to mock and deflate pretentiousness. They had a strong sense of community and loyalty to place, and the retention of a local accent showed their unwillingness to lose their roots, and reinforced their apparent 'naturalness', which made them forever seem a Lancashire lad and lass at heart. Here we think of Gracie Fields in films such as *Looking on the Bright Side* (1932), *Sing as We Go* (1934), *Keep Smiling* (1938) and *The Show Goes On* (1937) (see Richards, 1984: Ch. 10). George Formby likewise maintained an irrepressible cheerfulness: the 'cheeky chappie', the little man forever playing the fool, yet possessing local knowledge with which to outsmart the upper-class 'toffs' in films such as *Off the Dole* (1935), *Keep Fit* (1938) and *No Limit* (1935) (see Richards, 1984: Ch. 11). The films of both Fields and Formby showed Britain very much as a class-divided society, and both achieved fame through their ability to poke fun at middle- and upper-class decorum and the respectability, formality and reserve which the BBC typified.

The films were important in their attempt to present society from the bottom up, and their capacity to install a sense of pride in working-class localism. They presented a contrast to the accounts of working-class life provided by the middle and upper classes. For some in the upper echelons of society the working class was akin to an exotic tribe. Frances Donaldson, for example, remarks that the upper and middle classes regarded the working class as quasi-foreign, and when they moved amongst them with view to improving their lot 'they did so as anthropologists . . . or missionaries visiting a tribe more primitive than themselves' (Donaldson, 1975, quoted in Fussell, 1980: 74). George Orwell's famous *The Road to Wigan Pier* (1937) was written in this style: he had received an upper-class public school education at Eton which provided him with a keen sense of social distinctions.[2]

One memorable passage that sticks in the mind, and that epitomized Orwell's frequent discomfort with aspects of working-class life, was the uneasiness with which he received his daily breakfast slice of bread and dripping. Each time it was put on his plate it contained a black thumbprint, left by the coal miner he was lodging with who always cut the bread after lighting the coal fire and slopping out the chamber-pots. Here we have an example of what Elias (1978) refers to as the 'disgust function', the feeling of revulsion which those who have developed more refined taste and bodily controls can experience when they encounter the habits of common people (see also Bourdieu, 1984; Featherstone, 1991a: Ch. 9). In this type of writing, in which all is revealed about 'darkest England', we frequently get swings from emotional identification, the desire for the immersion in the directness, warmth and spontaneity of the local community, to revulsion, disgust and the desire for distance.

The audience for accounts of working-class life has a long history, going back to Engels and Charles Booth in the nineteenth century. It is still evident in the dramatic exposé style of many of the accounts written by 'one of us' about 'the people of the abyss', to mention the title of one of Jack London's books. This sense of an anthropologist parachuted into the alien depths of deepest working-class England was still to be found in the 1950s in the publicity for Richard Hoggart's *The Uses of Literacy*:

the inside cover of the first Penguin edition suggested that the book sought 'to remedy our ignorance' about 'how the other half lives' (Laing, 1986: 47).

Hoggart's book, as has been suggested, is noticeable for its sympathetic descriptions of traditional working-class life; but it also presents this life as threatened by modernization in the form of the mass media and com-mercialization. Many of these negative influences were seen as originating in the United States. Hoggart has little time for television, milk bars, jukebox boys and other elements of the 'candy-floss world' of mass culture. The tensions which developed within working-class culture as it encountered the forces of the affluent society, consumerism and mass culture were captured in a series of novels of the late 1950s and 1960s many of which were made into films. Here we think of Alan Sillitoe's *Saturday Night and Sunday Morning* (1958), Stan Barstow's *A Kind of Loving* (1960), David Storey's *This Sporting Life* (1960) and Ken Loach's films of Neil Dunn's *Up the Junction* (1965), *Poor Cow* (1967), and Barry Hine's *Kes* (1967) which explored the earthiness and richness of life within the closed working-class community with occasional glimpses of the modernizing processes (see Laing, 1986; Stead, 1989). Notable here is the central character in the much-acclaimed film version of *Saturday Night and Sunday Morning*, Arthur Seaton, a working-class hero if there ever was one, played by Albert Finney, who although he finally is entrapped into marriage, in the last moments of the film defiantly casts a stone at the newly built modern suburban housing estate which is to be his future.

As Bernice Martin (1981: 71) reminds us, many of the accounts of working-class life focus upon its directness and simplicity of emotional expression. To the middle-class observer it is too often the 'immediate gratification', the ritual swearing and the aggression, sexuality, drinking and violence which attract attention. Yet these features are actually liminal moments of working-class life, a part which is too often mistaken for a whole. The moments of brotherhood and 'communitas' are necessarily limited moments of 'framed liminality', moments of 'anti-structure' (Turner, 1969) in which celebration and taboo-breaking are planned for, in stark contrast to the careful budgeting, time management and concern for reputation and respectability in routine everyday life. It is the represen-tations of these liminal moments which provide a rich repertoire of images. Here one thinks of, for example, Ridley Scott's 'Hovis Bread' commercial which is packed with nostalgic images of a nineteenth-century northern English working-class town set to a mournful refrain from Dvořák's *New World Symphony* played by a brass band. Or the former British Prime Minister Harold Macmillan reminiscing about the people in his northern working-class constituency of Stockton-on-Tees: 'Wonderful people, the finest people in the world', he remarked in a television interview, in a voice heavy with emotion and a tear in the corner of his eye, which almost had us convinced he regarded the Stockton working class as his only true organic community.

Many of these images of working-class community help to foster myths of belonging, warmth and togetherness which suggest the mythical security of a childhood long relinquished. There is nothing so powerful as the image of an integrated organic community in the childhood one has left behind (Hall, 1991: 46). Geoffrey Pearson (1985) has provided an important account of the ways in which successive generations always have recourse to the myth of 'the good old days', the existence of a less violent, more law-abiding and harmonious community in the past of their childhood or parents' times. As one goes further and further back into history one finds successive displacements of this golden age back to the 1950s, 1930s, 1900s, 1870s and so on. Successive generations have invested in a form of nostalgia in which the past is viewed as the epitome of coherence and order, something which was more simple and emotionally fulfilling, with more direct and integrated relationships. The assumption, here, is that one's identity and those of one's significant others are anchored in a specific locale, a physical space which becomes emotionally invested and sedimented with symbolic associations so that it becomes a place. As Bryan Turner (1987) remarks, nostalgia, or the loss of a sense of home, is a potent sentiment in the modern world, particularly so for those groups who are ambivalent about modernity and retain the strong image of the alleged greater integration and simplicity of a more integrated culture in the past.

When we speak of a locality, then, we should be careful not to presume an integrated community. There are problems with establishing the extent to which localities were integrated in the past. We have to be aware of the location in time-space and social space of those who make such pronouncements and that they might be painting a nostalgic and over-unified picture. It is also important that we do not operate with the view that localities are able to change only through the working out of a one-way modernization process entailing the eclipse of community and the local culture.

Usually when we think of a locality we have in mind a relatively small place in which everyone can know everyone else; that is, social life is based upon face-to-face relations. It is assumed that the intensity of the day-to-day contacts will generate a common stock of knowledge at hand which makes misunderstandings less frequent. It is the regularity and frequency of contacts with a group of significant others which are held to sustain a common culture. While the existence of such an integrated set of 'core values' or common assumptions rooted in everyday practices may be overstated at both local and national levels (see Featherstone, 1991a: Ch. 9) there is a further dimension of cultural integration which must be referred to. This is the generation of powerful emotionally sustaining rituals, ceremonies and collective memories.

Durkheim (1961), in his *The Elementary Forms of the Religious Life*, placed particular emphasis upon the way in which a sense of the sacred was generated in emotionally bonding periods of 'collective effervescence'.

Over time the intense sense of involvement and excitement which bound people together tends to diminish; the use of commemorative rituals and ceremonies can be understood as acting like batteries which store and recharge the sense of communality. Outside the regular calendar of ceremonies which reinforce our family, local and national sense of collective identity, it is also possible to draw on collective memories. As Halbwachs (1992) reminds us, collective memories refer to group contexts in the past which are periodically reinforced through contact with others who shared the initial experience (see also Middleton and Edwards, 1990).

Nations as communities

Yet are there limits to the size of the group and place to be considered a local community? Could a nation be considered a local community? If we examine the origins of the term it refers not only to the modern nation-state, but also draws on the meaning of *natio*, a local community, domicile family condition of belonging (Brennan, 1990: 45). There is often a clear reluctance to accept that the nation could ever embody the type of bonding typically attributed to the local community, especially from Marxists with internationalist sympathies. Hence Raymond Williams remarks:

> 'Nation' as a term is radically connected with 'native.' We are *born* into relationships which are typically settled in a place. This form of primary and 'placeable' bonding is of quite fundamental human and natural importance. Yet the jump from that to anything like the modern nation-state is entirely artificial. (Williams, 1983: 180, quoted in Brennan, 1990: 45)

This contrasts with the position of Benedict Anderson (1991: 6), who argues that 'all communities larger than the primordial village of face-to-face contact (and perhaps even these are imagined). Communities are to be distinguished not by their falseness/genuineness, but by the style in which they are imagined.' In this sense a nation may be considered as an imagined community because it provides a quasi-religious sense of belonging and fellowship which is attached to those who are taken to share a particular symbolic place. The place is symbolic in that it can be a geographically bounded space which is sedimented with symbolic sentiments; the configuration of the landscape, buildings and people have been invested with collective memories which have sufficient emotional power to generate a sense of communality. Certain places may be enshrined with a particular emblematic status as national monuments and used to represent a form of symbolic bonding which overrides and embodies the various local affiliations people possess.

Indeed, this is an essential part of the nation-building process in which the nation-state actively encourages the cultivation and elaboration of the *ethnie*, or ethnic core (Smith, 1990). In this sense the creation of a national community is invented, but it is not invented out of nothing. Anthony

Smith emphasizes the need for a common repository of myths, heroes, events, landscapes and memories which are organized and made to assume a primordial quality. In the eighteenth century with the birth of nationalism in Europe there was a deliberate attempt by cultural specialists (or proto-intellectuals) to discover and record the vernacular customs and practices, legends and myths, the culture of the people, which it was assumed was fast disappearing (see Burke, 1978). In effect, the expanding strata of the indigenous intelligentsia sought to pull together and weave into a coherent form this body of popular cultural sources which could be used to give the past a sense of direction and construct a national identity.

This can be linked to what Gellner (1983), Anderson (1991) and others regard as a crucial factor in the construction of nationalism: the availability of a print culture which can interconnect people over time and space. The possibility of the nation therefore depends upon the development of the book and the newspaper alongside a literate reading public capable of using these sources throughout the territorial area and thus able to imagine themselves as a community. The development of the film industry facilitates this process even better, as film provides a sense of instanciation and immediacy which is relatively independent of the long learning process and institutional and other supports necessary to be able to assimilate knowledge through books (S.F. Moore, 1989; Higson, 1989).

The nation, therefore, becomes represented through a set of more or less coherent images and memories which deal with the crucial questions of the origins, difference and distinctiveness of a people. In this sense it has a quasi-religious basis, as it is able to answer some of the questions of theodicy in a world which is subject to processes of secularization. The sacrifice and suffering people are willing to undergo for the nation must in part be understood with respect to the capacity of the discourses, images and practices which sustain the nation to provide a sense of overarching significance which transcends death, or renders death meaningful through subsuming the individual under a sacred totality. Yet the fact that a national culture is constituted as a unique particularity points to the situation of the rise of the European nation-states which were locked into power struggles and elimination contests in which the mobilization of the population by the idea of the distinctiveness of the nation through its difference from its neighbours attained significance.

The external pressures of the figuration of significant others to which the nation-state belongs and the escalating power struggles can make the construction of an identity for the nation more important. It has been argued that conflicts heighten the sense of the boundary between the 'in-group' and the 'out-group'. Hence Georg Simmel, who had written at length about the capacity of external conflicts to unify the internal structure of a group, remarked on the way in which the German reaction to the First World War resulted in a strong wave of social ecstasy and intensification of social bonds which unified the nation (Watier, 1991).

Simmel's writings are important because he gives us a sense of the multidimensional and relational nature of social life. A local culture may have a common set of work and kinship relationships that reinforce the practical everyday lived culture which is sedimented into taken-for-granted knowledge and beliefs. Yet the articulation of these beliefs and sense of the particularity of the local place will tend to become sharpened and more well defined when the locality becomes locked into power struggles and elimination contests with its neighbours. In such situations we can see the formation of a local culture in which the particularity of its own identity is emphasized. In this case the locality presents an oversimplified unified image of itself to outsiders. This image, to use a metaphor of Cohen (1985), can be likened to the local community's face, or mask. This does not mean that inside the locality social differentiation has been eliminated and relationships are necessarily more egalitarian, simple and homogeneous; rather, its internal differences and discourses may very well be complex. Internally we may be able to consider the community as incorporating all sorts of independencies, rivalries, power struggles and conflicts. Many community studies document these conflicts: here one thinks of Elias and Scotson's (1994) account of the struggles between the established and the outsiders. Yet under certain circumstances such struggles may be forgotten, as, for example, when the locality is brought into conflict with another locality, or the region is involved in inter-regional disputes. In such situations one's own particularity is subsumed into some larger collectivity and appropriate cultural work is undertaken to develop an acceptable public face for it. This process entails the mobilization of the repertoire of communal symbols, sentiments and collective memories.

The shifts in the interdependencies and power balances increase the local people's consciousness of the symbolic boundary between themselves and others which is aided by the mobilization and reconstitution of symbolic repertoires with which the community can think and formulate a unified image of its difference from the opposite party (Cohen, 1985). It is the capacity to shift the frame, and move between varying range of foci, the capacity to handle a range of symbolic material out of which various identities can be formed and reformed in different situations, which is relevant in the contemporary global situation. Here we have the sense that the contemporary world has not seen a cultural impoverishment, an attenuation of cultural resources. Rather there has been an extension of cultural repertoires and an enhancement of the resourcefulness of various groups to create new symbolic modes of affiliation and belonging, as well as struggling to rework and reshape the meaning of existing signs, to undermine existing symbolic hierarchies, for their own particular purposes in ways that become difficult for those in the dominant cultural centres to ignore. This shift has been aided and abetted by various sets of cultural specialists and intermediaries with sympathies for the local.

The sense of the strength of the sentiments which become embodied in the nation and their resilience over time, it has been argued, have been underestimated by some theorists who miss the role of the nation in the nation-state and assume that the national sentiments were merely a by-product of the modernization process devised to facilitate the integration of the nation-state. These sentiments have subsequently been proved redundant and undermined by the modernizing process (Arnason, 1990). In addition, there are often tendencies to underestimate the ways in which the formation of the nation and nationalism draw upon cultural resources which have yet to be modernized, such as the cultural memories, symbols, myths and sentiment surrounding the ethnic core (Smith, 1990). This suggests that the stock sociological contrast between tradition and modernity may not be that useful. This is noticeable in the case of nation-states such as Japan which, it is argued, cannot easily be fitted into the assumed developmental logic of modernization (Sakai, 1989; Mitsuhiro, 1989). In effect Japan managed to impose a restrictive and particularistic project of modernity and was able to protect it against universalistic challenges (Maruyama, 1969; Arnason, 1987a, 1987b). This would point to the continuing importance of cultural factors in the development of nation-states and in their relations with other nation-states.

The bilateral interactions that occur between nation-states, especially those which involve increasing competition and conflict, can have the effect of unifying the self-image of the nation: the image or national face which is presented to the other. A growth in the regularity and intensity of contacts as nation-states become bound up in regional figurations (their reference group of significant others), can intensify the pressures to form a distinctive and coherent identity. It is important to emphasize that this is a process which, in addition to the external presentation of the national face, also has an internal dimension and depends upon the power resources particular groups possess to mobilize the ethnic core. They will endeavour to mobilize different aspects of the ethnic core to suit their own particular interests and aspirations; in effect the process of cultural formation of a national identity always entails a part being represented as a whole: a particular representation of the nation is presented as unanimous and consensual.

Here one thinks of Margaret Thatcher's Downing Street statement on news of victory in the Falklands War in 1982: 'We are one nation tonight.' Such statements also point to the fragility of particular formulations of national identity: while to be legitimate they have to draw upon a finite and recognizable repository of the ethnic core, they are also subjected to a continuous process of struggle to develop and impose alternative formulations. The fragility and volatility of the emotional sentiments embodied in the nation, and the struggle over the legitimacy of the representation, therefore suggest that we should consider national cultures in processual terms. When we consider processes of the formation and deformation of national identity we should also be clear that it is easier to identify a common ethnic core where there has been a long-term process of national formation in European nations, as is the case in Britain and France. That we should be wary of taking their individual cases as the model for nation formation is evident when we consider newer nations, especially those endeavouring to construct a multicultural sense of identity. The case of Australia is interesting in this context and there are now a number of studies about the attempts to generate a unified national identity: to 'invent Australia', through the cultivation of representations of particular places such as Ayers Rock or Bondi Beach, and historical events such as Gallipoli (see White, 1981; Fiske *et al.*, 1987; Game, 1990).

The images that are constructed through television and the cinema are a necessary part in the process of the formation of a nation, especially in their capacity to bridge the public and the private. A nation is an abstract collectivity which is far too big to be directly experienced by people. Hence it is not only the existence of civic rituals such as Remembrance Day that provide the sense of the sacred which binds the nation together; increasingly it is the representation of these events which is crucial (Chaney, 1986). For people whose knowledge of these events is restricted to viewing television in their living room, television does not merely represent such events, but also constructs them. Yet it is not just a question of a passive audience taking in the event, as Dyan and Katz (1988) have argued; it is also possible for individuals and families to reconstitute the ceremonial space in the home by observing rituals, dressing up and 'participating', in the knowledge that countless others are doing the very same thing. Hence an 'atomized' audience can occasionally be united via television media events.

Yet it is insufficient to see the process of imagining the nation as purely the product of internal factors. In the Second World War the British film industry played an important part in mobilizing a nation identity through the production of representations of the common foe (Higson, 1989). We should not consider cultures in isolation, but endeavour to locate them in the relational matrix of their significant others (c.f. Gupta and Ferguson, 1992). It is not the isolation of the nation which is the crucial factor in developing an image of itself as a unique and integrated national culture. Rather, it is the need to mobilize a particular representation of national identity, as part of the series of unavoidable contacts, interdependencies and power struggles which nation-states become locked into with their significant others.

This means we should not just focus on bilateral relations between nation-states. Nation-states do not just interact; they form a *world*. That is, increasingly their interactions take place within a global context: a context which has seen the development of its own body of formal and taken-for-granted procedures based upon processes and modes of integration which cannot simply be reduced to the interests and control of individual nation-states (see Arnason, 1990). The gradual development of diplomatic conventions and procedures, such as international law which emerged alongside and independent from nation-states to form a nexus of underpinning ground-rules for international conflicts, are one set of examples (Bergesen, 1990). Another would be the independent power of multinational corporations to act independently to weaken the integrity of national culture through their capacity to direct a range of flows of cultural goods and information from the dominant economic centres to the peripheries – the cultural imperialism thesis would be a strong case of this type of argument. The perception and extent of these processes can increase nation-states' sensitivity to the need to preserve the integrity of their own national traditions and can be used to promote counter- or deglobalizing and fundamentalist reactions.

One effect, then, of the globalization process – the increasing contact and sense of the finitude of the world, the consciousness that the world is one place – is to lead to a clashing of a plurality of different interpretations of the meaning of the world formulated from the perspective of different national and civilizational traditions. The density and multi-directionality of the talk which takes place on the global stage necessarily demands that nation-states take up a position as they increasingly find it impossible to silence the other voices or consider opting out. Hence we have a plurality of national responses to the process of globalization which cannot be conceived as reducible to the ideas generated by Western modernity. One of the problems entailed in mapping the contemporary global condition is this range of different national cultural responses which continue to deform and reform, blend, syncretize and transform, in various ways, the alleged master processes of modernity.

With respect to theories of modernity there is often the assumption that modernization necessarily entails the eclipse of the national tradition and cultural identity. Yet theories of modernity that emphasize a relentless process of instrumental rationalization which effectively 'empties out' a society's repository of cultural traditions and meanings are misconceived. Weber's notion of the imposition of an 'iron cage', a new bureaucratized serfdom or 'Egyptification' of life, and the related arguments about the progressive commodification, rationalization and disenchantment of the world by critical theorists such as Habermas, would seem to be difficult to substantiate (see Haferkamp, 1987; Knorr-Cetina, 1994).[3]

Knorr-Cetina (1994), for example, argues that if we examine everyday practices closely we find that they 'testify to the presence of "meaning", and "tradition", of "the body", of "intimacy", "local knowledge" and everything else that is often thought to have been bred out of "abstract systems."' In effect the everyday practices of participants, even if they work within highly technicized organizations, operate with and by means of fictions. Hence if we observe the practices in local environments we find that the shared, deeply cherished classifications people use are a form of the sacred. Modernity has not meant a loss of magic and enchantment, or the fictional use of symbolic classifications in local institutions.

Globalization and cultural identity

If globalization refers to the process whereby the world increasingly becomes seen as 'one place' and the ways in which we are made conscious of this process (Robertson, 1992a) then the cultural changes which are thematized under the banner of the postmodern seem to point in the opposite direction by directing us to consider the local. Yet this is to misunderstand the nature of the process of globalization. It should not be taken to imply that there is, or will be, a unified world society or culture – something akin to the social structure of a nation-state and its national culture, only writ large. Such an outcome may have been the ambition of particular nation-states at various points of their history, and the possibility of a renewed world state formation process cannot be discounted in the future. In the present phase it is possible to refer to the development of a global culture in a less totalistic sense by referring to two aspects of the process of globalization.

First, we can point to the existence of a global culture in the restricted sense of 'third cultures': sets of practices, bodies of knowledge, conventions and lifestyles that have developed in ways which have become increasingly independent of nation-states. In effect there are a number of trans-societal institutions, cultures and cultural producers who cannot be understood as merely agents and representatives of their nation-states. Second, we can talk about a global culture in the Simmelian sense of a cultural form: the sense that the globe is a finite, knowable bounded space, a field into which all nation-states and collectivities will inevitably be drawn. Here the globe, the planet earth, acts both as a limit and as the common bounded space on which our encounters and practices are inevitably grounded. In this second sense the result of the growing intensity of contact and communication between nation-states and other agencies is to produce a clashing of cultures, which can lead to heightened attempts to draw the boundaries between the self and others. From this perspective the changes which are taking place as a result of the current phase of intensified globalization can be understood as provoking reactions that seek to rediscover particularity, localism and difference which generate a sense of the limits of the culturally unifying, ordering and integrating projects associated with Western modernity. So in one sense it can be argued that globalization produces postmodernism.

If we examine the first aspect of the globalization process, it is evident that the problems of intercultural communication in fields such as law have led to the development of mediating 'third cultures' (Gessner and Schade, 1990). These were initially designed to deal with the practical problems of intercultural legal disputes, but as with the development of the European Court of Justice and other institutions and protocols in international law, they can achieve autonomy and function beyond the manipulation of individual nation-states. In addition we can point to the further integrating effects of the internationalization of the world financial markets following the move to 24-hour trading after the 'Big Bang' of October 1986 (Dezalay, 1990). The process of deregulation encouraged the demonopolization of national legal systems and a more meritocratic market ethos in which international lawyers became part of a group of new professionals, which includes corporate tax accountants, financial advisers, management consultants and 'design professionals'.

The deregulation of markets and capital flows can be seen to produce a degree of homogenization in procedures, working practices and organizational cultures. In addition there are some convergences in the lifestyle, habitus and demeanour of these various sets of professionals. There are also similarities in the quarters of the cities they live and work in. Yet it should be emphasized that such groups are not to be found in every city, or even national capital. They are concentrated in various world cities such as New York, Tokyo, London, Paris, Los Angeles, São Paulo (King, 1990b; Sassen, 1991; Zukin, 1991). It is the integration of the particular services located in particular quarters of these world cities which produces transnational sets of social relations, practices and cultures. The process of globalization is therefore uneven, and if one aspect of it is the consciousness of the world as a single place, then it is in these select quarters of world cities that we find people working in environments which rely upon advanced means of communications which overcome time-space separation. Here we find the most striking examples of the effects of time-space compression, as new means of communication effectively make possible simultaneous transactions which sustain 'deterritorialized cultures'.

It is when we take the next step and assume that such areas are the prototypes for the future and that the international economy and communications networks will produce similar homogenizing effects in other areas of national societies that we run into problems. Here some would make the mistake of assuming that the extension of various social and cultural forms to different parts of the world is necessarily producing a homogenization of content. That is, the globalization process is seen as producing a unified and integrated common culture. Hence we find that theories of cultural imperialism and media imperialism assume that local cultures are necessarily battered out of existence by the proliferation of consumer goods, advertising and media programmes stemming from the West (largely the United States).

Such theories share with theories of mass culture a strong view of the manipulability of mass audiences by a monolithic system and an assumption of the negative cultural effects of the media as self-evident, with little empirical evidence about how goods and information are adapted and used in everyday practices (Tomlinson, 1991). Of course it is possible to point to the availability of Western consumer goods, especially major brands of food, drink, cigarettes and clothing, following the business and tourist trails to the remotest part of the world. It is also clear that certain images – the tough guy hero fighting against innumerable odds – have a strong appeal in many cultures. Hence we find Rambo movies played

throughout southern and eastern Asia so that 'remote villagers in rural
Burma could now applaud Rambo's larger-than-life heroics only days
after they hit the screens of Wisconsin' (Iyer, 1989: 12). To take a
second example, one of the major contemporary travel writers, Paul
Theroux (1992: 178), in his book *The Happy Islands of Oceania* recounts
how in the remotest parts of the Pacific Islands he found men coming up
to him to tell him about the latest developments in the Gulf War they
had heard on the radio. In addition he found that in the tiny island of
Savo in the Solomons Islands group, Rambo was a big folk hero. The
one generator on the island had no use except as a source of power for
showing videos. One can surmise that it may not be too long before
Savo has its satellite TV receiver or personal computers which link it
into the worldwide 'net'. Such accounts are by now legion – yet how are
we to read them?

One possibility is to attempt to outline some of the absorption/
assimilation/resistance strategies which peripheral cultures can adopt
towards the mass and consumer culture images and goods originating
from metropolitan centres (Hannerz, 1991). In the first place it is apparent
that once we investigate actual cases the situation is exceedingly complex.
It is not just a question of the everyday practical culture of local
inhabitants giving way to globally marketed products. Such market
culture/local culture interactions are usually mediated by the nation-state,
which in the process of creating a national identity will educate and
employ its own range of cultural specialists and intermediaries. Some of
these may well have been educated in world cities and have retained strong
networks and lifestyle identifications with other transnational 'design
professionals', managers and intellectuals and para-intellectuals. Some of
these may even be official 'cultural animateurs' employed by the ministry
of culture, in some cases perhaps with one eye on national cultural
integration and one eye on the international tourist trade.

Hence, depending on the priority it gives to the nation-forming project
and the power resources that the nation-state possesses, it can reinvent
memories, traditions and practices with which to resist, channel or control
market penetration. Some nation-states, for example, will invest in locally
produced film and television programmes. Yet as we have previously
mentioned, such experiments in cultural engineering are by no means
certain to succeed unless they can find a base to ground themselves in local
forms of life and practices. Hence the scenario of 'cultural dumping' of
obsolete American television programmes on a powerless nation-state on
the periphery is only one possibility from a range of responses. It has to be
set alongside the activities of cultural gatekeepers, brokers and entrepreneurs within the major cities of the nation-state in conjunction with
colleagues abroad in the world cities collaborating in deciding what
aspects of the local popular culture – music, food, dress, crafts, etc. – can
be packaged and marketed in the metropolitan centres and elsewhere. In
many cases it may be that various forms of hybridization and creolization

emerge in which the meanings of externally originating goods, information and images are reworked, syncretized and blended with existing cultural traditions and forms of life.

In the case of the effects of global television it is important to move beyond oversimplified oppositionally conceived formulations which stress either the manipulation, or the resistance, of audiences. In recent years the pendulum has swung towards the latter populist direction and it is claimed that a new cultural studies orthodoxy has emerged around the assumption of the creativity and skilfulness of active audiences and consumers (Morris, 1990). Television and the new communications technology are frequently presented as producing both manipulation and resistance, and the homogenization and fragmentation of contemporary culture (Morley, 1991).

The new communications technology is presented as producing a global *Gemeinschaft* which transcends physical place through bringing together disparate groups who unite around the common experience of television to form new communities (Meyrowitz, 1985). This means that the locality is no longer the prime referent of our experiences. Rather, we can be immediately united with distant others with whom we can form a 'psychological neighbourhood' or 'personal community' through telephone or the shared experience of the news of the 'generalized elsewhere' we get from watching television. Hence as Morley (1991: 8) remarks, 'Thus, it seems, locality is not simply subsumed in a national or global sphere: rather, it is increasingly bypassed in both directions; experience is both unified beyond localities and fragmented within them.' Yet this is not to suggest that the fragmentation of experience within localities is random or unstructured. Access to power resources creates important differentials. Just as there are 'information rich' nations on a global level there are also 'information poor' ones. Within localities there are clear differentials, with the wealthy and well-educated most likely to have access to the new forms of information and communications technology through possession of the necessary economic and cultural capital (Morley, 1991: 10). Here we can also point to Mary Douglas and Baron Isherwood's (1980) concept of 'informational goods', goods which require a good deal of background knowledge to make their consumption meaningful and strategically useful, as is the case with personal computers.

On the other hand it is the sense of instanciation and immediacy that television presents which appears to make its messages unproblematically accessible. American soap operas, Italian football or the Olympic games all have an apparent immediacy and intelligibility which could be mis-understood as producing a homogeneous response. Yet these global resources are often indigenized and syncretized to produce particular blends and identifications which sustain the sense of the local (see Canevacci, 1992).[4]

A further problem with the homogenization thesis is that it misses the ways in which transnational corporations increasingly direct advertising towards various parts of the globe which is increasingly tailored to specific differentiated audiences and markets. Hence the global and the local cannot be neatly separated, as we find in the statement by Coca-Cola: 'We are not a multi-national, we are a multi-local' (quoted in Morley, 1991: 15). Here we can usefully refer to the term 'glocal', the fusion of the terms global and local to make a blend. Apparently the term is modelled on the Japanese *dochaku*, which derives from the agricultural principle of adapting one's farming techniques to local conditions, and which was taken up by Japanese business interests in the 1980s (Robertson, 1995; see also Luke, 1995).

The various combinations, blends and fusions of seemingly opposed and incompatible processes such as homogenization and fragmentation, globalization and localization, universalism and particularism, indicate the problems entailed in attempts to conceive the global in terms of a singular integrated and unified conceptual scheme. Appadurai (1990) has rejected such attempts at theoretical integration to argue that the global order must be understood as 'a complex, overlapping, disjunctive order'. It can be best conceived as involving sets of non-isomorphic flows of people, technology, finance, media images and information, and ideas. Individual nation-states may attempt to promote, channel or block flows with varying degrees of success depending upon the power resources they possess and the constraints of the configuration of interdependencies they are locked into.

It is, of course, important that we examine the evidence from systematic studies which focus upon specific localities to examine the effects of these flows on groups of people. One important site where the various flows of people, goods, technology, information and images cross and intermingle is the world city. World cities are the sites in which we find the juxtaposition of the rich and the poor, the new middle-class professionals and the homeless, and a variety of other ethnic, class and traditional identifications, as people from the centre and periphery are brought together to face each other within the same spatial location (Berner and Korff, 1992). The socio-spatial redevelopment of the inner areas and docklands of some large Western cities in the 1980s have been regarded by some as examples of 'postmodernization' (Cooke, 1988; Zukin, 1988).

Yet, many of the cultural factors associated with this process – the postmodern emphasis upon the mixing of codes, pastiche, fragmentation, incoherence, disjunction and syncretism – were characteristics of cities in colonial societies decades or even centuries before they appeared in the West (King, 1995). From this perspective the first multi-cultural city was not London or Los Angeles but probably Rio de Janeiro or Calcutta, or Singapore. At the very least this points to some of the problems involved in defining the modern and the postmodern and their family of associated terms. A more nuanced and elaborated notion of cultural modernity which goes beyond Eurocentric notions of the homogenizing effects of industrialization, urbanization and bureaucratization is needed. A global conception of the modern is required, which rather than being pre-occupied with the historical sequences of transitions from tradition to modernity and postmodernity, instead focuses upon the spatial dimension, the geographical relationship between the centre and the periphery in which the first multiracial and multi-cultural societies were on the periphery not the core. Cultural diversity, syncretism and dislocation occurred there first. The interdependencies and power balances which developed between Western nation-states such as England and France and colonial societies clearly form an important, yet neglected aspect of modernity; an aspect which is noticeably absent from those accounts which derive from those working in the classic tradition deriving from French and German theorists (see also Bhabha, 1991). These themes will be discussed more fully in the next chapter (see also Featherstone and Lash, 1995).

It is the very process of intensified flows of people from the ex-colonial countries to the Western metropolitan centres in the postwar era that has made us increasingly conscious of this colonial aspect of the development of modernity and the question of cultural identity. The inward movement of people, as well as images and information, from places which for many in the West were constructed through oversimplified racist and exotic stereotypes of 'the Other', means that new levels of complexity are introduced to the formulation of notions of identity, cultural tradition, community and nation. This challenges the notion of one-way flows from the centre to the peripheries, as the dominant centres in the West become not only importers of raw materials and goods, but of people too.[5] The visibility and vociferousness of 'the rest in the West' (Hall, 1992c) means that cultural differences once maintained between societies now exist within them. The unwillingness of migrants to passively absorb the dominant cultural mythology of the nation or locality raises issues of multiculturalism and the fragmentation of identity.

In some cases this has provoked intensified and extremist nationalist reactions, as has occurred in France (the racist campaigns of Le Pen) and Britain (the 1980s Falklands War and its associated 'little Englanderism'). This can lead to a complex series of reactions on the part of immigrants. For some ethnic groups this entails a retreat into the culture of origin (in Britain a re-identification with the Caribbean, Pakistan, India or Bangladesh); or a retreat into fundamentalist religions from the home country. For others this may entail the construction of complex counter-ethnicities as with young second generation Afro-Caribbeans who have developed identities around the symbols and mythologies of Rastafarianism (Hall, 1992b: 308). For yet others the prospect of a unified single identity may be impossible and illusory as they move between various identities. Some third-generation young blacks in Britain constantly shift between British, Caribbean, black, subcultural and various gender identifications. For example, the film My Beautiful Laundrette (1981), by Stephen Frears and

Hanif Kureishi, has central characters who are two gay men, one white, one brown, with the latter's Pakistani landlord uncle throwing black people out on to the street: characters who do not present positive unified identity images and who are consequently not easy to identify with (Hall, 1991: 60).

The problems involved in trying to live with multiple identities helps to generate endless discourses about the process of finding or constructing a coherent identity (see Marcus, 1992a, on multiple and dispersed identities; also Gupta and Ferguson, 1992, on cultural dislocation). Yet in contrast to those arguments which assume that the logic of modernity is to produce an increasingly narrow individualism, a narcissistic preoccupation with individual identity which was common in the 1970s, today we find arguments which emphasize the search for a strong collective identity, some new form of community, within modern societies.

Maffesoli (1995), for example, sees the process of development from modernity to postmodernity as entailing a movement from individualism to collectivism, from rationality to emotionality. In this sense postmodernity is seen as sharing with its premodern antecedents an emphasis on emotionality, the cultivation of intense feelings and sensory experiences such as were found in the spectacles of the baroque. Here Maffesoli speaks of postmodernity as bringing about a new tribalism, the emergence of ephemeral postmodern *tribes*, which are to be found especially amongst young people in large cities such as Paris. These groupings provide a strong sense of localism and emotional identification (*Einfühlung*) through the tactile embodied sense of being together. They are regarded as *neo*-tribes because they exist in an urban world where relationships are transitory, hence their identifications are temporary as people will necessarily move on and through the endless flow of sociality to make new attachments (see also discussions in Bauman, 1991, 1992). The subject of tribalism, both in its traditional sense of exclusive membership of a group based upon kinties and strong identification with a locality or region, and in the sense of the emergence of more transitory neo-tribes, has recently attracted a good deal of public interest (see Maybury-Lewis, 1992a, 1992b).

This interest too has been subjected to the process of global marketing by various arms of the tourist industry, which it has been predicted will become the world's leading industry by 1996 (Urry, 1992). Of course for many tourists the ease with which they can now travel to the more exotic and remote parts of the world amounts to a step into a tourist reservation in which they enjoy 'home plus'. In effect, they are locals whose contact with another set of locals in the tourist location is highly regulated and ritualized. It has been argued that this particular set of tourists is being replaced by more sophisticated post-tourists who seek a whole range of experiences and direct encounters with locals. Some of those post-tourists are not at all worried that what they are presented with is a simulation of a local culture; they are interested in the whole paraphernalia of the 'behind the scenes' and the construction of the performance and set (Urry,

1990). Such staged simulations of localities can vary from reassuring clear cartoon-style parodies (the Jungle Cruise in the Magic Kingdom), to small-scale 'walk-in, see and touch' simulations of the key buildings and icons which in the popular imagination are taken to represent a national culture (the World Showcase at EPCOT [the Experimental Prototype Community of Tomorrow]), to the whole heritage industry efforts to preserve and restore full-scale living and working examples of 'the past' (for discussion of Walt Disney World see Fjellman, 1992). Some would see this as part of a wider shift away from the imposition of abstraction and uniformity through modernist architecture to a postmodern struggle for place, to reinvent place and rehumanize urban space (Ley, 1989).

In yet other situations it is the locals themselves who are asked to take part in staged authenticity for tourists. Here the tourists are granted the privilege of moving around the living working locality in which the real inhabitants perform for them. Hence McCannell (1992: Ch. 8) discusses the case of Locke, California, a company town, the home of the last surviving Chinese farm labourers. The whole town was sold to tourist developers in 1977 who marketed it as 'the only intact rural Chinatown in the United States'. Here the inhabitants along with the town became museumified, presented as the last living examples of 'a way of life which no longer exists'.

McCannell (1992: 18) also discusses examples of 'enacted or staged savagery', such as the deal struck between MCI Incorporated and the Masai of Kenya covering wage rates, admission fees, television and movie rights, etc. which could allow the Masai to earn a living by perpetually *acting Masai*. Also interesting in this context is Dennis O'Rourke's film *Cannibal Tours* (1987) which follows a group of wealthy European and North American tourists up the Sepik River in Papua New Guinea abroad a luxury cruise ship (see the interview with O'Rourke by Lutkehaus, 1989; the review by Bruner, 1989; and discussion in McCannell, 1992). Such situations vary a great deal in both the objectives of the tourists and the relative power of the parties involved. In the case of New Guinea the tribespeople were well aware of the unequal exchange and of the hard bargains which the wealthy tourists invariably strike, and that the middle-men and local representatives of the tourist agencies had creamed off the money. The tribespeople here did not have sufficient power resources to manipulate the degree of openness and closure of the boundary of the locality in their own terms. In other cases this can lead to what MacCannell (1992: 31) refers to as 'the hostile Indian act', in which ex-primitives typically engage in hatred, sullen silence and freezing out. For their part, the cannibal tourists can achieve a safe package version replete with vicarious thrills of the 'heart of darkness', while fulfilling a theme in the popular imagination: a visit to the place of 'the Other' – with the proviso that at the end of each day they can return to their home comforts and familiar Western surroundings of the cruise ship.

There are cases, however, where it is possible for tourists, to take part in tribal life on a more complete basis, as is the case with some communities of Inuit in Alaska. Here the tourist lives with the tribe and takes part in a wide range of activities – there is no tour ship to retreat to and only individuals or small groups are admitted to the tribe on a strictly regulated basis under the supervision of government agencies. The Inuit use the money they get to buy essential supplies and equipment (bullets for hunting rifles, etc.) in order to maintain a partly modernized, yet independent version of their traditional way of life. They are in a situation in which they possess sufficient power resources to be able to manipulate the boundary of their community to their own advantage and maintain their sense of cultural identity. A further example would be of the Ainu. A 'hunter and gatherer' people, they largely inhabit the northern Japanese island of Hokkaido, which only became officially integrated into Japan after the Meiji Restoration (1868). During the 1970s an Ainu cultural movement developed which not only established schools for the teaching of their language and traditions, but also in certain areas established traditional village structures to produce handicraft goods, so that tourists could come to witness their traditional lifestyle (Friedman, 1990: 320). Tourism, then, has been consciously manipulated for the purposes of the reconstitution of Ainu cultural identity.

For other cultural movements tourism may cease to be seen as a resource, but may be identified as a major element in the process which is destroying localism and ethnic identities. The Hawaiian cultural movement which has developed since the 1970s has reacted against the long-term process that has incorporated Hawaii into the US economy. This has seen the development of a multi-ethnic Hawaii in which Hawaiians became a minority in their own land, with their numbers reduced from 600,000 to 40,000 during the first century of contact, along with the stigmatization and disintegration of the Hawaiian language and customs. The tourist industry, the dominant force since the decline of the plantation economy, became identified with the taking of land and the commodification and trivialization of Hawaiian culture as exotica. Instead of the old system with its homogeneous model of Western modernist identity at the top and backward and quaint Hawaiians at the bottom, and with those at the bottom threatened with assimilation, it is argued that in its place a polycentric system has emerged (Friedman, 1992). The new model revolves around the Hawaiian cultural movement's opposition to tourist development and attempts to establish and defend their authentic sense of the past, and the newer more upmarket tourism which seeks both to modernize and develop and define those who stand in its way as lazy and backward, and to recreate a nostalgic vision of the former plantation Hawaii. A vision that has little acceptance from the Hawaiian movement, which wishes to develop a particular identity and way of life which resists the whole enterprise of being an object for someone else's gaze (for a further account of the complexity of localized identities in Hawaii see Kirkpatrick, 1989).

Concluding remarks

Anthony King (1995) has remarked that all 'globalizing theories are self-representations of the dominant particular', acutely pointing to the problem of the location of the theorist who necessarily writes from a particular place and within a particular tradition of discourse which endow him or her with differential power resources not only to be able to speak, but also to be listened to. Many of our Western taken-for-granted assumptions about the world have immense power because their very self-evident quality does not encourage the possibility of dialogue. Hence we have a number of theories about the ways in which the West was able to impose its particular vision of the 'exotic Other' on distant parts of the world. Yet this should not allow us to remain bound to the view that our representations must remain trapped within the particularism of our fantasy-laden projections, for the question of evidence cannot be completely dispensed with.

It took an American anthropologist of Sri Lankan origins to raise doubts about one of the powerful Western myths about the Pacific: that Captain Cook was deified by the Hawaiians. Obeyeskere (1992) demonstrates through careful research that it wasn't the Hawaiians who deified Captain Cook, but the Europeans who projected the myth of native deification on to the Hawaiians to bolster their own civilizing myths. The discovery of this reversal was made possible in part through Obeyeskere's knowledge of Asian societies – he could find no local evidence to support assumptions of the deifications of Westerners by over-credulous natives – and in part by his attribution of commonsense practical rationality to the Hawaiians; the latter is in contrast to those who emphasize the enduring strength of their culture through the inflexibility of their cosmological categories. As members of 'the rest' come increasingly to reside in the West and are able to make their voices heard, we can expect many more accounts which challenge the 'self-representations of the dominant particular'. At the same time, important as the drive for deconceptualization is, there remains the problem of reconceptualization, the possibility of the construction of higher-level, more abstract general models of the globe. Here we can make a number of points.

The first is to do with how we conceptualize the globe. To identify it as a single place is perhaps to give it a sense of false concreteness and unity (see Tagg, 1991). For many of the people in the world the consciousness of the process of globalization, that they inhabit the same place, may be absent or limited, or occur only spasmodically. To some extent an appropriate model to represent this might be a heap, a congeries or aggregate (see Elias, 1987c; S.F. Moore, 1989). Clearly, this is one way of understanding the notion of a global culture: the sense of heaps, congeries and aggregates of cultural particularities juxtaposed together on the same field, the same bounded space, in which the fact that they are different and do not fit together, or want to fit together, becomes noticeable and a source of practical problems. The study of culture, our interest in doing justice to the description of particularities and differences, necessarily directs us towards an ideographic mode in which we are acutely aware of the danger of hypostatizations and over-generalizations.

At the same time there are clearly systemic tendencies in social life which derive from the expansive and integrating power of economic processes and the hegemonizing efforts of particular nation-states or blocs. From this perspective there is a need for practical knowledge which is modelled in systematic form and which yields technically useful information and rational planning; for models in which differences have to become domesticated, turned into variables to further integration. In this sense certain aspects of the world are becoming more amenable to systems analysis as the world becomes more integrated through systemic practices and takes on systemic properties. Yet when we consider the relationship between the system and culture, a shift away from the powerful hegemonic control over the system could be accompanied by a concomitant shift in cultural categories. Friedman (1988), for example, has argued that while all cultures are plural and creole in terms of their origins, whether or not they identify themselves as such depends upon further processes. Hence our capacity to notice, look for or advocate pluralism and the defence of particularity may not depend upon the actual extent of these characteristics, but be a function of relative changes in our situation which now gives us 'permission' to see them:

> In fact it might well be argued that the pluralist conception of the world is a distinctly western mode of apprehending the current fragmentation of the system, a confusion of our own identity space. When hegemony is strong or increasing cultural space is similarly homogenized, spaghetti becomes Italian, a plural set of dialects become a national language in which cultural differences are translated into a continuum of correct to incorrect, or standard to nonstandard. (Friedman, 1988: 458)

In some ways this conception is similar to that developed by Elias in which he argues that in situations in which established groups are firmly in control relationships with outsider groups are more hierarchical and the dominant group is able to colonize the weaker with its own pattern of conduct. The established are able to develop a collective 'we-image' based upon a sense of superiority and 'group charisma', an image which is inseparable from the imposition and internalization of a sense of 'group disgrace', a stigmatized sense of unworthiness and inferiority by the outsider group. The outsiders are invariably characterized as 'dirty, morally unreliable and lazy' (Mennell, 1989: 122). This colonization phase of the relationship between the established and the outsiders can give way with a shift in interdependencies and the relative power balance to a second phase, that of 'functional democratization'. In this second phase of differentiation and emancipation, people become enmeshed in longer and denser webs of interdependencies, which the established group finds difficulty in controlling. Outsider groups gain in social power and confidence and the contrasts and tensions in society increase. It can be added that in this second phase it is possible that many of the unified models which are seen as doing an injustice to particularity and complexity, become subjected to critique and rejection. Interest develops in constructing models and theories which allow for notions of syncretism, complexity and seemingly random and arbitrary patterns (Serres, 1991). These concluding remarks are, of course, speculative, and there are many difficulties in trying to use established-outsider models in situations where there are increasing numbers of participants in the global 'game' and the boundaries between collectivities can be breached or ignored, yet at the very least it perhaps does suggest that we should not be too hasty in dispensing with theories of social relations altogether.

Notes

1. For discussions of localism and locality see Cooke (1990b), Bell and Newby (1971) and Cohen (1985).

2. It is interesting to note that the term 'Wigan Pier' was coined by George Formby Sr, who ironically confounded the grime of a mining town with the delights of a seaside resort (Richards, 1984: 191).

3. Some of these criticisms apply to the recent work of Giddens (1990, 1991) on modernity. For a critique of his neglect of the cultural dimension and assumption that globalization is merely modernity writ large, see Robertson (1992b).

4. Canevacci (1992), for example, mentions how the Brasilian Indios at Iguacu Falls not only were fans of Italian football and identified with Rud Guillot of Milan, but also used video cameras both to communicate amongst themselves and to produce images for the outside world.

5. This is not just a question of the flow between the West as the centre and 'the rest' as the periphery. As Abu-Lughod (1991) has indicated, we have to consider the proliferation of multiple cores, and especially how the cultures of the rising cores in Asia are diffusing within their own circuits. This also means raising the question of the relations between the hosts and migrants into these new cores – e.g. Japan.

8
TRAVEL, MIGRATION AND IMAGES OF SOCIAL LIFE

Robert Park once remarked that human beings, like the higher types of animals – 'everything above the oyster, in fact' – are made for locomotion and action'.

(1923: 157, quoted in Suttles, 1991: xi)

All I ask is heaven above and the road before me.

(The Vagabond in Vaughan Williams, *Songs of Travel*, 1904)

History is always written from a sedentary point of view and in the name of a unitary State apparatus, at least a possible one, even when the topic is nomads. What is lacking is a Nomadology, the opposite of a history.

(Deleuze and Guattari, 1987: 23)

I hate travelling and explorers.

(Lévi-Strauss, 1976: 15)

In the literature on postmodernism there is a tendency to criticize notions of fixed identity and celebrate disorder, syncretism and hybridity. For some, the latter qualities are assumed to be in the nature of social life – somehow, despite the 'anti-foundational' rhetoric, a more basic and fundamental aspect of culture which became occluded. Alternatively, there is a hidden historical narrative in which the present phase is assumed to be distinct from the past – something which in its most inflated form is presented as a new age, postmodernity. In both cases there is the assumption that many of our existing models can no longer adequately handle the increasing complexity and fluidity of contemporary life. They are criticized for relying on, or seeking to establish, universal categories, unified identities and systemic models. In contrast to this perceived rigidity and inflexibility, in which theory seeks to speak for and about everyone everywhere, postmodern theories emphasize our limited horizons and the integrity of all the varieties of local knowledge.

Of particular interest in this context is the frequent use of metaphors of movement and marginality. There are references to travel, nomadism, migrancy, border-crossings, living on the borders. Nomadism and migrancy are seen not only as characteristics of the contemporary global condition, but as central to language. Chambers (1990, 1994), for example, refers to the nomadic experience of language which ceases to be an instrument of precision and clarity. Rather, thought wanders and migrates: instead of having a fixed base or home, it dwells in a mobile habitat which produces discontinuities and fragmented experiences. The nomad has become an important category in this type of cultural studies literature. Gabriel (1990: 396) reminds us that the nomadic way of life and art forms have two main aspects. First, 'the fundamental ideal that all life, experience and existence is without frontiers and boundaries'. Second, 'the foundational idea of not glorying fulfilment in terms of territory and resources'. The temporary existence of the nomad involves a rejection of the state apparatus and its laws. It is also assumed that a wandering life produces a wandering aesthetics, with a constant shift of form and content.

The theorists who have been particularly influential in this context are Deleuze and Guattari (1983, 1987), not only through their discussions of 'nomadic thought' and 'nomadic art', but through their general critique of fixed categories and identities. Deleuze and Guattari's celebration of a return to pre-cognitive forms of experience and their concept of 'flows' have been especially influential on a younger generation of theorists in cultural studies. This is found in some of the literature on cyberspace and 'the internet' (the computer information network) which has been influenced by their notions of dispersed power, rhizomes and flows (see Featherstone, 1995; Featherstone and Burrows, 1995). From one perspective Deleuze and Guattari can be seen as the latest writers in a tradition of intellectual and artistic thought which, while influenced by the philosophies of Bergson and Nietzsche with their valuation of immediate experience over form, draws upon the transgressive avant-garde and bohemian impulses that can be found in the tradition of artistic modernism since the nineteenth century. This tradition has often sought to provide a critique of the achievements and lifestyles of modernity and has strong sympathies for the outsider. The bohemian, for example, identified strongly with the wandering life of the gypsies, Murger's novel and Bizet's opera *Carmen* being key influences in the formation of the bohemian mythology in the mid-nineteenth century (Pels and Crebas, 1988). Yet there are clearly antecedents which can be traced back a long way. The increasing valuation of travel as experience, as in the case of educative self-formative projects (*Bildungsprozesse*) can be found, for example, in the Grand Tour in the Western tradition which rose to prominence in the eighteenth century. This notion of travel as experience can be traced back at least as far as the Renaissance and Middle Ages with the valuation of the life of the travelling scholar, artist and vagabond. This can also be linked into older notions of the heroic quest and life as a spiritual/creative journey (religious and secular forms of pilgrimage).[1] Nomadic themes and experiences, then, have often been valued by artists and intellectuals, as well as by the growing legions of bohemians and other camp-followers who since the nineteenth century have sought to imitate their lifestyles and have developed an interest in the aestheticization of life.

The linkage between mobility and the regenerative powers of travel is a powerful theme in Western culture, especially in art and literature. Travel has often been regarded as aiding the decentring of habitual categories, a form of playing with cultural disorder, something which can also be found in postmodern theory. While postmodernism can be seen to be a continuation of these neo-Romantic themes, there are further aspects of mobility in contemporary life to which it, along with postcolonial theory, draws attention. The first relates to the increasing flows of people around the world: the numbers of sojourners, refugees and migrant workers means that 'the other' is no longer something to be searched out in exotic locations in the distant parts of the world by adventurers, literary travellers and tourists; the others work and live alongside us in the metropolitan areas. The second relates to the flows of information and images which also further the process of global compression. We no longer need to travel to see and understand the other, the images flow into our living rooms and the problem ceases to become one of access to limited information about the other; rather it becomes a problem of selection, of managing and ordering the overload of information. The development of the new information technology in the direction of virtual reality and cyberspace have added to this problem through the potential which will soon be available, to access all the information and images in human history. In addition to images and information about the other, the technology also has the potential to increase the dialogue with the other: the various others around the world can now speak back to the West and dispute its various accounts, symbolic hierarchies and universalist claims. Ultimately, it is argued, we face a world of not just mobile subjects, but mobile objects; or rather a world in which the distinction between subjects and objects becomes narrowed and eclipsed as they both become joined and dispersed in an increasingly fluid informational field (Lash and Urry, 1993).

We therefore have a certain amount of category turmoil, as notions of mobility, movement and border-crossing are used to confront and decentre relatively established taxonomies, canons and symbolic hierarchies. In its most heightened form this can be found in the discipline cluster of cultural studies (see Grossberg *et al.*, 1992), but it is also to be found in anthropology (Clifford and Marcus, 1986; Clifford, 1988), political theory (Connolly, 1994), sociology (Game, 1991), psychology (Shotter, 1993), geography (Soja, 1989), women's studies (Nicholson, 1990) and in business studies (Clegg, 1989), as the implications of questions of cultural complexity, which are gathered under the catch-all term postmodernism, continue to be explored.

If we seek to investigate the place of mobility in social life we therefore cannot ignore the ways in which it has been represented culturally and the ways in which metaphors of travel and movement form an important part of the cultural tradition of modernism (van den Abbeele, 1992). This suggests we need to investigate the framing capacity of these metaphors and their ability not only to direct our gaze, but to form particular images of the world. In effect we not only need to investigate the process of theory-building in terms of the current phase, but also need to consider the formation of images of social life in the past. Why, for example, does sociology pay so little attention to mobility and migration? Why did it for so long, and still today in some quarters, perpetuate an image of sedentary Europe and the notion that traditional societies were made up of bounded, settled *Gemeinschaften*? The danger of confining sociology to the study of modernity, as some would advocate, is that it confines the premodern to the status of an inchoate traditional society. In effect it confirms all the limitations of what Elias (1987a) has referred to as 'the retreat of sociologists into the present'.

Society and the settled image of social life

One of the key terms in sociology is 'society'. Yet it is a term that has not always been subject to close scrutiny. In Nisbet's influential *The Sociological Tradition* (1967), while community, authority, status, the sacred and alienation make it into the list of the key unit-ideas of sociology, there is no place for society. This is because, Nisbet (1967: 5) informs us, such ideas must be *distinctive*, they must help to differentiate one discipline from another and ideas 'like "individual", "society", "order" are useless here . . . for these are elements of *all* the disciplines of social thought'. Yet perhaps Nisbet exaggerates the universal validity of these ideas in his assumption that they are so essential and fundamental that they can be taken for granted and need not be subjected to analysis. Such ideas have a history: they come into being and may very well fade away. Such at least would seem to be the implications of the recent arguments that we are now witnessing 'the end of the social' (Touraine, 1986; Baudrillard, 1993): arguments which are often made without specific reference to globalization. In Baudrillard's case, for example, it is the development of the commodity-form which has led to a superabundance of commodity-signs in today's consumer cultures, allied with technological developments, in particular the mass media, which has increased the capacity to produce simulations. The 'derealization of the real' is seen as producing social fragmentation, threatening normativity and social structures. In effect the solid base of the social bond in norm-reinforcing face-to-face social interactions has been removed in a general attenuation of social life. For Touraine (1986) the process of movement into the postindustrial society need not be seen as a totally negative one for it leads to a greater capacity for action. In effect politics, long suppressed in the sociological world-view to a derivative of the social, is resurrected with the fragmentation of long-existing social structures and by the increasing opportunity and capacity for individuals, collectivities and social movements to act.

While Nisbet, as mentioned above, is reluctant to explore the history of the concept 'society', he does make the telling point that 'the referent of "social" was almost invariably the communal. *Communitas*, not *societas* with its more impersonal connotations, is the real etymological source of the sociologist's use of the word "social" in his studies of personality, kinship, economy and polity' (Nisbet, 1967: 56). This is evident in the writings of one of the key figures in the establishment of sociology, Auguste Comte, whose view of social life was very much dominated by the goal of devising new institutional forms which would replace traditional modes of communal order. His views should be seen in the context of the conservative reaction to the French Revolution, out of which sociology was born. This also entailed a reaction to the optimism of the Enlightenment with its commitment to action and progress, which led to a revival of interest in traditional forms of order such as the medieval manor and the village. Durkheim followed Comte in regarding society as community writ large. Durkheim, is, of course, the sociologist *par excellence*, who stressed the power of society and the reality of the social. His concepts of the collective conscience, the sacred and the social bond stress the common beliefs and sentiments which are held to further social integration. Society was conceived as a bounded entity which was usually analysed at a high level of abstraction. If a broader understanding of the particularities of a given society was needed then it could be compared with another society. Societies were conceived as the basic units of social life and to understand social life entailed the use of a repertoire of societal concepts.

The social was seen as more fundamental to social life than the polity; indeed in the social science division of labour that was emerging, there was a marked hostility to political science with its emphasis upon power and action, nationalism and internationalism. As we will see below, while the focus of sociology has been predominantly on the internal relations of (nation-state) societies, the value position of sociologists has often been anti-nationalist – coupled in some cases with an internationalist attachment to the notion of humanity. For some sociologists nationalism and warfare belonged to an earlier stage of development now rapidly becoming surpassed (e.g. Spencer's sequence of movement from military to industrial societies); that is until the cataclysmic events of the First World War caused some to rethink their categories. Society, then, became regarded as the generic and fundamental unit of social life and in this sense did not need a history because history was in effect conceived as the development of society.

At the same time, we need also to focus upon the relation of society to space as well as time. In short where is 'the where' of society? Part of the answer may come from the implicit assumption of Comte and Durkheim that society is community writ large. It could be added that if society is not integrated and prey to the social disorganization of modernity, then it should be integrated and whether the mode of integration is to come from corporate groupings (Durkheim) or socialism (Tönnies), such integration is imperative. Society, then, should occupy a single bounded space with an integrated social structure and culture. Important in this context is

Tönnies's (1955) influential *Gemeinschaft und Gesellschaft*,[2] in which we are nominally presented with two fundamental ideal types of social life. Yet it is clear that Tönnies regarded community and association as forming a developmental sequence and that his sympathies lie with *Gemeinschaft*. Tönnies's depiction of *Gesellschaft* as atomized secondary relationships, social disintegration and cultural fragmentation is largely a negative one, constructed from the perspective of community. His views here were influenced by the late nineteenth-century Nietzsche revival in Germany, and especially by *The Birth of Tragedy* with its argument for a new Dionysian age (Liebersohn, 1988). His image of *Gemeinschaft* drew upon an idealized picture of medieval Germany in which the family household was the basic unit, with the strength of blood and kinship ties drawing people together into larger village and regional units. As we will see this is very much an image of a settled place with a common culture.

This image of the traditional community with its high level of normative integration and order, which has been so influential in constructing the image of society, is of course highly nostalgic. Its vision of prior harmony and simplicity presents a picture of a fall from grace which resonated with the popularity of depictions of childhood as a phase of lost innocence that became popular in the wake of the Romantic Movement of the nineteenth century. It reduced premodern societies to flatness and immobility. That social units might be able to exist adequately without a high level of normative integration and common values is hardly considered.

Tönnies (1955: 261) emphasizes that *Gemeinschaft*, based upon a consensus of wills and concord provided by common folkways, mores and religion, clearly has little room for power struggles, violence and war. These are features which are central to the investigations of preindustrial social life provided by Norbert Elias, Le Goff, Raymond Williams and others. Elias (1978, 1982), for example, emphasizes the slow process of the taming of violent impulses as warriors were gradually induced to become courtiers as part of the state formation process. His account of everyday life is one in which those with smaller, weaker, less trained bodies (women and children) were prey to the less constrained violent impulses of the more powerful (adults and men, especially specialists in violence such as warriors). A further non-nostalgic account which dissolves the harmonious depiction of 'traditional society' is provided by Raymond Williams (1975), who is scathing about the constant series of references to the 'organic communities' of Old England which successive generations see as imperilled and dying out (see also Pearson's [1985] critique of depictions of a golden age of family values which are constructed to make a sharp contrast to the alleged disorderly and violent present).

In addition to neglecting violence, conflict and war this harmonious communal image of social life gives little attention to mobility: not just the displacements of people through warfare, but the more routine movements of wayfarers, migrant workers, pilgrims, travellers, beggars and others (Jusserand, 1973). In contrast to the harmonious village in the mind where everyone lived and died within the confines of a settled place, Moch (1992: 1) argues that

> Our image of a sedentary Europe . . . is seriously flawed. People were on the move; and where and why they traveled tells us a good bit about the past and about the pressures and processes that produced the world with which we are familiar. Human movement is connected to every level of life in western Europe – from the intimacy of family decisions about how cash will be earned to the global scale, where it reflects Europe's place in the world economy. Migration, in short, connects the changes in European history with the lives of men and women in the past.

Western Europe is, of course, not the world and we should be aware that the peculiarities of the migration pattern were linked to the family structure which not only encouraged partner-centred marriage and the setting up of separate households, but encouraged a phase of independent youth in which young people (especially men) travelled over long distances to work. This contrasted with the pattern in southern and south-eastern Europe, and in many other parts of the world, where the young men remained in the family of origin before and after marriage (see Mitterauer, 1992: 22). The main point to emphasize, however, is that the model of society developed by sociologists which drew largely upon West European experience ignored mobility in its depiction of society as over-integrated and settled, an image which drew upon a nostalgic construction of community-based preindustrial society depicted as the polar opposite of modernity, with the latter perceived as entailing relentless change and social disorder.

This model assumes that societies reproduce themselves through a common set of values which induce a normative consensus. It has been heavily criticized in both its Parsonian and neo-Marxist variants by Abercrombie, Hill and Turner in their book *The Dominant Ideology Thesis* (1980). They find little evidence of a shared value system or a dominant ideology in either feudalism, market capitalism, or late capitalism. The assumption that a common culture is the social cement which makes social life possible has also been influential in anthropology, with the myth of isolated integrated tribal society which will be discussed shortly (see Featherstone, 1991a: 131ff.). In both cases the image of social life is of a bounded entity with a high level of social and cultural integration, models which assume that society has a high degree of functional interdependence of its various parts, as well as a high degree of unity and independence *vis-à-vis* other societies. There is little sense of power relations, conflicts and hybridity. There is little sense of leakages of people and culture: in effect all the elements of social and cultural life hang together to the extent that there are few cultural ambiguities or problems of conflicting or double identities. Sociology in its pursuit of the typical, average or normal has generally had little interest in the idiosyncratic and the exceptional. If there are inequalities, then the problem becomes how they are reproduced and transmitted across the generations, something which leads to a more general concern with behaviour as opposed to action. This has been emphasized by Lasch (1991: 135), who in a discussion of nostalgia argues that

> literary representations of small-town life often fall into a kind of sociological style of thought, concerning themselves with the repetitive cycle of births, marriages and deaths. In other words, they concern themselves with behaviour as opposed to action. As Arendt has shown, the concept of behaviour is closely linked, in turn, to the concept of society, since the social realm is distinguished from the political by the absence of conscious determination, the tenacity of customs and rituals the original significance of which has been lost to memory, and the accumulated weight of habits highly resistant to change. In the reaction against eighteenth century liberalism, 'society' became a rallying cry for those who condemned revolution on the grounds that deep-seated habits and prejudices could not be altered over-night, at least not without causing irreparable harm. For conservatives and socialists alike the discovery of society implied a devaluation of politics.

It has also been argued that the academic division of labour, which became established in the social sciences in the nineteenth century, resulted in sociology ceding the analysis not only of action and the state to politics, but of international relations as well (Wallerstein, 1987). With regard to the international field perhaps this view is a little oversimplified; it would seem to apply best to international politics, for it ignores the tradition which developed in European sociology (largely French influenced) which focused upon humanity. Saint-Simon, Comte and Durkheim, in addition to their focus upon society, were in their various ways aware of the linkages between industrialization and what we now call globalization (Turner, 1990a). In effect they were concerned about the ways in which the social disorganization and individualism which accompanied industrialization could be curbed by the development of a new set of moral bonds which would have universal validity. The tension between the societal and global focus of analysis emerged most noticeably in Durkheim's sociology. On the one hand he explored the possibility of new modes of moral individualism, which could become in effect a new religion which would be the sole common denominator for a highly differentiated humanity (Durkheim, 1969). On the other hand his concern with social order and solidarity, it has been argued, was influenced by the nationalist sentiments that increased after the 1870 French defeat in the Franco-Prussian War; in this context it has been suggested that the potential of nationalism, regarded as a source for the *conscience collective*, and the nation, as a source for the sacred in the modern world, became important themes running throughout his mature work (Turner, 1990a: 347).

Indeed, his discussion of the powerful emotional bonding between people and the resilience of the sacred in the modern world, would seem to have continuing relevance for the understanding of the contemporary resurgence of nationalism, new religious movements and even aspects of consumer culture (Featherstone, 1991a: Ch. 8; Alexander, 1988). At the same time Durkheim took seriously the moral and cultural mission of intellectuals to find some new means of ordering social life and regulating the relations between societies, hence his focus on humanity. Yet this emphasis upon humanity and the global dimension was not accompanied by a sociology of the emergent post- or supra-societal entities: this does not seem to have been a concern of Durkheim's. Rather, the focus was on the moral and cultural level, with the emphasis given to the cultivation of new forms of solidarity which would enable modes of common identification between different people and lessen xenophobia as well as egoism and selfish individualism. Hence there is a tension within the work of Durkheim between the focus upon society as the basic unit of social life and the delineation of its mechanisms for normative and moral regulation, and the focus upon humanity driven by the need to discover new types of moral integration which will supersede the loyalties generated by nation-state societies in the phase of intensified globalization and national rivalries which occurred in the late nineteenth and early twentieth centuries.

It has been argued that this tension which was evident within the major classical sociologists has ceased to operate amongst their successors. Moore (1966), for example, in making a plea for the revival of this broader focus, criticizes the Americanization of sociology for its narrow focus upon society, the unstated subtext of which, as we have argued, is the bounded nation-state. The critique of this focus upon society as the final unit of social life in which it is regarded as the basic generic category of sociology has been elaborated by Tenbruck (1994). He argues that

> Sociology tends to suggest the idea of societies as entities, requiring their study as *sui generis* objects and conceives of their structure as merely internal. In this way it establishes an artificial object that only admits of a one-sided selection, consideration and explanation of fact. (Tenbruck, 1994: 78)

Concepts like 'subsystem', 'subcultures', 'levels' and 'dimensions' remain within this perspective of the dominance of society as an integrated holistic entity. Likewise the general categories frequently used within sociology such as 'structure', 'differentiation' and 'complexity' are assumed to be general variables which operate in all time and places.

This focus upon the intra-societal dimension leads to a neglect of inter- and trans-societal processes such as: the reciprocal influences of societies on each other; the religious, political, economic and cultural processes which occur across boundaries; the flows of migrants, exiles and refugees; military, cultural and economic expansion. Where aspects of the above phenomena are studied, the tendency within sociology is to see them from the perspective of their intra-societal linkages and effects – e.g. migrants are examined from the perspective of assimilation and integration into the host society. When social change is considered the tendency is to focus upon the internal constitution of societies which are assumed to parallel each other in terms of their major structural mechanisms which produce change. Hence theories of modernization are based upon the assumptions that societies change along common lines of internal development. From this perspective differences between countries are just different states of a process which is seen everywhere as directed and straining towards some notion of normal development (for a critique of the notion of development see Tenbruck, 1990). Yet this misses the way in which European modernization arose in unique conditions of a network, or figuration, of interrelated nation-state societies which from their early stages of formation were bound together in interdependencies and power struggles. Needless to say, the particularities of this historically unique reference group can hardly be assumed to be replicable in other times and places.

Following Weber, Tenbruck emphasises that societies are always shaped by the external situation.[3] Important here is the permanent preparedness for war and defence of borders. Even those societies which have sought to maintain isolation, such as Tokagawa Japan, have had to go to great efforts in terms of military preparedness and surveillance to regulate their inhabitants and to manipulate the 'valve' through which interchanges with outsiders through trade, warfare, migration, etc. could occur. Indeed it is not possible to understand the development of Japanese society without paying attention to the long-term relationship with China as its major significant other. The cultural borrowings and syncretisms which have resulted from this process, as we shall see shortly in our discussion of culture, cannot but put a big question mark against the long-held notions of culture within sociology and anthropology which emphasize organic or aesthetic unity.

This suggests that sociology needs to adopt not only a relational understanding of the shifting place of what have come to be known as 'societies' within their particular reference group, but also a long-term processual perspective which considers 'societies' as temporary phenomena. Societies then as processual entities should be considered as always in the process of formation and deformation: they do not always have to exist for social relations to take place, they come into being and fade away – perspectives which one can glean from the writings not only of Weber, but of Simmel and Elias. But it is not just societies which are in the process of formation and deformation; the larger reference group within which they are born, grow and change is also significant. This is a process of which Weber and Elias were clearly aware through their focus upon the state and the power balances between nation-states. Indeed they can hardly be considered sociological imperialists given their capacity to shift from a sociological frame of reference to discuss what some would wish to separate out as political, economic (and in Elias's case) psychological data from a perspective which was always sensitive to historical particularities. Hence their mode of analysis was always pointing towards the global, the sense that all the nation-states and other forms of association in the world would become increasingly bound together in power struggles and interdependencies. As Elias indicates in his synopsis to *The Civilizing Process* (1982) the creation of larger nation-states and blocs and the nature of the power balances, interdependencies and linkages between and across them will influence the types of identity formation and personality structure which develop in various parts of the world.

It is only relatively recently and in response to the current phase of intensified global competition and interdependencies that we have started to think that there might be a sociological problem here: how to develop a series of concepts which are adequate to understand this process. Concepts which in the first place are not based upon the assumptions of the set gathered together under the master concept 'society', so that the perspective of those who talk about 'world society' as some form of emergent 'great unifier', modelled on the nation-state, is rejected. Second, concepts which are sensitive to the cultural and social dimensions of these processes and do not reduce them to derivations from, or reactions to, the economic. The process of globalization, then, can be understood as the increasing extension of the reference group of societies which are established in a process of contact which necessarily form a world, however inchoate and limited that world might be when compared to the sense of the finite known world we inhabit. This larger trans- and supra-societal process forms the context within which societies are able to develop. The process of state formation in Europe, for example, produced a series of power struggles, rivalries, alliances and elimination contests. The competition for additional power resources to draw upon and use in these struggles increasingly became widened to take in the whole world. It should be added that the development of modernity cannot be understood in isolation from this process, despite the tendencies to conceive it in terms of the unfolding of an inner logic which is immanent to society. We will return to a discussion of modernity shortly, after considering the images of culture and society that have been developed within anthropology.

Cultural integration and rootedness

Anthropology since its inception has always sought to talk about the characteristics of 'man' in general (or 'humanity', as this remaining connection to philosophical anthropology is depicted today). At the same time it has sought to be sensitive to the particularities of the tribal collectivity addressed. An assumption, influenced by German Romanticism and late nineteenth-century hermeneutics (for example Dilthey, who influenced Boas), has been that tribes possess distinctive cultures that form a unique complex which needs to be interpreted in their own terms. The assumed isolation of the tribal societies, which were scattered around the distant parts of the world before they were 'discovered' by Europeans and North Americans, is assumed to lessen the problem of 'contamination', and preserve in a purer form the unique features which can be assumed to cohere into an integrated whole. The term 'culture' is often used to apply to the totality encompassing social and cultural life; in this sense culture has often been used to refer to 'the whole way of life' of a people.[4] The distinctiveness of the cultural practices of different peoples has been linked to the construction of the other culture as 'strange' and the anthropologist represented as a 'merchant of astonishment' who dips into the world showcase of cultures to titillate our sensibilities (Friedman, 1987).

This notion of a culture as a unique separate totality in which all the various intricate and bizarre parts fit together to make a unified whole is, for example, found in the work of Ruth Benedict. Benedict (1934) was influenced by the work of Boas with his assumptions that the main creative force of culture is the tendency towards consistency, which in turn derives from the drive for emotional consistency (Hatch, 1973: 81). The difference between cultures is conceived as similar to the difference between people. A culture is a combination of elements within an overall distinguishing pattern of organization which effectively makes each cultural configuration singular and incommensurable. This orientation to culture is captured in the following remarks from *The Chrysanthemum and the Sword*:

> As a cultural anthropologist also I started from the premise that the most isolated bits of behaviour have some systematic relation to each other. I took seriously the way hundreds of details fall into over-all patterns. A human society must make for itself some design for living. It approves certain ways of meeting situations, certain ways of sizing them up. People in that society regard these solutions as foundations of the universe. They integrate them, no matter what the difficulties. Men who have accepted a system of values by which to live cannot without courting inefficiency and chaos keep for long a fenced-off portion of their lives where they think and behave according to a contrary set of values. They try to bring about more conformity. They provide themselves with some common rationale and some common motivations. Some degree of consistency is necessary or the whole scheme falls to pieces. (Benedict, 1946: 12)

Benedict's assumptions about the unity and separateness of cultures meet with little sympathy from many contemporary anthropologists, who are more sensitive to disunities, fragmentation, contestation, pluralism and the processual nature of culture.[5] As Eric Wolff (1990: 110) informs us: 'Anthropology has treated signification mainly in terms of encompassing cultural unities such as patterns, configurations, ethos, eidos, epistemes, paradigms, cultural structures'. The tendency has been for these unities to be conceived as the outcomes of processes of logico-aesthetic integration. Here the assumption is that there is some underlying logical or aesthetic force at work in the drive towards integration and reintegration; it is as if these cognitive processes were guided by a *telos* all their own. This perspective, which assumes the replication of uniformity, misses the problem of 'the organization of diversity'. The assumption that there is some inherent patterning to culture, then, is not only difficult to apply to open as opposed to closed societies, or pluralistic and differentiated as opposed to unified societies.

There is an important sense, Wolff (1990) reminds us, in referring to the work of Wallace (1970), in which all societies are, in a radical sense, plural societies. They are comprised of the diverse cognitive perspectives of men, women and children, males and females, masters and slaves, warriors and priests, all of which will have different models of social life. This echoes the view of feminist anthropologists that men and women do not share the same cultural understandings. It is wrong to assume that such divergent perspectives will somehow be harmoniously integrated within some overarching framework driven by a cultural logic. Rather we need to ask the questions, 'Which groups will want to represent the social world as coherent and consistent?' and, 'Why and how do they seek to develop and proliferate their particular representations of the world?' We need to investigate the reasons why cultural specialists (priests, artists, intellectuals, academics and cultural intermediaries) seek at various times to produce models of social life which emphasize consistency and at other times (e.g the current wave of interest in postmodernism) develop theories which stress disunity and disorder (see Featherstone, 1991a). The shift from a perception of the social world as relatively integrated and centred to one in which the foundations are cracked and 'the centre cannot hold' may well be related to shifts in the power balances and interdependencies of various groups of cultural specialists both in terms of their internal outsider–established struggles and their more general relations to other more powerful and less powerful groups who offer them employment, protection, admiration, endorsement and even indifference and contempt, as masters and publics. When establishments become destabilized the selectivity of the particular view of the world and their conceptual apparatus becomes apparent as its particularity as opposed to universality emerges when it is ranged alongside the alternative schemata which are busy surfacing and being resurrected. Hence as Wolff (1990) reminds us, power should never be conceived as external to signification, as something which only comes in afterwards, for power essentially inhabits meaning. Here we should also mention the approach of Norbert Elias (1987a) who argues for a process-sociology which through focusing upon changes over time becomes sensitive to the formation and deformation of bodies of knowledge in the shifting interdependencies and balances of power between various social groups.

A further problem with the unified vision of culture is highlighted by Renato Rosaldo (1993: 91ff.). This is the tendency to present culture at one pole of a stark Manichaean choice between order and chaos. Culture, then, is often presented as a necessary corrective normative regulation to underlying violence and selfish egoism. Influential contemporary anthropologists such as Geertz and Turner, he argues, inherit this position from Durkheim. For Rosaldo, the basic problem with Durkheim's sociology is that it is built upon the twin imperatives of integration and regulation which keep at bay a 'what-would-happen-if' vision of chaos, which is rarely articulated. In effect Durkheim leaves little room between order and chaos, and has little sense that people can live with ambiguity, uncertainty, spontaneity and improvisation. It is possible to regard Durkheim's concern to develop a univocal theory of society as part of a more general movement within modernity to produce a systematic and ordered vision of the world which eliminates ambiguity (Levine, 1985). Foucault's work points to the development of the human sciences as part of a project to order, dissect and regulate human social life.

Yet however suspicious we should be about the concept of post-modernity read as an epochal break, we should be aware that both the theories and models it develops and the features of the contemporary world it constructs as evidence of new tendencies in social life, direct our attention towards the question of the extent to which disorder has always been a feature of social life, and the degree to which order/disorder varies in different parts of history and places in the world. It would seem hard to dispute that human social life depends upon the use of symbols with which the world is not only structured, but demarcated and classified in taken-for-granted evaluative ways. Classification entails the use of boundaries, which although taken for granted as we move through the everyday world, vary in their degree of absoluteness, rigidity and tolerance of ambiguity (see Zerubavel, 1991). What would seem to fit with the arguments of those who suggest that we are moving into a new era of postmodernity is the assumption that we are seeing the generation of global conditions in which certain groups of people are becoming involved in situations demanding more flexible classifications, situations in which it is not possible to refer to one set of overriding cultural rules which can arbitrate without ambiguity. This is not to suggest that we live in societies with an open public sphere with equal access for participants; far from it. Rather, it is to argue that more people are seeking access to public platforms and demanding citizen rights for minorities and outsider groups. The politics of multiculturalism demands a certain degree of respect and tolerance, not without its own aporias (Taylor, 1992), but it leads to a questioning of the modes of classification and categorization devices of other groups.

The argument for a greater reflexivity in the construction of tribal life, as societies and cultures, has developed around the close scrutiny of the practice of ethnography. Here the ethnographer ceases to be permitted to remain invisible, but the whole process of interpretation and construction of categories is subjected to a critique which emphasizes that ethnography is essentially a mode of 'writing culture': this is constrained by literary devices, tropes and metaphors which act in the text to produce the effect of unity and a closed narrative. This 'postmodern turn' in anthropology can be found in the writings of Clifford (1988), Clifford and Marcus (1986), Marcus and Fischer (1986), Marcus (1992b), Crapanzo (1980, 1992), Taussig (1980, 1987) and others. Marcus and Fischer (1986) for example identify their project as driven by the 'crisis of representation', which highlights the problem of adequately depicting cultural differences. In this they have sought to build on the writings of Said (1978), White (1973) and others who question the possibility of the adequate recovery of another culture – the 'salvage paradigm' so long influential in anthropology. The model of culture which has operated since E. B. Tylor's famous definition of culture as 'that complex whole' (quoted in Kroeber, 1948: 60), not only suggests an organic or mechanical image of culture, it is also premised upon the assumption of 'the existence of an initially unperceived coherence, a surprising meaningfulness, a covert rationality' (Thornton, 1992: 22). The aim here is to bring to the surface the rhetorical devices used to construct this idealized image of society and culture which gives the anthropologist the sense of a coherent reality which he or she has the authority to capture and distil (this can apply equally to history, and in addition to White, 1973 we should point to the work of Bann, 1984).

Instead of the genre convention of realism with its intention to totalize and represent the reality of a whole world or form of life, Marcus and Fischer (1986: 23) favour a more experimental approach in which a number of rhetorical devices are used to create a text which is intentionally and openly incomplete. Such texts lay bare their own processes of construction and reveal the various elements which were brought into and excluded from the final frame. Crapanzo (1980), for example, in his *Tuhami: Portrait of a Moroccan* refuses to produce a unified narrative and sense of cultural coherence. The book departs from the traditional life-history framework by self-consciously using modernist techniques to present the edited transcripts of interview as a puzzle requiring the reader's interpretation. He holds back the authority of the ethnographer by deliberately manipulating form to capture mood, fantasy and emotion to produce a fragmented almost surrealist text (see discussion in Marcus and Fischer, 1986: 71ff.).

The use of such devices is hardly new, and they clearly have a modernist rather than postmodernist origin. This is emphasized by Clifford (1988) who discusses surrealism's impact on anthropology, with its valuation of an aesthetics of fragments, unexpected juxtapositions and the mixing of the unconscious, dream images and extraordinary experiences with mundane everyday life. Of particular interest in this context are those French ethnographers who were influenced by the Collège de Sociologie, a loose informal grouping of intellectuals which developed in Paris in the 1930s around the work of Bataille (see Richardson, 1992). They developed a neo-Durkheimian interest in the sacred combined with ritual expressions of transgression, excess and sacrifice. In effect, it was argued, cultures should not be seen as unified, but are deeply ambivalent in structure. Cultures include instructions on both the rule *and* the transgression. Marcel Griaule, one of this group, argued that the ethnographic surrealist should delight in cultural impurities and disturbing syncretisms (Clifford, 1988: 131). Michel Leiris, another member of the group, became preoccupied with the problem of the appropriate narrative form for the material he was collecting which eventually led to *L'Afrique fantôme*, an open-ended 'anti-book' which was a series of entries comprised of facts and images which he refused to unify by letting his imagination work over them. His advice to the reader ran: 'Warning this book is unreadable' (cited in Clifford, 1988: 167).

Surrealism, then, used techniques of collage, cutting and assemblage with the cuts left visible and not blended into a unified representation. It sought to destabilize the authority of the artist/scientist/narrator and the myth of the gifted special person who could bring back for us more fundamental knowledge of reality. The confident monologue of the singular voice gives way to an inchoate polyphony. It is also interesting to note that Walter Benjamin (1982) who laboured on his massive *Passagenwerk*, a surrealist-inspired fragmentary account of the rise of mass culture and consumer dreamworlds in mid-nineteenth-century Paris, frequented the Collège de Sociologie in the late 1930s. Benjamin's writings have been particularly influential amongst postmodern theorists, and have also been used in ethnography (e.g. Taussig, 1980, 1987). We might add wryly, that the opposition to strong conceptual unities and preference for weaker frames, which are somehow held to be nearer to unmediated life itself, has long been a tradition within artistic and intellectual movements (such as *Lebensphilosophie* around the turn of the century; see the discussion of its relevance to Georg Simmel's writings in Featherstone, 1991b). It reappeared in the postmodernism of the 1960s, where one only has to think of the 'non-action' films of Andy Warhol such as *Sleep* (1963; a six-hour film of a man sleeping) and *Mario Banana* (1964; a male transvestite eating a banana [for a discussion of the films see O'Pray, 1989]). Its reverence for the unmediated particularity of life, or the re-presenting of cultural representations without commentary, points towards an inherent tension within the social sciences. That is, on the one hand the pressure to generalize, to construct general theories which have as universal relevance as possible, and on the other hand the tendency to particularize, to do justice to the assumed unique singularity of people, institutions and culture and to break down even further the alleged identities of these particularities to reveal the multiple voices and conflicting perspectives which inhabit them.

Before we leave the discussion of the assumption of cultural integration in anthropology it is worth raising the question: 'What does the notion of an integral tribal society with a separate culture do for us?' One answer is given by Baudrillard (1993), who comments on the tremendous fuss made of the discovery of an unknown tribe in the Philippines. His argument is that the reason why every effort was made to keep them isolated from contact in a sort of reservation (unknown to the tribe) is that as we become increasingly sucked into a simulational culture and mourn the loss of the real, the existence of a set of 'real' human beings somewhere on earth makes us feel more human (again).

It has been suggested that after Malinowski anthropology tended to focus upon the village as a bounded site of residence, effectively using the rhetorical device of synecdoche in which a part (the village) could be taken to represent the whole (the culture) (Clifford, 1992). The focus is on the village as a place of local dwelling. Any notion of movement or mobility tends to be restricted to the village and surrounding area constructed as 'the field'. Yet according to Clifford (1992: 100) this misses a number of factors, which slip out of the account constructed. In the first place there are the means of transport and communication: the boat, the car, the telephone which links the village to the outside world. Second, there is the relationship with the capital city and the national context – the places the ethnographer has to visit in order to get permission to visit the village. Third, there is the university home of the researcher and all the sorts of comings and goings in and out of the field by both natives and researchers that take place with relative ease in the contemporary world. In addition the central role of 'the informant', which has often been occluded and undertheorized in the past, needs to be made more central. In doing so the informant should not be thought of as a passive writer/inscriber who resides in the field, but as a traveller too. It is therefore far from adequate to localize non-Western people as 'natives' by freezing part of their lives and using it to represent the whole. This static depiction of native peoples confined to their local areas is very much a fiction. Indeed Appadurai (1988: 37) uses the stronger term 'incarcerated' and goes on to remind us: 'Natives, people confined to and by the places to which they belong, groups unsullied by contact with a larger world have probably never existed' (Appadurai, 1988: 39).

Yet if it is a fiction, it is a very powerful one which has become deeply entrenched in social life and we need to enquire into the process of its formation. Here it should be understood as related to two parallel processes. The first is the 'discovery' of native peoples with the opening up of the New World from the sixteenth century onwards and the problems this made for existing systems of classification. If this process of colonialism and the development of mercantile capitalism opened up a phase of greater travel, mobility and mixing of peoples, goods and categories, then it should also be placed alongside a second process, the development of the nation. The formulation of the people in a territorial area into a nation was a part of the state-formation process, which gathered impetus with the intensification of rivalries as states became drawn together into a tighter figuration through war, colonial expansion and economic competition. In the late eighteenth and nineteenth centuries artists and intellectuals rediscovered and invented ethnic histories and national traditions which helped to develop a national identity (see Burke, 1978). This may well have helped to formulate the organic metaphor of culture as something integrated, bounded and distinct. National identities have emphasized blood and soil. They have also drawn upon arborescent metaphors of rootedness. Keith Thomas (1983: 220) has traced the history of the oak tree as an emblem of the British people (see Malkki, 1992: 27). National identities by their emphasis upon natural metaphors of roots, soil, motherland and fatherland have provided a sense not only of rootedness, but also of exclusivity – it is only possible to belong to one national genealogical tree.[6] These brief remarks would suggest that it is possible to reconstruct the formation of sedentary metaphors in the territorialization of our identities alongside the growth of the nation-state and the development of assumptions about the rights and obligations of citizens and subjects. The notion of the nation as 'homeland', of the home as a place of residence from which one ventures out but always seeks to return, is a powerful related metaphor, as is the opposite notion that modernity induces an unhappy state of 'homelessness', which will be discussed below.

There is not the space to consider here the important question of the relationship between the process of the generation of strong national identities in the phase of intensified competition between nation-states after 1870 which produced strong images of nations as 'imagined communities', each with its own homeland and heritage, and migration. The 'great swarmings', the intensified migration of the period 1880–1920, was also a phase in which nation-states developed panics about 'immigration crises', and the need to construct strong boundaries and identities (see Zolberg, 1995). Heated debates took place within the United States in the late nineteenth century about the merits of the assimilation model versus more plural models of tolerance to ethnic diversity (Lasch, 1991). The phase of intensified mobility was therefore also a phase of concern about 'home' and identity; yet it is difficult to encounter positive images of mobility and migration, although they doubtless exist. The various countercultural currents of modernity, such as artistic modernism, bohemias, etc. with their interest in travel and the outsider, and the tales of migrants, slaves and refugees would provide some sources.

The relationship between travel and home is a complex relational one. Certain peoples have also developed, alongside the formation of the nation-state, various positive and negative depictions of travel and the degree of boundedness and closure of the nation-state. The Portuguese, for example, since the exploratory voyages of the fifteenth and sixteenth centuries, developed a much greater sense of the world, as opposed to the nation-state, as their spatial unit. The term *saudade*, roughly translated as longing or nostalgia, has for the Portuguese long been associated with unending wanderlust (Feldman-Bianco, 1992). It points to the double sense of a concern with travel and wandering and the collective memory of Portugal as an imagined community. Other parts of the world may well share this sense of national identity as movement and mobility, as Wang Gungwu (1993) has argued is the case with South East Asia. This is in marked contrast to East Asia, where mobility and migration are seen as limited and marginal in the context of a static agrarian society reinforced by Confucian pietism and bureaucratic structures. It would be interesting to reconstruct aspects of the national identities of various Western nations in the light of these remarks. For a preliminary contrast between the United States and Sweden in terms of their attitude towards the lure of 'the road' based upon road movies see Eyerman and Lofgren (1995).

A further point needs to be made before we turn to modernity. This is the assumption that communities (tribal or preindustrial), societies, or nations are spatially separated entities. This, as we mentioned earlier, misses the grounds within which these entities are situated. In effect their identities are formed in a figuration of communities or societies. Yet the danger with this approach is that it assumes a fixed level of coherence and identity formation of the basic units. Likewise when nation-states are conceived as actors on the international stage, with one state engaging another. As Bergesen (1990) has pointed out in a critique of Wallerstein's work, there is a methodological individualist assumption evident in his assumption that nation-states acquire their properties prior to their participation in the world-system. In effect they seem 'born whole'.

Yet nation-states only developed within a figuration which acted as a ground and constraint to their actions. All sorts of contacts were occurring between nascent proto-nation-states through the Church, dynastic ties and other forms of association, which helped to develop a cultural complex of interchanges and transactions; this acted as a developing field or ground within which nation-states could begin to form their identities. For the vast majority of nation-states which emerged in the nineteenth and twentieth centuries this international cultural complex, or transnational field, formed a gradually extending world whose significance became increasingly salient with the intensification of contact. The space within which local communities, societies and nation-states developed has always been hierarchically interconnected through the power balances and interdependencies which were unavoidably developing alongside the very formation of these entities. In the same way as we cautioned to be suspicious of the use of the term 'tradition', it should be apparent that we should also be cautious about the positing of a primeval state of autonomy of peoples, communities or societies which was violated by the development of modernity, capitalism or colonialism. As Gupta and Ferguson (1992: 8) remark: 'Instead of assuming the autonomy of the primeval community, we need to examine how it was formed *as a community* in the first place'.

To be aware of the construction of local communities, societies and nation-states as sedentary homelands does not mean that we should switch to the opposite assumption that the normal condition of human beings is, or should be, one in which everyone is a 'nomad' or a 'traveller'. Rather, we need to develop theories of culture which do justice to its processual and relational aspects. We need to enquire into the grounds for the formation of images of the world as a hybrid motion of displaced nomads as well as the persistence of images of localities as integrated and settled communities. The challenge to theorizing today is how to construct theories of communal living in localities which do not merely represent sedentariness as the norm, but seek to consider its various modalities, including displacements into images of imaginary homes/homelands. Such theories also need to take into account the ways in which those inhabitants who engage in various modes of travel manage to construct and live out their various affiliations and identities.[7]

Global modernities

Today the term 'modernity' is widely used in the social sciences. There are many reasons for this: the dissatisfaction with the ability of other terms such as 'capitalism' to cover all the aspects of contemporary social life that have accompanied the decline of interest in the various forms of Marxism and neo-Marxism since the 1980s; the growth of interest in post-modernism, which tends to circumscribe modernity by pointing to its limits and directs our attention back to the question of what it was; the upsurge of interest in culture and the nature of contemporary and modern experience. From a sociological perspective modernity is usually defined as 'a post-traditional order' (Giddens, 1991: 2). Its main features include: industrialism based upon machine production; capitalism based upon commodity production and the commodification of labour power; a massive increase in organizational power based upon the surveillance of populations; the control of the means of violence and the industrialization of war; the development of the nation-state, the basic referent for what we call 'society' (Giddens, 1990: 15ff.; 1991: 10ff.; for a slightly different list see S. Hall, 1992a; B. Turner, 1990b). For Giddens these factors help to generate the characteristic sense of dynamism in modern institutions, the sense that the modern world is a runaway world. This is based upon: the separation of time and space, which means that activities are no longer confined to place and that simultaneous communication can take place over distance; the disembedding of social institutions from tradition through the use of abstract systems and media such as money; the increasing use of reflexive knowledge.

Giddens concentrates on the institutional dimension of modernity and gives little attention to the cultural dimension. He does (1991: 137ff.), however, suggest that two images of modernity have dominated socio-logical literature: the first, taken from Weber, is that of 'the iron cage' bureaucratization of life and the second, taken from Marx, is that of modernity as a monster, which while irrational in the form of capitalism, can in principle be tamed. Against these Giddens proposes his own image of the 'juggernaut – a runaway engine of enormous power which collectively as human beings, we can drive to some extent but which also threatens to rush out of our control and which could rend itself asunder'. Common to all three images is the assumption that there is a singular modernity which detraditionalizes the world. In effect the basic mech-anisms that bring about modernity will produce more or less similar effects throughout the world. Culture will follow and adapt to these more basic economic, political and institutional processes.

The relationship between the various aspects of modernity is very complex. On the one hand there is the question of the validity of delineating modernity in terms of a number of key dimensions (social, economic, political and cultural) which are analysed separately and then shown to interlink (see, for example, S. Hall, 1992a). As Elias (1984) reminds us, we cannot assume this division of social life into separate spheres each with its separate discipline to be in the nature of things; rather they should be seen as emergent categories which depend upon a process of formation. Elias examines the growth of economics in the eighteenth century as the first science of society which was premised upon the emergence of a distinctive economic sphere, which in turn depended upon the accumulation of both the numbers and the power potential of economic specialists. I have made some tentative steps towards examining the development of the cultural sphere in the same way in Chapter 2 in the present book: 'The Autonomization of the Cultural Sphere'.

The second point relates to the relationship between the institutional and cultural dimensions of modernity. While the distinctions between the two aspects are not always easy to make, Tibi (1995) for example would see the institutional dimension in terms of the characteristics outlined by Giddens (1990, 1991) which we have already discussed, and the cultural complex as the unfinished project of modernity as described by Habermas (1988). Giddens assumes the former to be eminently globalizable, indeed he assumes that modernity produces globalization in a manner which does not take into account the independent force of cultural factors in this process, and does not see that in important respects the imputed causality could be reversed and globalization could be seen to produce modernity (see Robertson, 1992a, 1992b for this argument). Habermas's project of modernity entails the realization of the Enlightenment vision of a good society in which not only have traditional dogmatic authority structures been criticized and abolished, but the negative aspects of modern science, technology and instrumental rationality (the domination of nature and the domination of man by man, which are in effect the 'dark side' of the Enlightenment) have been curbed and held in check by an active public of reflexive and responsible people.

While Tibi (1995) and many others have detected the 'Eurocentric' nature of Habermas's depiction, the same could also be said for Giddens in terms of his assumptions about the experiential, cultural and subjective changes in modern life which allegedly follow from the accelerated institutional changes as we move into 'high modernity'. In addition Giddens shows little sensitivity to the culture/power complex, the ways in which the various images of 'the other' and the West, which were generated through the process of colonialism led to a range of selective appropriations of modernity. Not only can we see a series of different entry-points into modernity (Therborn, 1995), but a series of different projects were also developed as well as demands for selective appropriation of the institutional parameters. Tibi (1995), for example, has referred to the contemporary Muslim dilemma as the 'Islamic dream of semi-modernity'.

Speaking about Japan, Miyoshi and Harootunian (1989a: 146) has suggested that 'the signifier "modern" should be regarded as a regional term peculiar to the West'.

For all Giddens's discussions of time-space, the spatial dimension of modernity is underplayed. We need to ask the question of the spatial dimension of modernity, or 'where is modernity?', not just in terms of some superior logic emanating from the Western centre (versions of Weber's rationalization thesis) but in terms of the spatial relationship of the non-West to the West. Modernity, then should not be seen exclusively in temporal terms, as an epoch, but in spatial and relational terms too: terms that entail power relationships in the very construction and implementation of the set of categories which are now only beginning to surface as the non-West accumulates the power resources to speak back and be listened to in the West. Postmodern and postcolonial theories are symptoms of this process which point to this shift in power balances. To dismiss them as hypostatized temporal or epochal categories (e.g. postmodernity) is to miss this important cultural dimension of the process.

This is very much a view from the Western centre which discounts the possibility that, despite the integrating and unifying tendencies, there could be the development of global modernities in the plural and that there could also be many projects of modernity (to play off a phrase of Habermas's) which are yet to be completed. In short we need to attend to the spatial dimension of modernity and its particular cultural embedding in the West. The process of separation of the West from the rest of the world and its subsequent attempted imposition of its version of the project of modernity on to the rest of the world, suggests a movement from the belief in its capacity to hierarchize and order flows of communication and people, to one in which mixing, movement and dislocation become the norm as the interchange between the rest and the West can no longer be regulated. But perhaps it is wrong to conceive these two aspects as merely sequential stages: perhaps they should be understood as long co-present within the development of Western modernity.

The first image of modernity is one of order and entails the progressive control, domination and regulation of the natural and social worlds through the application of rational knowledge. In this image the Enlightenment faith in science and technology is seen as flawed, for instead of delivering the good society and human happiness, the secret inner logic of history is a narrative of the fall, one which points to the realization of a dystopia rather than a utopia. This has been a particularly strong theme in German social thought and those influenced by Nietzsche's writings. Weber's vision of the refeudalization of social relationships and the bureaucratization of the world, in which machine-like routines govern human beings and drive out all creativity, is echoed in Horkheimer and Adorno's image of 'a totally administered world'. This also resonates with Foucault's emphasis on the application of knowledge from the human sciences to produce increasing surveillance, panopticism and discipline.[8]

Zygmunt Bauman (1991) has likewise emphasized that a central feature of modernity is the production of order, yet he points to the limits of this process and our inability to complete the project. Modernity is a time when the ordering of nature, the social world and the self, and the connections between all three, is reflected upon. Yet the quest for order needs to feed off the notion of the opposite of order: chaos. This is the sense that we are threatened by incoherence, incongruity, irrationality, ambiguity, contingency, polysemy, confusion and ambivalence; in effect modern existence is saturated by a 'without us the deluge' feeling as we strive for control (Bauman, 1991: 7). Modern consciousness is governed by the urge to extend outwards, to map and classify, which means it has to discover or reveal ever new layers of chaos beneath its constructed order to feed its Sisyphean restlessness. In effect Bauman is reading modernity from the point of view of postmodern theory in teasing out its inherent limits and contradictions. Bauman's reflections are helpful here in drawing attention to the way which our two images of modernity as order and chaos are linked.

If the first image emphasizes the dark side of Enlightenment and reason to present an image of modernity as fixed, static and closed, the second image emphasizes modernity as continual change driven by the need to deal with the disorder which it both seeks out and generates. This second image is of modernity producing endless disruption and social disorganization as it pacifies and controls nature for human purposes and tears down the old structures of social life to make way for the new. It is an heroic Promethean image of human life captured by Goethe in *Faust* Part 2, where the social and physical landscape is transformed in the name of progress (see Berman, 1982). This image became particularly influential in social thought in Germany and the United States in the late nineteenth and early twentieth centuries as both countries experienced rapid industrialization and the expansion of cities such as Berlin and Chicago into metropolises. The picture presented of Chicago by Robert Park and his group of associates, who became known as the Chicago School of Sociology, was one of a constant inflow of immigrants which had to be processed by the city. The model of the city was based upon human ecology and stressed competition for territory and constant movement as the city expanded and pulled in more migrants whose assimilation process entailed spatial movement through the city's natural areas to accompany their movement through life time. Hence social disorganization (the slum, crime, delinquency, the hobo) was seen as a necessary part of the dynamics of modern urban life. Park's notion of modern urban life was influenced by the time he spent working with Georg Simmel in the last decade of the nineteenth century in Berlin, a city which experienced a parallel phase of rapid growth.

It is with Simmel that we can start to build a picture of the experiential and cultural dimensions of modernity. Simmel's writings on money and the metropolis are well known and it has been argued that he developed a

non-nostalgic approach to modern life which made him 'the first sociologist of modernity' (Frisby, 1985a, 1985b).[9] Simmel emphasized the
fragmentary dynamic nature of modern life as people in large cities were
bombarded by a range of impressions and sensations which threatened to
overwhelm them. This could lead to neurasthenia, a defence against which
was the blasé attitude of the urbanite, which Simmel (1971d) speaks of in
his famous essay on the metropolis and mental life. It is this battle with
the dissolution of fixed contents, to discover some capacity to adequately
unify, frame or form the excess of fluidity and motion which is central to
modern life. As Simmel (1923, quoted in Frisby, 1985b: 46) remarks

> The essence of modernity as such is psychologism, the experiencing [*das Erleben*]
> and interpretation of the world in terms of the reaction of our inner life and
> indeed as an inner world, the dissolution of fixed contents in the fluid element of
> the soul, from which all that is substantive is filtered and whose forms are
> merely forms of motion.

While the linkage of fluidity and motion with modernity is something we
will return to shortly, it is worth emphasizing that there is a further aspect
of modern culture which can be drawn from Simmel's work: this is the
tragic accumulation of culture. The accumulation of objective culture, the
production of knowledge in various media, has expanded tremendously in
modern times and is beyond the capacity of individuals to assimilate into
their subjective cultures. In Goethe's time perhaps there was a better
balance between subjective and objective culture, but Simmel holds that
this is something we have lost. In modernity, therefore, we are left with a
sense of cultural fragmentation and an over-optioned life in which there is
an absence of certainty and guidelines. Hence any selection becomes
a wager on a particular body of culture which we hope will provide *the*
ultimate meaningful framework for our lives. The fragmentation of
experience in our everyday lives in the streets of the metropolis is mirrored
by the fragmentation of the knowledge base which we endlessly traverse, in
an effort to find some lasting and justifiable perspective, to give a more
than fleeting coherence to our lives. This specifically modern experience of
temporality was particularly evident in the phenomenon of fashion. The
constant parade of new fashions provided a permanent sense of change in
which the new styles provided shocks and an accelerated sense of the
tempo of life (see Simmel, 1995; Lichtblau, 1995).
    Simmel was not of course the first person to attempt to chart the
aporias of modern culture and it would seem that his interest in charting
the sense of the transitory experience of modernity and 'the aestheticization of everyday life' (see Featherstone, 1991a: Ch. 5) builds upon some
of the motifs which are to be found in the writings of Baudelaire, who is
generally credited with introducing the concept of *modernité*. For
Baudelaire (1972) the key feature of the experience of modern life was the
sense of 'newness'. The fact that modern societies produced an endless
parade of commodities, buildings, fashions, social types and cultural

movements, and that they were all destined to be rapidly replaced by others, reinforced the sense of the transitoriness of the present moment (see Benjamin, 1973; Frisby, 1985b; Osborne, 1992). The *flâneur*, or stroller, in the public spaces of the large cities was able to experience these kaleido-scopic images and fragments whose novelty, immediacy and vividness, coupled with their fleeting nature and often strange juxtaposition, provided a range of aesthetic sensations and experiences (see Mazlish, 1994 for a discussion). Baudelaire is sometimes regarded as the founder of artistic modernism, which emerged in reaction to classicism and Romanticism. Modernism not only sought to capture the fragmentary quality of modern life in all its everyday banality and ugliness; it also became associated with the countercultural and transgressive impulses which developed the bohemian critique of the bourgeois lifestyle. It was associated too with formal innovations and strong avant-gardist impulses. We have already mentioned how the sensitivity to the problem of representation and more complex notions of unity found in modernism have been taken up in the various adaptations of postmodernism in sociology, anthropology and cultural studies. Walter Benjamin (1973) not only devoted considerable space to the analysis of the Paris of Baudelaire and the birth of mass consumer culture, but also showed a methodological sensitivity in the use of modernist as opposed to realist modes of representation (e.g. montage, juxtaposition) in his writings (see Buck-Morss, 1989).[10]

If we wish to understand the culture of modernity, then we need to consider both the impulse to generate a culture of order through the colonization and domestication of the world defined as disorder, and the critique of this ordering impulse through the celebration of the ability to live with disorder, fragmentation and mixing which is to be found in modernism. The first approach not only seeks to oppose chaos with order (Bauman, 1991) it also seeks to oppose mixing and hybridization with separation and purification with a view to the creation of strict classifications (Latour, 1993). The second approach develops an interest in the types of experience and ways of life which develop in the modern city and seeks to grapple with the problem of representation, to enable such experience to be adequately expressed in artistic terms, or made intelligible through a theoretical discourse. Hence the growth of artistic modernism and the culture of modernity are (unsurprisingly) inextricably linked.

Yet the sense of cultural disorder, the overload of sensory impressions and sign-play cannot be confined to modernity – they have forerunners in the upside-down world and sign-play of the carnivals and fairs of the Middle Ages (Featherstone, 1991a: Ch. 5).[11] The consumer culture of sign-play and spectacles can also be traced back to the designs of the seventeenth-century European absolutist state (most notably Spain) to produce the aestheticization and spectacles which became known as the culture of the baroque (Maravall, 1986). It may well be possible to discover a similar sensitivity to sign-play, the mixing of codes, fleeting impressions and a concern with aestheticization, style and fashion in the 'floating worlds' of cities such as Edo and Kyoto which developed in Tokogawa Japan between the seventeenth and the nineteenth centuries. If, then, we attempt to break down some of the elements of the experience of modernity which were associated with the problematic of cultural modernism, we may well find that they existed, albeit in different forms, in other times and places.

The nascent consumer cultures which developed in the modern European cities, such as eighteenth-century London and nineteenth-century Paris and Berlin, were places into which commodities, new exotic goods, information and people from various parts of the world flowed. They were places of social and cultural mixing generated as much by their capacity to take in things from the outside, be it their own national hinterlands or the world at large, as through the working out of an internal dynamic of restless modernity. Yet most accounts of modernity have focused upon its chronological unfolding and particular experiential and cultural qualities, either without reference to spatial location other than a vague or unstated assumption that it took place in the West (understandable when one considers the writers and audiences), or in European cities or nation-states. There is little sense of the relational basis of this process in the sense of the formation of relationships between the West and other parts of the world. For example, the collection of essays entitled *The Culture of Capital: Art, Power and the Nineteenth Century Middle Class* (Seed and Wolff, 1988) focuses largely on the city of Manchester's art and class structure with little reference to the countries whence the cotton came and the colonial and trade relations that tied Manchester, the place we are taught in history was the first industrial capitalist city, into a world.[12] It is therefore important to consider the spatial dimension of modernity in terms of the process of globalization which developed in parallel to it. But first we must return briefly to consider the experience of modernity.

The *flâneur*, the stroller or idler in the big cities described by Baudelaire, Benjamin and Simmel, enjoyed the immersion in the crowd, the variety of faces, body types and fashions as well as a flood of images on the advertising hoardings and billboards, in window displays, department stores, exhibitions and world fairs which made up the urban landscape. He or she experienced a sense of mixing and sign-play as formerly sealed apart categories of people and culture were juxtaposed, setting off half-remembered memories and allegories. The *flâneur* usually moved around a known urban world, yet one in which the shock of new encounters was potentially present, as the dynamic of modernity brought in new things, people and places as the old and present were torn down to make way for the new. The *flâneur* experienced swings between immersion in the immediacy of life and the distanced voyeuristic contemplation of it from a seemingly invisible perspective as people moved around amongst others who also adopted the 'distanced' blasé attitude which acted as a defence against overstimulation (neurasthenia). The *flâneur* was a traveller, albeit of a limited sort, who played with the idea of genuine experience and its aesthetic recovery.

Travel can be understood as paradigmatic of experience and we should remember that the root of the word 'experience' is *per*, which means to try, to test, to risk. Travel, of course, can be routine and mundane, or something to be endured as an impediment until one is settled back at home. Seneca, for example, saw Roman travel as distracted wandering and held that it was better to stay at home. It has been argued that it was not until modern times that travel was celebrated as a voyage of self-discovery (Leed, 1991: 7). Yet it is too simple to see the experiential side of travel and the pleasures of discovery and new sensations as a product of modernity, for it is possible to reverse the relationship and argue that what we regard as the specific experience of modernity was experienced in premodern times by travellers. This is the argument of Leed (1991: 6–7), who addresses the question 'How do the transformations of travel produce the mind of the traveler, a certain mentality that has often been termed "modern", post-Renaissance, but that is as old as civilized travel?' Travel, then thrusts the new into the middle of life, it opens up life to contingency and creates 'exotica' (matter out of place).

Travel is closely bound to the notion of modernity. The Renaissance voyages which took place since the sixteenth century enabled Europeans to encounter people of different ethnicities and encouraged them to make comparisons between themselves and others. The encounters and comparisons helped to change Europeans' self-image of Europe from being a periphery to ancient centres, to being a centre in its own right which was at the cutting edge of the 'modern' (Leed, 1991: 21). This increasing contact helped to generate the production and exchange of differences. As Todorov (1984: 49) reminds us, the discovery of the New World saw the production of two apparently contradictory myths, one whereby the 'other' is a 'noble savage', and one whereby he is a 'dirty dog', a potential slave.[13] Columbus effectively imposed his own values upon alterity and did not seek to know the other on its own terms. Yet the treasures and specimens, the plants, animals and people Columbus sent back to Spain and the various accounts of the voyages had a profound impact upon the existing bodies of knowledge and modes of classification. It has been argued by Grafton (1992) that between 1550 and 1650 Western thinkers moved away from assuming that they could find all-important truths in ancient books towards empirical knowledge. The Ancient view of a coherent and ordered universe now ran up against countless inconvenient facts. Francis Bacon's *Great Instauration* (1620) sought to produce knowledge that no longer relied upon the Ancient authorities. He used a wealth of information from the various voyages to argue that we should test out theories and establish knowledge on the basis of experiment and observation. The title page of the book shows a ship sailing past classical columns which represent the Pillars of Hercules, the ancient limits of navigation and knowledge. Against those who would caution not to go too far, Bacon urged his readers: 'too far is not enough' (Grafton, 1992: 198).[14]

A consequence of this process was that differences in space became associated with differences in time. This temporalization of difference was used to produce an evolutionary hierarchy. This in turn allowed Europeans to produce a moral justification of the exploitation, now seen as a necessary *Bildungsprozess*, which it was imperative for those designated children or 'minors' to go through if they were ever to develop and attain enlightenment. It was this confinement of other cultures to past history, to lower stages on the same ladder of history, which enhanced the sense of the threshold-advancing presentness of the European nations, a sense of modernity which in actuality developed out of the occluded spatial encounters with non-Western others.

It is of course this sense of a unified humankind converging on the common path beaten by the advancing Western modernity which was heavily criticized by elements of artistic modernism whose sympathies were for those who were the victims of this process. We have already discussed the ways in which anthropological and other theories adopted some of the techniques of artistic modernism such as collage and montage to produce a sense of a more complex multivocal process in which the boundedness of the locality is deconstructed. Yet it is a more significant move when not only are the others' perspectives and voices considered alongside those of the anthropologist/writer to problematize the process of cultural formation, but theories of modernity are produced from different parts of the world which dispute the Western account. When it is a part of the world such as Japan and East Asia which is rapidly gaining power potential in the shifting global balance of power, then we can assume that in the future this could lead to a revision of the long-established conceptual set: tradition and modernity, to which we can add postmodernity.[15] European colonialism therefore played an important role in the spatial totalization of Western modernity,[16] which resulted in modernity providing the standpoint for historical totalization, the standpoint from which all other cultures were to be judged and hierarchically ordered (see Osborne, 1992).

Modernization theory merely represents a continuation of this logic, with progress now defined as Americanization to replace Europeanization, in tune with the shifting global balance of power in the second half of the twentieth century. But this post-Second World War era also began a phase of decolonialism, and the growth in the global power of the non-West ushered in a process of the relativization of the modern world. That is, the modern world was revealed to be the Western world, and to be only a world among many worlds, which began a process of re-forming the various 'we-images', and 'they-images' of Western and other nations. As Sakai (1989: 106) remarks:

> What this simple but undeniable recognition pointed to was that history was not only temporal or chronological but also spatial and relational. The condition for the possibility of conceiving of history as a linear and evolutionary series of

incidents lay in its not as yet thematized relation to other histories, other *coexisting* temporalities. Whereas monistic history . . . did not know its implicit reliance on other histories and thought itself autonomous and total, 'world' history conceived of itself as the spatial relations of histories. In world history, therefore, one could not think of history exclusively in those terms which referred back only to that same history; monistic history could not deal with the world as it was apprehended in world history since the world is primarily a sphere of heterogeneity and others.

It is the series of challenges in the various dimensions of international and transnational contact between nation-states, not a benevolent gesture on the part of the more powerful Western nations, which results in a shift in the fantasy base of the 'we- and they-images'. This inaugurates a process of enforced listening for the Western nations. Modernity, then, began as a process of the self-recognition of Europe in which the Orient and other parts of the world became confined to an image of premodern traditionalism. The spatial expansion of Europe through colonialism, with the resultant inflow of goods, people and information, helped to produce various modes of mixing and disorder within a range of social and cultural life forms and practices which helped to generate an enhanced sense of 'the new', 'presentness' and the transitory nature of time. This disorder and mixing in one area of cultural life became reconstituted as a new symbolic hierarchy in which the various peoples of the world were rank-ordered as part of an assumed universal evolutionary history. This aspect of the project of modernity becomes relativized through two main factors: the shifts in the global balance of power away from the West in the second half of the twentieth century; and the increased intensity of transnational flows of commodities, people, images and information which are bypassing the boundaries of the nation-states (Lash and Urry, 1993). It is this latter aspect, in particular the extent of global migration, that is producing intensified contact which is undermining the once secure fantasy-based 'we- and they-images', and changing the nature of identity formation to the extent that categories of people are emerging who live more mobile lives and are at ease with more fluid identities. It is this process of mobility and migrancy, now labelled postmodern by some, which is held to be both the methodological key and the actuality of the contemporary world.

Notes

1. This is, of course, largely a male ideal. As Janet Wolff (1993) reminds us, it is men who have predominantly travelled and women who have remained at home.

2. The first edition of the book appeared in 1887. *Gemeinschaft und Gesellschaft* has been referred to as 'the founding charter of modern sociology' (Lasch, 1991: 139). It has been important in structuring the contrasts between tradition and modernity, community and urban life which have been influential in the development of sociology in the United States (especially the Chicago School). In addition it has been regarded as one major source of Talcott Parsons's 'pattern variables'.

3. Tenbruck's perspective has also been influenced by Simmel who, like Weber, argued against those who sought to understand social life from idealized comprehensive concepts

such as society, seeing the latter as having the role of a preliminary 'emergency-shelter', which should soon be discarded. For Simmel our focus of attention should be on the forms of as sociation and interactions between individuals (see Frisby and Sayer, 1986: 54ff.). For a discussion of Tenbruck's ideas in the context of a critique of the comparative method see Axtman (1993).

4. For a discussion of the different uses of the term 'culture' in anthropology see Boon (1973). The notion of culture as 'the whole way of life' of a people was formulated by Raymond Williams (1981) and has been influential in the field of cultural studies (see G. Turner, 1990).

5. Benedict's (1946) book has been subjected to a strong critique by the current generation of Japanese Studies scholars. Not only do many of these follow some of the assumptions about fragmentation and pluralism associated with postmodernism we have discussed, they also refuse to see these changes as just a product of a post-1960s consumer culture. Hence the supposed ethnic and cultural homogeneity of Japan is now being challenged as social movements and scholars alike rediscover, and are able to voice their views on, the outsiders allegedly incorporated and blended into Japaneseness. This is not to say that *Nihonjinron* (Japanese exclusiveness) has ceased to be the most powerful national image in Japan – far from it. Rather it is to suggest that groups like the Okinawans and the Ainu, as well as long-resident groups such as the Koreans are now discovering their public voice, suggesting a slight shift in the established/outsiders power balance.

6. Deleuze and Guattari (1987: 18) remark: 'It is odd how the tree has dominated Western reality and all of Western thought, from botany to biology and anatomy, but also gnosiology, theology, ontology, all of philosophy . . .: the root-foundation, *Grund, racine, fondement*. The West has a special relation to the forest and deforestation' (cited in Malkki, 1992: 28). The place of the forest in German intellectual thought and popular culture is particularly important.

7. The problems of multiple identifications in the contemporary world, which are to be found in the remotest areas, are captured in the film *Black Harvest* (Robin Anderson/Bob Connolly, 1992) which follows the initial success and eventual failure of a half-Australian businessman/half-New Guinea tribesman to organize a tribe to raise a crop of coffee.

8. In Foucault's case it is the increase in population pressure which encourages the state to regulate and control the excess of bodies. It is interesting to note that in his earlier *Madness and Civilization* (1971) he romantically draws a positive picture of the pre-modern madman who is free to wander and intervene in social life without the threat of incarceration or treatment, both of which emerge with modernity. Influenced by Nietzsche, his image of the pre-modern is one of individuality, difference and mobility with the modern life being engulfed by an increasingly homogenized mass of narrowly individuated people whose real differences are minimal. Weber and Adorno's writings show similar traces of the influence of Nietzsche.

9. As we have already mentioned, the loss of *Gemeinschaft* was an important theme not only in the writings of Tönnies and other German sociologists, but in literature and the humanities as well. Yet Tönnies was not only harking back to a traditional *Gemeinschaft*; his image of modern society, *Gesellschaft*, emphasizes that its very transitoriness and newness meant that it could not be considered as a fixed end state. In effect *Gesellschaft* itself should be considered as only a transitional and superficial phenomenon (Frisby, 1985b: 13). Tönnies did not use the term postmodern, although like other German theorists influenced by the Hegelian and Marxist traditions he could envisage something beyond the modern. This something typically entailed an *Aufhebung* of capitalist modernity, which sought to utilize technological developments to create some form of communal living that would provide social and moral integration and realization of freedom and individuality.

10. The use of the term 'modern' can be traced back, much further than nineteenth-century metropolises, or the eighteenth-century Enlightenment, or the early eighteenth-century 'battle of the books', the quarrel between the Ancients and the Moderns. The term 'modern', Habermas (1981) reminds us, derives from the late fifth-century Latin term *modernus*, which was used to demarcate a Christian present from a pagan past (Smart, 1990: 17). In this

context it points to a break in continuity, to the emergence of something new. Here we find that the modern seems to suggest the destabilization of old categories and the sense of a new start òr new era. Vattimo (1988) suggests that modernity's key notion of progress was a secularization of the Judaic-Christian notions of salvation and redemption. Postmodernity entails the abandonment of this belief in development and perfectibility through scientific and technological progress.

11. It has been argued that the sign-play and cultural fragmentation which some want to see as a central feature of postmodernism is very much evident in the depictions of *modernité*, that we find in the accounts of the experience of the modern city in the writings of Benjamin, Baudelaire and Simmel (Featherstone, 1991a: Ch. 5). From this perspective there are strong continuities between modernism and postmodernism, as Lyotard has argued. See the oft-quoted remark of Lyotard (1984: 79) that postmodernism 'is not modernism at its end but in the nascent state, and this state is constant', which points to the transitoriness of the new and the avant-garde impulses that are characteristic of artistic modernism (see also Frisby, 1985b; Lichtblau, 1995). This stance, however, gives insufficient emphasis to the 'end of history' arguments in postmodern theory in which while there is an endless parade of styles and images these are merely replays of images taken from the imaginary museum of cultures and histories (for a version of this perspective see Vattimo, 1988).

12. This is not to belittle the book, which is a work of careful scholarship. Rather it is to suggest that it represents perhaps the end point of a particular approach to history which would conceive social, cultural or local history in strictly local terms with the cut-off boundary being the locality or nation-state. What does seem to be apparent is that the movement towards postcolonial theory, world-systems theory and postmodernism which gathered pace during the 1980s, has expanded the frame of reference towards the global and encouraged a more relational focus. A book published only four years later by Catherine Hall, *White, Male and Middle Class* (1992), not only focuses on gender relations like the Seed and Wolff collection, but also considers the way in which English identities have been rooted in imperial power. In this context one could also mention that an essay from the founder of world-systems theory, Immanuel Wallerstein (1990) who has attacked the narrow focus upon the nation-state, begins with a citation from Sidney Mintz's writings on sugar, *The Power of Sweetness and the Sweetness of Power* (1988). One could envisage a similar book on cotton, which would focus on the relations between Manchester capitalism and imperialist presence in the Indian subcontinent and other colonies. Or, rather, we should add that this and similar topics (chocolate, tea, etc.) are being addressed as student projects on cultural studies and communications courses. We could also mention Said's *Culture and Imperialism* (1993) with its relational interpretation of Jane Austen's novels to highlight the rare occluded references she makes to the colonial source of the wealth on which the eighteenth-century English country house society was based. In effect the premises and categories of taken-for-granted worlds are challenged by these types of analysis.

13. For an account of the implications of the slave trade and the shipping of millions of blacks across the Atlantic which emphasizes the hybrid nature of cultural identity and argues that the enforced black migrations developed a counterculture to modernity see Gilroy, 1993. This is intrinsic to modernity but is invariably left out of conventional accounts, which readily take modernity's self-image as a starting point and have little conception of the integral rather than aberrant nature of slavery, the 'dark side of modernity.'

14. Bacon is presented as one of the key figures in the development of modern science in Horkheimer and Adorno's *Dialectic of Enlightenment* (1972). He is seen as obsessed by the scientistic vision of dominating nature and controlling the world through scientific knowledge. In common with other members of the Frankfurt School, Horkheimer and Adorno largely concentrate on the 'internal' (i.e. capitalist modernity) narrative of the domination of instrumental reason and do not focus on the place in this process of the West's relationship to others.

15. Here we should attempt to think through a set of categories which includes the various possible meanings of the 'Japanization of the West', and not just the 'modernization of Japan' (Miyoshi and Harootunian, 1989a).

16. Sociology has long neglected the analysis of the colonies. There is little sense of the relational dependence of Western societies on colonies in accounts of the formation of modernity (among the exceptions are King, 1990b, 1995; Hall, 1992c). In *The Sociology of the Colonies* Maunier (1949: xi) takes a typically top-down, nation-state-inspired perspective when he argues: 'The contact of groups or of peoples becomes a contact of civilizations, or of cultural spheres, when it occurs between communities which have not the same form, the same constitution, the same laws: which are therefore not on the same rung of the social ladder. If they are obliged to live together, their problem is how best to pass from diversity to uniformity, to reconcile difference and resemblance, to start from isolation and arrive at fusion. Assimilation or adaption marks the path to unification'.

REFERENCES

Abercrombie, N., Hill, S. and Turner, B. S. (1980) *The Dominant Ideology Thesis*. London: Allen & Unwin.

Abu-Lughod, J. (1991) 'Going beyond the global babble', in A. D. King (ed.) *Culture, Globalization and the World-system*. London: Macmillan.

Albrow, M. (1990) *Max Weber's Construction of Social Theory*. London: Macmillan.

Alexander, J. (ed.) (1988) *Durkheimian Sociology*. Cambridge: Cambridge University Press.

Anderson, B. (1991) *Imagined Communities*, revised edn, London: Verso.

Appadurai, A. (1986) 'Introduction: commodities and the politics of value', in A. Appadurai (ed.) *The Social Life of Things*. Cambridge: Cambridge University Press.

Appadurai, A. (1988) 'Putting hierarchy in its place', *Cultural Anthropology*, 3 (1).

Appadurai, A. (1990) 'Disjunction and difference in the global cultural economy', *Theory, Culture & Society*, 7 (2–3).

Arensberg, C. M. (1968) *The Irish Countrymen*. Garden City, NY: Natural History Press, orig. publ. 1937.

Arensberg, C. M. and Kimball, S.T. (1940) *Family and Community in Ireland*. London: Peter Smith.

Arnason, J. (1987a) 'The modern constellation and the Japanese enigma', Part I, *Thesis Eleven*, 17.

Arnason, J. (1987b) 'The modern constellation and the Japanese enigma', Part II, *Thesis Eleven*, 18.

Arnason, J. (1990) 'Nationalism, globalization and modernity', in M. Featherstone (ed.) *Global Culture*. London: Sage.

Axtman, R. (1993) 'Society, globalization and the comparative method', *History of the Human Sciences*, 6 (2).

Banck, G. A. (1994) 'Mass consumption and urban contest in Brazil: some reflections on lifestyle and class', *Bulletin of Latin American Research*, 13 (1): 45–60.

Bann, S. (1984) *The Clothing of Clio: A Study of Representations of History in Nineteenth Century Britain and France*. Cambridge: Cambridge University Press.

Barthes, R. (1982) *Empire of Signs*. London: Cape.

Battersby, C. (1989) *Gender and Genius*. London: Women's Press.

Baudelaire, C. (1972) 'The painter of modern life', in *Selected Writings on Art and Literature*. Translated with an introduction by P. E. Charvet. Harmondsworth: Penguin.

Baudrillard, J. (1970) *La société de consommation*, Paris: Gallimard.

Baudrillard, J. (1983a) *Simulations*. New York: Semiotext(e).

Baudrillard, J. (1983b) *In the Shadow of the Silent Majorities*. New York: Semiotext(e).

Baudrillard, J. (1993) *Symbolic Exchange and Death*. London: Sage.

Bauman, Z. (1973) *Culture as Praxis*. London: Routledge.

Bauman, Z. (1988a) 'Is there a postmodern sociology?', *Theory, Culture & Society*, 5 (2–3).

Bauman, Z. (1988b) *Legislators and Interpreters*. Cambridge: Polity.

Bauman, Z. (1990) 'Philosophical affinities of postmodern sociology', *Sociological Review*, 38 (3).

Bauman, Z. (1991) *Modernity and Ambivalence*. Cambridge: Polity.

Bauman, Z. (1992) *Intimations of Postmodernity*. London: Routledge.

Bell, D. (1976) *Cultural Contradictions of Capitalism*. London: Heinemann.

Bell, D. (1980) 'Beyond modernism, beyond self', in *Sociological Journeys: Essays 1960–1980*. London: Routledge.

Bell, C. and Newby, H. (1971) *Community Studies*. London: Allen & Unwin.

Bendix, R. (1970) 'Culture, social structure and change', in *Embattled Reason: Essays on Social Knowledge*. New York: Oxford University Press.

Benedict, R. (1934) *Patterns of Culture*. Boston: Houghton Mifflin.

Benedict, R. (1946) *The Chrysanthemum and the Sword*. Boston: Houghton Mifflin.

Benjamin, W. (1973) *Charles Baudelaire: A Lyric Poet in the Era of High Capitalism*. London: New Left Books.

Benjamin, W. (1977) *The Origin of German Tragic Drama*. London: New Left Books.

Benjamin, W. (1982) *Das Passagenwerk*, 2 vols, ed. R. Tiedermann, Frankfurt: Suhrkamp.

Bennett, T. *et al.* (1977) *The Study of Culture*. Milton Keynes: Open University Press.

Bennett, T., Martin, G., Mercer, C. and Woollacott, T. (eds) (1981) *Culture, Ideology and Social Process*. London: Batsford.

Bergesen, A. (1990) 'Turning world-system theory on its head', in M. Featherstone (ed.) *Global Culture*. London: Sage.

Berman, M. (1982) *All That is Solid Melts into Air*. New York: Simon & Schuster.

Berner, E. and Korff, R. (1992) 'Strategies and counterstrategies: globalization and localization from the perspective of the sociology of group conflict', University of Bielefeld, mimeo.

Bhabha, H. K. (1991) '"Race", time and the revision of modernity', *Oxford Literary Review*, 13.

Bhabha, H. K. (1994) *The Location of Culture*. London: Routledge.

Blundell, V., Shepherd, J. and Taylor, I. (eds) (1993) *Relocating Cultural Studies*. London: Routledge.

Bologh, R. W. (1990) *Love or Greatness. Max Weber and Masculine Thinking – a Feminist Inquiry*. London: Unwin Hyman.

Boon, J. (1973) 'Further operations of culture in anthropology', in L. Schneider and C. Bonjean (eds) *The Idea of Culture in the Social Sciences*. Cambridge: Cambridge University Press.

Bourdieu, P. (1977) *Outline of a Theory of Practice*, trans. Richard Nice. Cambridge: Cambridge University Press.

Bourdieu, P. (1979) 'The production of belief: contribution to an economy of symbolic goods', *Media, Culture & Society*, 2: 261–93.

Bourdieu, P. (1980) 'Sartre, or the invention of the total intellectual', *London Review of Books*, 2 (22), 20 Nov–3 Dec.

Bourdieu, P. (1983a) 'The field of cultural production', *Poetics*, 12: 311–56.

Bourdieu, P. (1983b) 'The philosophical institution', in A. Montefiore (ed.) *Philosophy in France*. Cambridge: Cambridge University Press.

Bourdieu, P. (1984) *Distinction: A Social Critique of the Judgement of Taste*, trans. R. Nice. London: Routledge.

Bourdieu, P. (1985) 'The market of symbolic goods', *Poetics*, 14: 13–44.

Bourdieu, P. (1992) 'Thinking about limits', in M. Featherstone (ed.) *Cultural Theory and Cultural Change*. London: Sage.

Bourdieu, P. and Darbel, A. (1966) *L'Amour de l'art*. Paris: Minuit.

Bourdieu, P. and Passeron, J. C. (1971) *La Reproduction*. Paris: Minuit.

Bourdieu, P., Boltanski, L., Castel, R. and Chamboredon, J. C. (1965) *Un Art moyen*. Paris: Minuit.

Bovone, L. (1989) 'Theories of everyday life: a search for meaning or a negation of meaning', *Current Sociology*, 37 (1).

Bradbury, M. and McFarlane, J. (eds) (1976) *Modernism 1890–1930*. Harmondsworth: Penguin.

Brennan, T. (1990) 'The national longing for form', in H. Bhabha (ed.) *Nation and Narration*. London: Routledge.

Brombert, V. (1960) *The Intellectual Hero: Studies in the French Novel 1880–1955*. London: Faber & Faber.

Bruner, E. M. (1989) 'Of cannibals, tourists and ethnographers', *Cultural Anthropology*, 4 (4).

Buci-Glucksmann, C. (1994) *Baroque Reason*. London: Sage.

Buck-Morss, S. (1989) *Dialectic of Seeing: Walter Benjamin and the Arcades Project*. Cambridge, MA: MIT Press.

Burger, P. (1984) *Theory of the Avant-Garde*. Manchester: Manchester University Press.

Burke, P. (1978) *Popular Culture in Early Modern Europe*. London: Temple Smith.

Burke, P. (1989) 'New reflections on world history', *Culture and History*, 5.

Campbell, C. (1987) *The Romantic Ethic and the Spirit of Modern Consumerism*. Oxford: Blackwell.

Canevacci, M. (1992) 'Image accumulation and cultural syncretism', *Theory, Culture & Society*, 9 (3).

Castells, M. (1994) 'European cities, the informational society and the global economy', *New Left Review*, Issue 204: 19–32.

Chambers, I. (1987) 'Maps for the metropolis: a possible guide for the postmodern', *Cultural Studies*, 1 (1).

Chambers, I. (1990) *Border Dialogues: Journeys in Postmodernity*. London: Routledge.

Chambers, I. (1994) *Migrancy, Culture and Identity*. London: Routledge.

Chaney, D. (1986) 'The symbolic form of ritual in mass communication', in P. Golding (ed.) *Communicating Politics*. Leicester: Leicester University Press.

Chatterjee, P. (1993) *The Nation and its Fragments*. Princeton: Princeton University Press.

Clarke, J., Critcher, C. and Johnson, R. (eds) (1979) *Working Class Culture*. London: Hutchinson.

Clegg, S. (1989) *Frameworks of Power*. London: Sage.

Clifford, J. (1988) *The Predicament of Culture*. Cambridge, MA: Harvard University Press.

Clifford, J. (1989) 'Notes on travel and theory', *Inscriptions*, 5: 177–88.

Clifford, J. (1992) 'Traveling cultures', in L. Grossberg, C. Nelson and P. Triechler (eds) *Cultural Studies*. London: Routledge.

Clifford, J. and Marcus, G. (eds) (1986) *Writing Culture*. Berkeley: California University Press.

Cohen, A. (1985) *The Symbolic Construction of Community*. London: Tavistock.

Connerton, P. (1989) *How Society Remembers*. Cambridge: Cambridge University Press.

Connolly, W. (1994) 'Tocqueville, territory and violence', *Theory, Culture & Society*, 11 (1).

Cooke, P. (1988) 'Modernity, postmodernity and the city', *Theory, Culture & Society*, 5 (2–3).

Cooke, P. (1990a) *Back to the Future: Modernity, Postmodernity and Locality*. London: Unwin Hyman.

Cooke, P. (1990b) 'Locality, structure and agency: a theoretical analysis', *Cultural Anthropology*, 5 (1).

Cornwall, A. and Lindisfarne, N. (eds) (1994) *Dislocating Masculinity*. London: Routledge.

Coser, L. (1977) 'George Simmel', in *Masters of Sociological Thought*, 2nd edn. New York: Harcourt Brace Jovanovich.

Crane, D. (1987) *The Transformation of the Avant-Garde*. Chicago: Chicago University Press.

Crapanzo, V. (1980) *Tuhami: Portrait of a Moroccan*. Chicago: Chicago University Press.

Crapanzo, V. (1992) *Hermes' Dilemma and Hamlet's Desire. On the Epistemology of Interpretation*. Cambridge, MA: Harvard University Press.

Critcher, C. (1979) 'Sociology, cultural studies and the postwar working class', in J. Clarke, C. Critcher and R. Johnson (eds) *Working Class Culture*. London: Hutchinson.

Culler, J. (1983) *On Deconstruction*. London: Routledge.

Dahrendorf, R. (1987) 'Max Weber and modern social science', in W. J. Mommsen and J. Osterhammel (eds) *Max Weber and his Contemporaries*. London: Allen & Unwin.

Darnton, R. (1983) *The Literary Underground of the Old Regime*. Cambridge, MA: Harvard University Press.

Davidoff, L. (1973) *The Best Circles: Society, Etiquette and Season*. London: Croom Helm.

Davis, F. (1974) *Yearning for Yesterday: A Sociology of Nostalgia*. New York: Free Press.

Davis, M. (1992) 'Beyond *Blade Runner*: urban control and the ecology of fear', Westfield, NJ: Open Magazine Pamphlet Series.

de Certeau, M. (1981) 'The discovery of everyday life, a sample', *Tabloid*, 3: 24–30.

de Certeau, M. (1984) *The Practice of Everyday Life*. Berkeley: California University Press.

Debord, G. (1970) *Society of the Spectacle*. Detroit: Red & Black.

Deleuze, G. and Guattari, F. (1983) *Anti-Oedipus*. Minneapolis: Minnesota University Press.

Deleuze, G. and Guattari, F. (1987) *A Thousand Plateaus: Capitalism and Schizophrenia*. Minneapolis: Minnesota University Press.

Dennis, N., Henriques, F. and Slaughter, C. (1956) *Coal is Our Life*. London: Tavistock.

Derrida, J. (1973) *Speech and Phenomena (and Other Essays) on Husserl's Theory of Signs*. Evanston: Northwestern University Press.

Dezalay, Y. (1990) 'The big bang and the law', in M. Featherstone (ed.) *Global Culture*. London: Sage.

Donaldson, P. (1975) *Edward VIII*. Philadelphia.

Dorfman, A. and Mattelart, A. (1975) *How to Read Donald Duck*. New York: International General Editions.

Douglas, M. and Isherwood, B. (1980) *The World of Goods*. Harmondsworth: Penguin.

Dumont, L. (1986) 'Collective identities and universalist ideology: the actual interplay', *Theory, Culture & Society*, 3 (3): 25–34.

Durkheim, E. (1961) *The Elementary Forms of the Religious Life*. New York: Collier.

Durkheim, E. (1969) 'Individualism and the intellectuals', *Political Studies*, 17.

Dyan, D. and Katz, E. (1988) 'Articulating consensus: the ritual and rhetoric of media events', in J. C. Alexander (ed.) *Durkheimian Sociology: Cultural Studies*. Cambridge: Cambridge University Press.

Dyer, R. (1979) *Stars*. London: British Film Institute.

Eagleton, T. (1984) *The Function of Criticism*. London: Verso.

Eckstein, M. (1990) *The Rites of Spring. The Great War and the Birth of the Modern Age*. New York: Doubleday.

Elias, N. (1971) 'Sociology of knowledge: new perspectives, part 1', *Sociology*, 5.

Elias, N. (1978) *The Civilizing Process, Volume 1: the History of Manners*. Oxford: Blackwell.

Elias, N. (1982) *The Civilizing Process Volume 2: State Formation and Civilization*. Oxford: Blackwell.

Elias, N. (1983) *The Court Society*. Oxford: Blackwell.

Elias, N. (1984) 'On the sociogenesis of sociology', *Sociologisch Tijdschrift*, 11 (1).

Elias, N. (1987a) 'The retreat of sociologists into the present', *Theory, Culture & Society*, 4 (2–3).

Elias, N. (1987b) 'The changing balance of power between the sexes', *Theory, Culture & Society*, 4 (2–3).

Elias, N. (1987c) *Involvement and Detachment*. Oxford: Blackwell.

Elias, N. (1987d) Interview with M. Featherstone *et al.*, University of Teesside, mimeo.

Elias, N. and E. Dunning (1987) *Quest for Excitement: Sport and Leisure in the Civilizing Process*. Oxford: Blackwell.

Elias, N. and Scotson, J. L. (1994) *The Established and the Outsiders*, revised edn. London: Sage.

Enloe, C. (1989) *Bananas, Beaches and Bases: Feminism and International Politics*. Berkeley: California University Press.

Ewen, S. (1976) *Captains of Consciousness: Advertising and the Social Roots of the Consumer Culture*. New York: McGraw-Hill.

Ewen, S. and Ewen, E. (1982) *Channels of Desire*. New York: McGraw-Hill.

Eyerman, R. and Lofgren, O. (1995) 'Road movies', *Theory, Culture & Society*, 12 (1).

Featherstone, M. (1990) 'Global culture: an introduction', in M. Featherstone (ed.) *Global Culture*. London: Sage.

Featherstone, M. (1991a) *Consumer Culture and Postmodernism*. London: Sage.

Featherstone, M. (1991b) 'Georg Simmel: an introduction', *Theory, Culture & Society*, 8 (3): 1–16.

Featherstone, M. (1995) in M. Featherstone and A. Wernick (eds) *Images of Ageing*. London: Routledge.

Featherstone, M. and Burrows, R. (eds) (1995) *Cyberbodies, Cyberspace and Cyberpunk*. London: Sage. (Also special issue of *Body & Society* 1 (3), 1995.

Featherstone, M. and Lash, S. (1995) 'Globalization, modernity and the spatialization of social theory', in M. Featherstone, S. Lash and R. Robertson (eds) *Global Modernities*. London: Sage.

Fechter, P. (1948) *Menschen und Zeiten*. Gutersloh: Berdelsmann.

Feldman-Bianco, Bella (1992) 'Multiple layers of time and space: the construction of class, ethnicity and nationalism among Portuguese immigrants', in N. G. Schiller, L. Basch and C. Blanc-Szanton (eds.) *Towards a Transnational Perspective on Migration: Race, Class, Ethnicity and Nationalism Reconsidered*. Annals of the New York Academy of Science, Vol. 645. New York: New York Academy of Sciences.

Fiefer, M. (1985) *Going Places*. London: Macmillan.

Fiske, J. and Hartley, J. (1978) *Reading Television*. London: Methuen.

Fiske, J., Hodge, B. and Turner, G. (eds) (1987) *Myths of Oz*. Sydney: Allen & Unwin.

Fjellman, S. J. (1992) *Vinyl Leaves: Walt Disney World and America*. Boulder, CO: Westview Press.

Foucault, M. (1971) *Madness and Civilization*. London: Tavistock.

Foucault, M. (1986) 'What is enlightenment?', in P. Rabinow (ed.) *The Foucault Reader*. Harmondsworth: Penguin.

Foucault, M. (1987) *The Use of Pleasure*. Harmondsworth: Penguin.

Frankenberg, R. (1966) *Communities in Britain*. Harmondsworth: Penguin.

Friedman, J. (1987) 'Prolegomena to the adventures of Phallus in Blunderland: an anti-anti discourse', *Culture & History*, 1 (1).

Friedman, J. (1988) 'Cultural logics of the global system', *Theory, Culture & Society*, 5 (2–3), special issue on postmodernism.

Friedman, J. (1990) 'Being in the world: globalization and localization', in M. Featherstone (ed.) *Global Culture*. London: Sage.

Friedman, J. (1992) 'Narcissism, roots and postmodernity: the constitution of selfhood in the global crisis', in S. Lash and J. Friedman (eds) *Modernity and Identity*. Oxford: Blackwell.

Frisby, D. (1981) *Sociological Impressionism: A Reassessment of Georg Simmel's Social Theory*. London: Heinemann.

Frisby, D. (1985a) 'Georg Simmel, first sociologist of modernity', *Theory, Culture & Society*, 2 (3).

Frisby, D. (1985b) *Fragments of Modernity*. Cambridge: Polity.

Frisby, D. and Sayer, D. (1986) *Society*. London: Tavistock.

Frith, S. (1983) *Sound Effects: Youth, Leisure and the Politics of Rock 'n' Roll*. London: Constable.

Frith, S. and Horne, H. (1987) *Art into Pop*. London: Methuen.

Fussell, P. (1980) *Abroad. British Literary Travelling between the Wars*. Oxford: Oxford University Press.

Fussell, P. (1982) *The Great War and Modern Memory*. Oxford: Oxford University Press.

Gabriel, T. H. (1990) 'Thoughts on nomadic aesthetics and the black independent cinema: traces of a journey', in R. Ferguson, M. Gever, T. T. Minh-ha and C. West (eds) *Out There: Marginalization and Contemporary Culture*. Cambridge, MA: MIT Press.

Game, A. (1990) 'Nation and identity: Bondi', *New Formations*, 11.

Game, A. (1991) *Undoing the Social*. Milton Keynes: Open University Press.

Gay, P. (1973) *The Enlightenment*, vol. 1. London: Wildwood House.

Geertz, C. (1983) *Local Knowledge*. New York: Harper.

Gellner, E. (1983) *Nations and Nationalism*. Oxford: Blackwell.

Gerth, H. H. and Mills, C. W. (1948) *From Max Weber*. London: Routledge.

Gessner, V. and Schade, A. (1990) 'Conflicts of culture in cross-border legal relations', *Theory, Culture & Society*, 7 (2–3).

Giddens, A. (1990) *The Consequences of Modernity*. Cambridge: Polity Press.

Giddens, A. (1991) *Modernity and Self-Identity*. Cambridge: Polity Press.

Giddens, A. (1994) 'Living in a post-traditional society', in U. Beck, A. Giddens and S. Lash (eds) *Reflexive Modernization*. Cambridge: Polity.

Gilroy, P. (1993) *The Black Atlantic*. London: Verso.

Gledhill, C. (1991) *Stardom: Industry of Desire*. London: Routledge.

Goldman, H. (1988) *Max Weber and Thomas Mann*. Berkeley: California University Press.

Goldman, R. and Wilson, J. (1983) 'Appearance and essence: the commodity form revealed in perfume advertisements', *Current Perspectives in Social Theory*, 4.

Goldscheid, R. (1904) 'Review of *Philosophie des Geldes*', *Archiv für systematische Philosophie*, 10.

Gooding-Williams, R. (1987) 'Nietzsche's pursuit of modernism', *New German Critique*, 41.

Gouldner, A. (1975) 'Sociology and the everyday life', in L. Coser (ed.) *The Idea of Social Science*. New York: Harcourt, Brace and World.

Grafton, A. (1992) *New Worlds, Ancient Texts: the Power and Shock of Discovery*. Cambridge, MA: Harvard University Press.

Green, B. S. (1988) *Literary Methods and Sociological Theory: Case Studies of Simmel and Weber*. Chicago: Chicago University Press.

Green, M. (1976) *The von Richthoven Sisters*. New York: Basic Books.

Grossberg, L., Nelson, C. and Triechler, P. (eds) (1992) *Cultural Studies*. London: Routledge.

Gungwu, Wang (1993) 'Migration and its enemies', in B. Mazlish and R. Builtjens (eds) *Conceptualizing Global History*. Boulder, CO: Westview Press.

Gupta, S. (ed.) (1993) *Disrupted Borders*. London: Rivers Oram Press.

Gupta, A. and Ferguson, J. (1992) 'Beyond "culture": space, identity, and the politics of difference', *Cultural Anthropology*, 7 (1): 6–23.

Habermas, J. (1974) 'The public sphere', *New German Critique*, 3.

Habermas, J. (1981) *Theorie des Kommunikativen Handelns*, Frankfurt am Main: Suhrkamp.

Habermas, J. (1984a) *The Theory of Communicative Action Volume 1*. London: Heinemann.

Habermas, J. (1984b) 'Remettre le mobile en mouvement', *Le monde d'aujourd'hui*, 6 August.

Habermas, J. (1988) *The Philosophical Discourse of Modernity*. Cambridge: Polity.

Habermas, J. (1989) *The Structural Transformation of the Public Sphere*. Cambridge: Polity.

Haferkamp, H. (1987) 'Beyond the iron cage of modernity', *Theory, Culture & Society*, 4 (1).

Halbwachs, M. (1992) *On Collective Memory*. Chicago: Chicago University Press.

Hall, C. (1992) *White, Male and Middle Class*. Cambridge: Polity.

Hall, S. (1991) 'Old and new identities', in A. King (ed.) *Culture*. London: Sage.

Hall, S. (1992a) 'Introduction', to S. Hall and B. Gieben (eds) *Formation of Modernity*. Cambridge: Polity.

Hall, S. (1992b) 'The question of cultural identity', in S. Hall, D. Held and T. McGrew (eds) *Modernity and its Futures*. Cambridge: Polity.

Hall, S. (1992c) 'The rest and the West: discourse and power', in S. Hall and B. Gieben (eds) *Formation of Modernity*. Cambridge: Polity.

Hall, S., Hobson, D., Lowe, D. and Willis, P. (eds) (1980) *Culture, Media and Language*. London: Hutchinson.

Hannerz, U. (1990) 'Cosmopolitans and locals in world culture', *Theory, Culture & Society*, 7 (2–3).

Hannerz, U. (1991) 'Scenarios for peripheral cultures', in A. King (ed.) *Culture, Globalization and the World-System*. London: Macmillan.

Harvey, D. (1989) *The Condition of Postmodernity*. Oxford: Blackwell.

Hatch, E. (1973) *Theories of Culture*. New York: Columbia University Press.

Hebdige, D. (1979) *Subculture: The Meaning of Style*. London: Methuen.

Hebdige, D. (1982) 'The cultural politics of pop', *Block*.

Hebdige, D. (1988) *Hiding in the Light*. London: Routledge.

Held, D. (1980) *Introduction to Critical Theory*. London: Hutchinson.

Heller, A. (1978) *Renaissance Man*. London: Routledge.

Heller, A. (1984) *Everyday Life*. London: Routledge.

Heller, A. (1990) *Can Modernity Survive?* Cambridge: Polity.

Hennis, W. (1988) *Max Weber: Essays in Reconstruction*. London: Allen & Unwin.

Henrich, D. (1987) 'Karl Jaspers: thinking with Max Weber in mind', in W. J. Mommsen and J. Osterhammel (eds) *Max Weber and his Contemporaries*. London: Allen & Unwin.

Higson, A. (1989) 'The concept of national cinema', *Screen*, 30 (4).

Hirsch, F. (1976) *The Social Limits to Growth*. London: Routledge.

Hoggart, R. (1957) *The Uses of Literacy*. Harmondsworth: Penguin.

Hohendahl, P. U. (1982) *The Institution of Criticism*. Ithaca, NY: Cornell University Press.

Horkheimer, M. and Adorno, T. (1972) *Dialectic of Enlightenment*. New York: Herder & Herder.

Huyssen, A. (1986) 'Mass culture as women: modernism's other', in *After the Great Divide*. Bloomington: Indiana University Press.

Iyer, P. (1989) *Video Nights in Kathmandu: Reports from the Not-So-Far East*. London: Black Swan.

Jackson, B. (1968) *Working Class Community*. London: Routledge.

Jacoby, R. (1987) *The Last Intellectuals*. New York: Basic Books.

Jameson, F. (1979) 'Reification and utopia in mass culture', *Social Text*, 1 (1).

Jameson, F. (1984a) 'Postmodernism or the cultural logic of late capitalism', *New Left Review*, 146: 52–92.

Jameson, F. (1984b) 'Postmodernism and the consumer society', in H. Foster (ed.) *Postmodern Culture*. London: Pluto.

Jaspers, K. (1989) *Karl Jaspers on Max Weber*. New York: Paragon House.

Jusserand, J. J. (1973) *English Wayfaring Life in the Middle Ages*. Boston: Milford House.

Kamper, D. (1990) 'After modernism: outline of an aesthetics of posthistory', *Theory, Culture & Society*, 7 (1).

Kaplan, E. A. (1987) *Rocking around the Clock*. London: Methuen.

Kasson, J. F. (1990) *Rudeness and Civility*. New York: Hill & Wang.

Kellner, D. (1983) 'Critical theory, commodities and the consumer society', *Theory, Culture & Society*, 3 (3): 66–83.

Kern, S. (1983) *The Culture of Time and Space 1880–1918*. Cambridge, MA: Harvard University Press.

King, A. D. (1990a) 'Architecture, capital and the globalization of culture', in M. Featherstone (ed.) *Global Culture*. London: Macmillan.

King, A. D. (1990b) *Global Cities*. London: Routledge.

King, A. D. (1995) 'The times and spaces of modernity (or who needs postmodernism?)' in M. Featherstone, S. Lash and R. Robertson (eds) *Global Modernities*. London: Sage.

Kirkpatrick, John (1989) 'Trials of identity in America', *Cultural Anthropology*, 4 (3): 301–11.

Kitto, H. D. F. (1951) *The Greeks*. Harmondsworth: Penguin.

Klapp, O. E. (1969) *The Collective Search for Identity*. New York: Holt, Rinehart & Winston.

Knorr-Cetina, K. (1981) *The Manufacture of Knowledge. An Essay on the Constructivist and Contextual Nature of Science*. Oxford: Pergamon.

Knorr-Cetina, K. (1994) 'Primitive classification and postmodernity: towards a sociological notion of fiction', *Theory, Culture & Society*, 11 (3).

Krauss, R. (1984) 'The originality of the avant-garde: a postmodern repetition', in B. Wallis (ed.) *Art after Modernism*. New York: Museum of Contemporary Art.

Kroeber, A. L. (1948) 'The nature of culture', in *Cultural Patterns and Processes*. New York: Harcourt, Brace and World.

Kroker, A. and Cook, D. (1988) *The Postmodern Scene*. New York: St Martin's Press.

Laing, S. (1986) *Representations of Working Class Life 1957–1964*. London: Macmillan.

Lamont, M. and Lareau, A. (1988) 'Cultural capital: elisons, gaps and glissandos in recent theoretical developments', *Sociological Theory*, 6 (2): 153–68.

Las Casas, B. de (1992) *A Short Account of the Destruction of the Indies*. Harmondsworth: Penguin.

Lasch, C. (1991) *The True and Only Heaven: Progress and Its Critics*. New York: Norton.

Lash, S. (1988) 'Discourse or figure', *Theory, Culture & Society*, 5 (2–3).

Lash, S. and Urry, J. (1987) *The End of Organized Capitalism*. Cambridge: Polity.

Lash, S. and Urry, J. (1993) *Economies of Signs and Spaces*. London: Sage.

Lassman, P. and Velody, I. with Martins, H. (eds) (1989) *Max Weber's Science as a Vocation*. London: Unwin Hyman.

Latour, B. (1987) *Science in Action*. Milton Keynes: Open University Press.

Latour, B. (1993) *We Have Never Been Modern*. Hemel Hempstead: Harvester Wheatsheaf.

Leed, E. J. (1991) *The Mind of the Traveler*. New York: Basic Books.

Lefebvre, H. (1971) *Everyday Life in the Modern World*. Harmondsworth: Penguin, orig. publ. 1968.

Leiss, W. (1978) *The Limits to Satisfaction*. London: Marion Boyars.

Leiss, W. (1983) 'The icons of the marketplace', *Theory, Culture & Society*, 1 (3).

Leiss, W., Kline, S. and Jhally, S. (1986) *Social Communication in Advertising*. London: Methuen.

Levine, D. (1965) *Wax and Gold: Tradition and Innovation in Ethiopian Culture*. Chicago: Chicago University Press.

Levine, D. (1985) *The Flight from Ambiguity*. Chicago: Chicago University Press.

Levi-Strauss, C. (1976) *Tristes Tropiques*. Harmondsworth: Penguin.

Ley, D. (1989) 'Modernism, post-modernism and the struggle for place', in J. A. Agnew and J. A. Duncan (eds) *The Power of Place*. London: Unwin Hyman.

Lichtblau, K. (1995) 'Sociology and the diagnosis of the times: or the reflexivity of modernity', *Theory, Culture & Society*, 12 (1).

Liebersohn, H. (1988) *Fate and Utopia in German Sociology 1870–1923*. Cambridge, MA: MIT Press.

Liebersohn, H. (1989–90) 'Review of Marianne Weber *Max Weber: A Biography*, with a new Introduction by Guenther Roth', *Telos*, 78.

Liu, A. (1990) 'Local transcendence: cultural criticism, postmodernism and the romanticism of detail', *Representations*, 32.

Linder, H. S. (1970) *The Harried Leisure Class*. New York: Columbia University Press.

Lindholm, C. (1990) *Charisma*. Oxford: Blackwell.

Lowenthal, L. (1961) *Literature, Popular Culture and Society*. Palo Alto: Pacific Books.

Luke, T. (1995) 'New world order or new world orders? Power, politics and ideology in the informationalizing glocal order', in M. Featherstone, S. Lash and R. Robertson (eds) *Global Modernities*. London: Sage.

Lunn, E. (1986) 'Cultural populism and egalitarian democracy', *Theory and Society*, 15: 479–517.

Lutkehaus, N. C. (1989) '"Excuse me, everything is not all right": an interview with film-maker Dennis O'Rourke', *Cultural Anthropology*, 4 (4).

Lynd, D. and Lynd, H. (1929) *Middletown*. New York: Harcourt Brace.

Lynd, D. and Lynd, H. (1937) *Middletown in Transition*. New York: Harcourt Brace.

Lyotard, J.-F. (1984) *The Postmodern Condition*. Manchester: Manchester University Press.

MacCannell D. (1992) *Empty Meeting Grounds. The Tourist Papers*. London: Routledge.

McGrane, B. (1989) *Beyond Anthropology: Society and the Other*. New York: Columbia University Press.

McKendrick, N., Brewer, J. and Plumb, J. H. (1982) *The Birth of a Consumer Society*. London: Europa.

MacIntyre, A. (1981) *After Virtue*. London: Duckworth.

Maffesoli, M. (1988) *Le Temps des tribus*. Paris: Meridiens Klincksiek.

Maffesoli, M. (1989) 'The sociology of everyday life (epistemological elements)', *Current Sociology*, 37 (1).

Maffesoli, M. (1991) 'The ethic of aesthetics', *Theory, Culture & Society*, 8 (1).

Maffesoli, M. (1995) *The Time of the Tribes*. London: Sage.

Malkki, Liisa (1992) '*National Geographic*: the rooting of peoples and the territorialization of national identity among scholars and refugees', *Cultural Anthropology*, 7: 24–44.

Manasse, E.M. (1957) 'Jaspers' relation to Weber', in P. A. Schlipp (ed.) *The Philosophy of Karl Jaspers*. New York: Tudor Publishing.

Mandel, E. (1975) *Late Capitalism*. London: New Left Books.

Mannheim, K. (1956) 'The problem of the intelligentsia', in E, Mannheim and P. Kecskennseti (eds) *Essays on the Sociology of Culture*. London: Routledge.

Maravall, J. A. (1986) *Culture of the Baroque*. Manchester: Manchester University Press.

Marcus, G. (1992a) 'Past, present and emergent identities: requirements for ethnography in late twentieth century modernity', in S. Lash and J. Friedman (eds) *Modernity and Identity*. Oxford: Blackwell.

Marcus, G. (ed.) (1992b) *Rereading Cultural Anthropology*. Durham, NC: Duke University Press.

Marcus, G. and Fischer, M. M. J. (1986) *Anthropology as Cultural Critique*. Chicago: Chicago University Press.

Marcuse, H. (1964) *One-dimensional Man*. London: Routledge.

Marshall, G. (1982) *In Search of the Spirit of Capitalism*. London: Hutchinson.

Martin, B. (1981) *A Sociology of Contemporary Cultural Change*. Oxford: Blackwell.

Maruyama, M. (1969) *Thought and Behaviour in Japanese Politics*. London: Oxford University Press.

Mattelart, A. (1979) *Multinational Corporations and the Control of Culture*. Brighton: Harvester.

Maunier, J. (1949) *The Sociology of the Colonies*. London: Routledge.

Maybury-Lewis, D. (1992a) 'On the importance of being tribal', *Utney Reader*, 52 (July–August).

Maybury-Lewis, D. (1992b) *Millennium: Tribal Wisdom and the Modern World*. New York: Viking Penguin.

Mazlish, B. (1994) 'The *flâneur*: from spectator to representation', in K. Tester (ed.) *The Flâneur*. London: Routledge.

Mellencamp, P. (ed.) (1990) *The Logics of Television*. Bloomington: Indiana University Press.

Mennell, S. (1985) *All Manners of Food*. Oxford: Blackwell.

Mennell, S. (1987) 'On the civilizing of appetite', *Theory, Culture & Society*, 4 (2–3): 373–403.

Mennell, S. (1989) *Norbert Elias*. Oxford: Blackwell.

Merleau-Ponty, M. (1964a) 'The eye and the mind', in *The Primacy of Perception*. Evanston: Northwestern University Press.

Merleau-Ponty, M. (1964b) *Sense and Non-Sense*. Evanston: Northwestern University Press.

Meyrowitz, J. (1985) *No Sense of Place*. Oxford: Oxford University Press.

Middleton, D. and Edwards, D. (eds) (1990) *Collective Remembering*. London: Sage.

Minh-ha, Trinh T. (1989) *Woman, Native, Other. Writing Postcoloniality and Feminism*. Bloomington: Indiana University Press.

Minchinton, W. (1982) 'Convention, fashion and consumption: aspects of British experience since 1750', in H. Baudel and H. van der Meulen (eds) *Consumer Behaviour and Economic Growth*. London: Croom Helm.

Mintz, S. (1988) *The Power of Sweetness and the Sweetness of Power* (8th Duiker Lecture). Deventer: Van Loghum Slaterus.

Mitsuhiro, Y. (1989) 'Postmodernism and mass images in Japan', *Public Culture*, 1 (2).

Mitterauer, M. (1992) *A History of Youth*. Oxford: Blackwell.

Miyoshi, M. (1991) *Off Center: Power and Culture Relations between Japan and the United States*. Cambridge: Harvard University Press.

Miyoshi, M. and Harootunian, H. (1989a) 'Introduction', in H. Harootunian and M. Myoshi (eds) *Postmodernism and Japan*. Durham, NC: Duke University Press.

Miyoshi, M. and Harootunian, H. (eds) (1989b) *Postmodernism and Japan*. Durham, NC: Duke University Press.

Moch, L. P. (1992) *Moving Europeans. Migrations in Western Europe Since 1650*. Bloomington: Indiana University Press.

Mollenkopf, J. and Castells, M. (eds) (1991) *Dual City: Restructuring New York*. New York: Russell Sage Foundation.

Monk, R. (1990) *Ludwig Wittgenstein*. London: Cape.

Moore, P. (ed.) (1989) *Genius: The History of an Idea*. Oxford: Blackwell.

Moore, S. F. (1989) 'The production of cultural pluralism as a process', *Public Culture*, 1 (2).

Moore, W. E. (1966) 'Global sociology: the world as a singular system', *American Journal of Sociology*, 71.

Morley, D. (1991) 'Where the global meets the local: notes from the sitting room', *Screen*, 32 (1).

Morris, M. (1990) 'Banality in cultural studies', in P. Mellencamp (ed.) *Logics of Television*. Bloomington: Indiana University Press.

Morris, M. (1992) 'The man in the mirror: David Harvey's *Condition of Postmodernity*', in M. Featherstone (ed.) *Cultural Theory and Cultural Change*. London: Sage.

Moscovici, S. (1990) 'Questions for the twenty-first century', *Theory, Culture & Society*, 7 (4).

New Formations (1983) *Formations of Pleasure*. London: Routledge.

Nicholson, L. J. (ed.) (1990) *Feminism/Postmodernism*. London: Routledge.

Nisbet, R. (1967) *The Sociological Tradition*. London: Heinemann.

Obeyeskere, G. (1992) *The Apotheosis of Captain Cook*. Princeton: Princeton University Press.

O'Pray, M. (ed.) (1989) *Andy Warhol Film Factory*. London: British Film Institute.

Osborne, P. (1992) 'Modernity is a qualitative, not a chronological category', in F. Barker, P. Hulme and M. Iverson (eds) *Postmodernism and the Re-reading of Modernity*. Manchester: Manchester University Press.

Pearson, G. (1985) 'Lawlessness, Modernity and Social Change', *Theory, Culture & Society*, 2 (3).

Pels, D. and Crebas, A. (1988) '*Carmen* or the invention of a new feminine myth', *Theory, Culture & Society*, 5 (4). Reprinted in M. Featherstone, M. Hepworth and B. S. Turner (eds) *The Body: Social Process and Cultural Theory*. London: Sage [1991].

Portis, E. B. (1973) 'Max Weber's theory of personality', *Sociological Inquiry*, 48 (2).

Preteceille, E. and Terrail, J. P. (1985) *Capitalism, Consumption and Needs*. Oxford: Blackwell.

Reddy, W. M. (1984) *The Rise of Market Culture*. Cambridge: Cambridge University Press.

Richards, J. (1984) *The Age of the Dream Palace: Cinema and Society in Britain 1930–1939*. London: Routledge.

Richardson, M. (1992) 'The sacred and the Collège de Sociologie', *Theory, Culture & Society*, 9 (3).

Rieff, P. (1990) 'The impossible culture: Wilde as a modern prophet', in *The Feeling Intellect*. Chicago: Chicago University Press.

Ritzer, G. (1993) *The McDonaldization of Society*. London: Sage.

Robertson, R. (1982) 'Review of D. Frisby *Sociological Impressionism*', *Theory, Culture & Society*, 1 (1).

Robertson, R. (1990a) 'Mapping the global condition', in M. Featherstone (ed.) *Global Culture*. London: Sage.

Robertson, R. (1990b) 'After nostalgia? Wilful nostalgia and the phase of globalization', in B. S. Turner (ed.) *Theories of Modernity and Postmodernity*. London: Sage.

Robertson, R. (1991) 'Social, theory, cultural relativity and the problem of globality', in A. D. King (ed.) *Culture, Globalization and the World System*. New York: Macmillan.

Robertson, R. (1992a) *Globalization*. London: Sage.

Robertson, R. (1992b) 'Globality and modernity', *Theory, Culture & Society*, 9 (2).

Robertson, R. (1995) 'Glocalization: time–space and homogeneity–heterogeneity', in M. Featherstone, S. Lash and R. Robertson (eds) *Global Modernities*. London: Sage.

Rojek, C. (1995) *Decentring Leisure*. London: Sage.

Roth, G. (1988) 'Introduction to Marianne Weber', *Max Weber: A Biography*. 2nd edn. New York: Wiley.

Rorty, R. (1986) 'Freud and moral reflection', in J. H. Smith and W. Kerrigan (eds) *Pragmatism's Freud*. Baltimore: Johns Hopkins University Press.

Rosaldo, R. (1993) *Culture and Truth: the Remaking of Social Analysis*. London: Routledge.

Sahlins, M. (1976) *Culture and Practical Reason*. Chicago: Chicago University Press.

Said, E. W. (1978) *Orientalism*. Harmondsworth: Penguin.

Said, E. W. (1993) *Culture and Imperialism*. New York: Vintage.

Sakai, N. (1989) 'Modernity and its critique: the problem of universalism and particularism', in M. Miyoshi and H. D. Harootunian (eds) *Postmodernism and Japan*. Durham, NC: Duke University Press.

Sassen, S. (1991) *Global Cities: New York, London, Tokyo*. Princeton: Princeton University Press.

Sayre, H. M. (1989) *The Object of Performance: The American Avant-Garde since 1970*. Chicago: Chicago University Press.

Scaff, L. A. (1989) *Fleeing the Iron Cage: Culture, Politics and Modernity in the Thought of Max Weber*. Berkeley: California University Press.

Scaff, L. A. (1990) 'Georg Simmel's theory of culture', in M. Kaern, B. S. Phillips and R. S. Cohen (eds) *Georg Simmel and Contemporary Sociology*. Dordrecht: Kluwer.

Scheff, T. J. (1990) 'Language acquisition versus formal education: a theory of genius', in *Microsociology: Discourse, Emotion and Social Structure*. Chicago: Chicago University Press.

Schiller, H. I. (1976) *Communications and Cultural Domination*. New York: Sharpe.

Schiller, H. I. (1985) 'Electronic information flows: new basis for global domination?', in P. Drummond and R. Patterson (eds) *Television in Transition*. London: British Film Institute.

Schor, N. (1987) *Reading in Detail: Aesthetics and the Feminine*. London: Methuen.

Schutz, A. (1962) 'On multiple realities', in *Collected Papers Volume 1*. The Hague: Nijhoff.

Schutz, A. (1964) 'Don Quixote and the problem of reality', in *Collected Papers Volume 3*. The Hague: Nijhoff.

Schwentker, W. (1987) 'Passion as a mode of life: Max Weber, the Otto Gross Circle and eroticism', in W. J. Mommsen and J. Osterhammel (eds) *Max Weber and his Contemporaries*. London: Allen & Unwin.

Seed, J. and Wolff, J. (eds) (1988) *The Culture of Capital: Art, Power and the Nineteenth-Century Middle Class*. Manchester: Manchester University Press.

Seigel, J. (1986) *Bohemian Paris*. New York: Viking.

Serres, M. (1991) *Rome: the Book of Foundations*. Stanford, CA: Stanford University Press.

Sharrock. W. and Anderson, B. (1986) *The Ethnomethodologists*. London: Tavistock.

Shils, E. (1960) 'Mass society and its culture', *Daedalus*, 89 (2): 288–314.

Shotter, J. (1993) *Cultural Politics of Everyday Life*. Milton Keynes: Open University Press.

Shusterman, R. (1988) 'Postmodern aestheticism: a new moral philosophy?', *Theory, Culture & Society*, 5 (2–3).

Simmel, G. (1923) 'Rodin', in *Philosophische Kultur*, 3rd edn. Potsdam.

Simmel, G. (1968) 'On the concept of the tragedy of culture', in *The Conflict in Modern Culture and Other Essays*. New York: Teachers College Press.

Simmel, G. (1971a) 'The adventurer' in D. L. Levine (ed.) *Georg Simmel on Individuality and Social Forms*. Chicago: Chicago University Press.

Simmel, G. (1971b) 'Sociability', in D. L. Levine (ed.) *Georg Simmel on Individuality and Social Forms*. Chicago: Chicago University Press.

Simmel, G. (1971c) 'Subjective culture', in D. L. Levine (ed.) *Georg Simmel on Individuality and Social Forms*. Chicago: Chicago University Press.

Simmel, G. (1971d) 'The metropolis and mental life', in D. Levine (ed.) *Georg Simmel on Individuality and Social Forms*. Chicago: Chicago University Press.

Simmel, G. (1977) *The Problem of a Philosophy of History*, trans. and ed. G. Oakes, New York: Free Press.

Simmel, G. (1978) *The Philosophy of Money*, trans. T. Bottomore and D. Frisby. London: Routledge.

Simmel, G. (1983) *Philosophische Kultur*. Berlin: Wagenbach.

Simmel, G. (1986) *Schopenhauer and Nietzsche*. Amherst: Massachusetts University Press.

Simmel, G. (1990) *The Philosophy of Money*, 2nd edn, trans. D Frisby. London: Routledge

Simmel, G. (1991) 'The Berlin Trade Exhibition', *Theory, Culture & Society*, 8 (3).

Simmel, G. (1995) 'Fashion', in D. Frisby and M. Featherstone (eds) *Simmel on Culture*. London: Sage.

Smart, B. (1990) 'Modernity, postmodernity and the present', in B. S. Turner (ed.) *Theories of Modernity and Postmodernity*. London: Sage.

Smith, A. D. (1990) 'Towards a global culture?' *Theory, Culture & Society*, 5 (2–3).

Soja, E. (1989) *Postmodern Geographies*. London: Verso.

Springborg, P. (1981) *The Problem of Human Needs and the Critique of Civilisation*. London: Allen & Unwin.

Stallybrass, P. and White, A. (1986) *The Politics and Poetics of Transgression*. London: Methuen.

Staude, J. R. (1967) *Max Scheler: An Intellectual Portrait 1874–1928*. New York: Free Press.

Staude, J. R. (1990) 'George Simmel and Max Scheler', University of Teesside, mimeo.

Stauth, G. and Turner, B. S. (1988a) *Nietzsche's Dance*. Oxford: Blackwell.

Stauth, G. and Turner, B. S. (1988b) 'Nostalgia, postmodernism and the critique of mass culture', *Theory, Culture & Society*, 5 (2–3): 509–26.

Stead, P. (1989) *Film and the Working Class*. London: Routledge.

Stein, M. (1960) *Eclipse of Community*. New York: Harper.

Suttles, G. (1991) 'Preface', to *Kamikaze Biker*. Chicago: Chicago University Press.

Swanson, G. E. (1992) 'Modernity and the postmodern', *Theory, Culture & Society*, 9 (2).

Swingewood, A. (1977) *The Myth of Mass Culture*. London: Methuen.

Tagg, J. (1991) 'Globalization, totalization and the discursive field', in A. King (ed.) *Culture, Globalization and the World-System*. London: Macmillan.

Taussig, M. (1980) *The Devil and Commodity Fetishism in South America*. Chapel Hill: North Carolina University Press.

Taussig, M. (1987) *Shamanism, Colonialism and the Wild Man: A Study of Terror and Healing*. Chicago: Chicago University Press.

Taylor, C. (1992) *The Politics of Multiculturalism*. Princeton: Princeton University Press.

Tenbruck, F. (1980) 'The problem of thematic unity in the work of Max Weber', *British Journal of Sociology*, 31.

Tenbruck, F. (1990) 'The dream of a secular ecumene: the meaning and politics of development', in M. Featherstone (ed.) *Global Culture*. London: Sage.

Tenbruck, F. (1994) 'History of society or universal history', *Theory, Culture & Society*, 11 (1).

Therborn, G. (1995) 'Routes to/through modernity', in M. Featherstone, S. Lash and R. Robertson (eds) *Global Modernities*. London: Sage

Theroux, P. (1992) *The Happy Isles of Oceania: Paddling the Pacific*. New York: Putnam.

Theweleit, K. (1987) *Male Fantasies Volume 1: Women, Floods, Bodies, History*. Cambridge: Polity.

Thomas, K. (1983) *Man and the Natural World*. Harmondsworth: Allen Lane.

Thornton, R. J. (1992) 'The rhetoric of ethnographic holism', in G. Marcus (ed.) *Rereading Cultural Anthropology*. Durham, NC: Duke University Press.

Tibi, B. (1995) 'Culture and knowledge: the politics of Islamisation of knowledge as a postmodern project? The fundamentalist claim to de-Westernisation', *Theory, Culture & Society*, 12 (1).

Todorov, T. (1984) *The Conquest of America*. New York: Harper.

Tomlinson, J. (1991) *Cultural Imperialism*. London: Pinter.

Tönnies, F. (1955) *Community and Association*. London: Routledge.

Touraine, A. (1986) *Le Retour de l'acteur*. Paris. Traus. *The Return of the Actor*. Minneapolis: Minnesota University Press, 1988.

Turner, B. S. (1987) 'A note on nostalgia', *Theory, Culture & Society*, 4 (1).

Turner, B. S. (1990a) 'Two faces of sociology: global or national', in M. Featherstone (ed.) *Global Culture*. London: Sage.

Turner, B. S. (ed.) (1990b) 'Introduction', to B. S. Turner (ed.) *Theories of Modernity and Postmodernity*. London: Sage.

Turner, C. (1990) 'Lyotard and Weber: postmodern rules and neo-Kantian values', in B. S. Turner (ed.) *Theories of Modernity and Postmodernity*. London: Sage.

Turner, G. (1990) *British Cultural Studies*. London: Unwin Hyman.

Turner, V. (1969) *The Ritual Process: Structure and AntiStructure*. Harmondsworth: Allen Lane.

Tyssen, L. van Vucht (ed.) (1995) *Modernization and the Search for Fundamentals*. Dordrecht: Kluwer.

Urry, J. (1990) *The Tourist Gaze*. London: Sage.

Urry, J. (1992) 'The tourist gaze and the "environment"', *Theory, Culture & Society*, 9 (3).

Van den Abbeele, G. (1992) *Travel as Metaphor*. Minneapolis: Minnesota University Press.

Vattimo, G. (1988) *The End of Modernity*. Cambridge: Polity.

Vaughan, M. (1984) 'Intellectuals, nationalism and modernity', unpublished paper, University of Lancaster.

Veblen, T. (1953) *The Leisure Class*. New York: New American Library, orig. publ. 1891.

Viddich, A. and Bensman, J. (1958) *Small Town in Mass Society*. Princeton, NJ: Princeton University Press.

Vowinckel, G. (1987) 'Command or refine? Culture patterns of cognitively organizing emotions', *Theory, Culture & Society*, 4 (2–3): 489–514.

Walker, J. A. (1987) *Crossovers: Art into Pop/Pop into Art*. London: Methuen.

Wallace, A. F. C. (1970) *Culture and Personality*. New York.

Wallerstein, I. (1974) *The Modern World-System I*. London: Academic Press.

Wallerstein, I. (1980) *The Modern World-System II*. London: Academic Press.

Wallerstein, I. (1987) 'World-systems analysis', in A. Giddens and J. Turner (eds) *Social Theory Today*. Cambridge: Polity.

Wallerstein, I. (1990) 'Culture as the ideological battleground of the modern world-system', in M. Featherstone (ed.) *Global Culture*. London: Sage.

Warner, W. L. and Lunt, P. S. (1941) *The Social Life of a Modern Community*. New Haven: Yale University Press.

Wasielewski, P. L. (1985) 'The emotional basis of charisma', *Symbolic Interaction*, 8 (2).

Watier, P. (1991) 'The war writings of Georg Simmel', *Theory, Culture & Society*, 8 (3), special issue on Georg Simmel.

Weber, Marianne (1975) *Max Weber: A Biography*. New York: Wiley. (2nd revised edition edited by G. Roth, 1989.)

Weber, Max (1948a) 'Politics as a vocation', in H. H. Gerth and C. W. Mills (eds) *From Max Weber*. London: Routledge.

Weber, Max (1948b) 'Science as a vocation', in H. H. Gerth and C. W. Mills (eds) *From Max Weber*. London: Routledge.

Weber, Max (1948c) 'Religious rejections of the world and their directions', in H. H. Gerth and C. W. Mills (eds) *From Max Weber*. London: Routledge.

Weber, Max (1948d) 'The sociology of charismatic authority', in H. H. Gerth and C. Wright Mills (eds) *From Max Weber*. London: Routledge.

Weber, Max (1949) 'The meaning of "ethical neutrality" in sociology and economics', in *The Methodology of the Social Sciences*. New York: Free Press.

Weber, Max (1951) *The Religion of China*. Glencoe, IL: Free Press.

Weingartner, R. H. (1962) *Experience and Culture: The Philosophy of Georg Simmel*. Middletown, CT: Wesleyan University Press.

Weinstein, D. and Weinstein, M. (1990) 'Georg Simmel: sociological flâneur/bricoleur', *Theory, Culture & Society*, 8 (3).

Weinstein, D. and Weinstein, M. (1991) 'Georg Simmel', *Canadian Journal of Political and Social Theory*.

Whimster, S. (1987) 'The secular ethic and the culture of modernism', in S. Whimster and S. Lash (eds) *Max Weber, Rationality and Modernity*. London: Allen & Unwin.

Whimster, S. (1989) 'Heidelberg man: recent literature on Max Weber', *Theory, Culture & Society*, 6 (3).

White, H. (1973) *Metahistory*. Baltimore: Johns Hopkins University Press.

White, R. (1981) *Inventing Australia*. Sydney: Allen & Unwin.

White, R. (1983) 'A backwater awash: the Australian experience of Americanization', *Theory, Culture & Society*, 1 (3).

Wilensky, H. L. (1964) 'Mass society and mass culture: interdpendencies or dependencies', *American Sociological Review*, 29 (2): 173–97.

Williams, R. (1961) *Culture and Society 1780–1950*. Harmondsworth: Penguin, publ. orig. 1958.

Williams, R. (1975) *The Country and the City*. London: Chatto & Windus.

Williams, R. (1981) *Culture*. London: Fontana.

Williams, R. (1983) *Towards 2000*. London: Chatto & Windus.

Williamson, B. (1982) *Class, Culture and Community*. London: Routledge.

Wohl, R. (1980) *The Generation of 1914*. London: Weidenfeld & Nicholson.

Wolfe, T. (1989) *The Right Stuff*. London: Black Swan.

Wolff, Eric R. (1990) 'Distinguished lecture: facing power – old insights, new questions', *American Anthropologist*, 92 (3).

Wolff, J. (1993) 'On the road again: metaphors of travel in cultural criticism', *Cultural Studies*, 7 (2).

Yeats, W. B. (1991) *Selected Poetry*. Harmondsworth: Penguin.

Zerubavel, E. (1991) *The Fine Line: Making Distinctions in Everyday Life*. Chicago: Chicago University Press.

Zolberg, A. (1995) 'The Great Wall against China: responses to the first immigration crisis, 1885–1925', in Wang Gungwu (ed.) *Global History and Migrations*. Boulder, CO: Westview Press.

Zukin, S. (1988) 'The postmodern debate over urban form', *Theory, Culture & Society*, 5 (2–3).

Zukin, S. (1991) *Landscapes of Power. From Detroit to Disney World*. Berkeley: California University Press.

INDEX